W9-CNW-367

John Knox Christian School
82 McLaughlin Rd. S.
Brampton, ON L6Y 2C7

The Story of God and His People
A Light to the Gentiles

Second edition by
Jesslyn De Boer
Hazel Timmer

First edition by
Hazel Timmer
Nancy Groom
Steven Baxendale
Olga Vasquez
Ellen Weber

CHRISTIAN SCHOOLS
INTERNATIONAL

CHRISTIAN SCHOOLS INTERNATIONAL
3350 East Paris Ave., SE
Grand Rapids, Michigan 49512-3054

Second Edition
© 1998 CHRISTIAN SCHOOLS INTERNATIONAL
Printed in the United States of America
All rights reserved

10   9   8   7   6

ISBN 0-87463-968-9

The development of *The Story of God and His People* was made possible with grants from Christian Schools International Foundation and Canadian Christian Education Foundation, Inc.

Photographs by Neal and Joel Bierling, Phoenix Data Systems.
Illustrations: Archive Photos: 201, 250, 254–256, 271; Art Resource/Scala: 284; Corbis/Bettman: 37, 251, 274, 278, 286, 289; Kenneth D. Bratt: 275; Gustave Doré: 31, 66, 70, 104, 108, 111, 148, 175, 184, 244; Albrecht Dürer: 76; Granger: 221; SuperStock: 10, 12, 23, 26, 32, 34, 40, 46, 47, 51, 65, 73, 78, 79, 93, 96, 102, 116, 150, 203, 238, 240; all other illustrations and maps by Teresa Wyngarden.

Contents

The Message of the Gospels

1 — — ➤ Introduction to the Gospels

> **Bible Reference: Luke 1:1–4; 2:25–32;**
> **John 1:6–8; 20:31**

Therefore God exalted him to the highest place
and gave him the name that is above every name,
that at the name of Jesus every knee should bow,
in heaven and on earth and under the earth,
and every tongue confess that Jesus Christ is Lord,
to the glory of God the Father.

Philippians 2:9–11

The name of Jesus, the name above every name, has spread throughout the world. But during the days of the early church few people knew the name. In fact, it is difficult to find mention of Jesus in the writings of the Roman or Jewish historians. The Gospels are our primary source of information on the life of Jesus of Nazareth, but even these writings don't cover his entire life.

A Written Record

The Gospels were not written down for at least 30 years after Jesus ascended to heaven. There were probably two main reasons for this. First, history and traditions at this time were commonly passed down orally. When Jesus said in the Sermon on the Mount, "You have heard that it was said . . . ," he was referring to the Jewish oral tradition. Second, the apostles were eyewitnesses to Jesus' life, death, and resurrection. When the apostles grew old and Jesus still had not returned to earth, it became clear that their witness should be given a more permanent form and shared with the growing church.

The Gospels' Witness

The four Gospels tell us almost all that we know about Jesus. But they are not biographies of Jesus, at least not the kind of biographies we are familiar with. Even after reading all four Gospels, we cannot write down the story of Jesus' life from beginning to end in exact sequence.

Of course, the Gospels do give us facts about Jesus' life, death, and resurrection. And they record many of Jesus' teachings and sayings (for example, his parables). But their main purpose is not to tell everything that happened in his life. Their main purpose is to witness to who Jesus is—the Christ, the Messiah, the Son of God. The Gospels were written to convert unbelievers and to build up the faith of believers.

The Gospels' Testimony

A witness called to testify at a trial is sworn to tell the truth. Each witness, however, can describe the truth only as he or she has seen or experienced it. The Holy Spirit guided each Gospel writer to write the truth, yet each writer chose certain information to include, emphasized certain facts or teachings, arranged the material in a certain order, and added his own comments. Together the four Gospel accounts build a persuasive case for Jesus as the Son of God. Each Gospel confirms, complements, and adds to the body of evidence.

The Synoptic Gospels

What does *synoptic* mean? The prefix *syn* means "at the same time or together with"; the root word *optic* refers to seeing. Put the two together, and you have something like "seeing at the same time" or "seeing together with."

Three of the Gospels—Matthew, Mark, and Luke—share many similar stories written in very similar language. They are called the synoptic Gospels. They look at Jesus with much the same vision. John's Gospel is distinctly different.

2 ▬ ▬ ▬ ➤ The Gospel of Matthew

Bible Reference: The Gospel of Matthew

The Author and His Audience

The Gospel of Matthew was apparently written by the apostle Matthew. Matthew, also known as Levi, was a tax collector before Jesus called him to be a disciple. Although nothing in the Gospel of Matthew specifically tells us that he wrote it, the Christian church since the second century has accepted Matthew as its author.

Matthew seems to have written especially for Greek-speaking Jews. His main purpose was to demonstrate to them that Jesus was the Messiah. You know that the Jews were longing for a messiah to come. (The Jews of Qumran expected two messiahs, one a king like David and the other a priest like Aaron.) Many Jews wondered if Jesus really was the Messiah. Jews who had

Saint Matthew by Ghilberti, 1419.

become Christians were surrounded by Jews who were hostile to Jesus and his followers. Matthew wrote to convince and reassure them that Jesus was indeed the one the Jews had been waiting for.

A Flavor of the Old Testament

Matthew included ingredients in his writing that his audience would find particularly meaningful. While all of the Gospel writers quoted the Old Testament to prove that Jesus is the Messiah, Matthew did so 65 times. Matthew also spiced up his Gospel with Jewish terms and referred to Jewish customs without making explanations. The result was a New Testament book with an Old Testament flavor. Matthew designed his writing for readers with Jewish tastes.

Earlier versions of Old Testament writings, used heavily by Matthew, were discovered here in the Qumran Caves.

The Kingdom of Heaven

While Matthew tried to convince his readers that Jesus was the Messiah, he also made it very clear that Jesus was not the kind of messiah that most of them were expecting. Since Jews were expecting a king like David, one who would drive out the Romans just as David had driven out the Philistines, Matthew explained exactly what Jesus' kingdom, the "kingdom of heaven," was all about. (Matthew used the phrase "kingdom of heaven" instead of "kingdom of God.") He laid out Jesus' teachings on the true nature of the kingdom of heaven by including the Sermon on the Mount and Jesus' parables.

The Old Testament authors never wrote about a kingdom of God, but they did anticipate a day when God would reveal his glory and all people would acknowledge his rule. Many Jews understood the Old Testament prophecies to mean an earthly kingdom ruled by God.

Matthew wanted his readers to clearly understand the kingdom of God as Jesus described it. His Gospel contains 10 parables that are not included anywhere else; each of these parables reveals something about the kingdom of heaven. Jesus' life and ministry mark the beginning of the kingdom of God. The kingdom parables call for a response to Jesus and his mission.

Disciples of All Nations

Matthew was careful to point out that the kingdom is open to Gentiles as well as Jews. His evidence begins in the family tree in Matthew 1, which lists two Gentile women, Rahab and Ruth, as part of the covenant family—a sign of God's grace. Matthew also recorded the visit of the Gentile Magi to worship the child Jesus. And he ended his Gospel with Jesus' commission to his disciples to tell all nations the good news.

3 ‒ ‒ ‒ ‒ ➤ The Gospel of Mark

Bible Reference: The Gospel of Mark

Who Was Mark?

Mark was not one of the 12 apostles. In fact, he is not mentioned by name anywhere in the Gospels. A common belief, however, is that the

Saint Mark by Giusto di Giovanni Menabuoi, c. 1376–1378.

author of the Gospel of Mark is the same John Mark mentioned in other parts of the New Testament. John would have been his Jewish name; Mark is a Latin name.

Mark's Gospel is the shortest of the four Gospels. Quick-paced and action-packed, Mark's story begins and ends abruptly. In it Jesus moves quickly from place to place. The Greek word that means "immediately" keeps the action moving. It is also translated as "at once," "quickly," or "just then." The word appears 41 times in Mark, compared to seven times in Matthew and only once in Luke.

For Persecuted Christians

The Christians in Rome were suffering severe persecution under the emperor Nero. When a fire burned down half of Rome in A.D. 64, Nero accused the Christians of setting it.

Mark wrote to these Christians. He answered their questions by explaining that Jesus also suffered—not only at the end of his life but through all of it. In fact, one major theme of Mark is the need for the Messiah's suffering and death. Mark chose this theme to give courage and hope to those who were suffering and dying for Christ.

Nero.

In keeping with his theme, Mark chose stories that would encourage the persecuted believers in Rome, stories in which they could see Jesus as the suffering servant, unrecognized as the Messiah, persecuted and misunderstood by many.

In Mark 8:31–38 Mark wrote Jesus' own prediction of his death on a cross. Remember that Matthew had to convince the Jews that Jesus was not the kind of messiah that they were expecting. Mark's audience would also have had difficulty understanding the idea of a suffering, crucified Savior. To the Jews crucifixion meant a person was cursed; to the Romans it was scandalous. Mark taught that crucifixion was the way for the Messiah and that it might also be the way for some Roman Christians.

Mark 10:45 summarizes the central truth of Mark's Gospel: "For even the Son of Man did not come to be served, but to serve, and to give his life as a ransom for many."

Focused on Action

Mark lived and wrote in a world of action and crisis. There was no time to think about genealogies, meditate on fulfilled prophecies, or add a lot of human details. People were suffering and dying. They needed to know the truth—immediately! That's why Mark focused on Jesus' actions instead of on his teachings.

Mark recorded 18 miracles that Jesus performed but only 4 parables. He didn't comment much on Jesus' works, either. He let the actions speak for themselves, convincing us that Jesus is the Son of God, a Savior whose greatest glory and victory came at the world's greatest shame and defeat—the cross.

Along with the suffering Savior theme, Mark paid a lot of attention to the actions required of disciples. In Mark 8:34 Jesus says, "If anyone would come after me, he must deny himself and take up his cross and follow me."

4 – – – – ➤ The Gospel of Luke

Bible Reference: The Gospel of Luke

Luke

The Gospel of Luke is the first volume of the two-volume work "Luke-Acts." Although Luke does not identify himself as the author of this work, the earliest church traditions agree that he wrote it.

Saint Luke by Giusto di Giovanni Menabuoi, c. 1376–1378.

Luke was a doctor. He was not an eyewitness to Jesus' life and ministry, but he accompanied Paul on his second missionary journey. A well-educated person, Luke wrote in the Greek language. He was a skillful writer with a large vocabulary, an eye for details, and good sense of order.

Besides his contact with Paul, Luke must have had access to many oral traditions and writings about Jesus. Before Luke composed his own book about Jesus, he investigated these sources to ensure that the stories he used were trustworthy and accurate.

The Holy Spirit inspired Luke to choose from authentic stories and to arrange them in such a way that they would witness to the truth about Jesus. Luke was not trying to write Jesus' biography. Rather, he wanted to write a book that would strengthen the faith of those who believed so they could be sure of themselves when unbelievers attacked them.

Theophilus

Theophilus was probably a Roman official (since Luke addresses him as "most excellent") or at least a person with high position and wealth. He may have been Luke's patron or publisher. But Luke also intended this Gospel to be read by all believers, both Jews and Gentiles. Luke himself was probably a Gentile, so he was especially sensitive to Gentiles and others who were not in the mainstream of Jewish society. Because his audience included many Gentiles who didn't know about Palestine and Jewish customs, Luke often explained geographical, historical, and religious details. When he quoted the Old Testament, Luke used the Greek version, which Gentiles would understand, rather than the Hebrew.

The Universal Gospel

The Gospel of Luke makes it clear that Jesus came to save all who are lost—both Jews and Gentiles. Luke showed that Jesus also included the poor and weak in his kingdom—and women, too. Although in Jesus' day women were considered inferior to men, Jesus didn't treat them that way.

The content of Luke's Gospel relates to his profession. As a doctor he was concerned about all kinds of people. Luke showed this attitude through the stories he chose and the way he told those stories.

The Gospel of Luke highlights the human details of the story of Jesus. It lets us see the concerns and problems that surrounded Jesus' entry into this world. It draws us into the anticipation and wonder at Jesus' miraculous birth. It even gives us the words to the joyful songs of Mary, Zechariah, the angels, and Simeon so that we can sing along in praise to God.

5 ▬ ▬ ▬ ▬ ➡ The Gospel of John

Bible Reference: The Gospel of John

John: Fisherman, Disciple, Church Leader

Although the writer of this Gospel didn't identify himself, we can be fairly sure that this John was the disciple whom Jesus called from fishing

The Island of Patmos.

on the Sea of Galilee. He was called "the disciple whom Jesus loved" and was part of the inner circle of disciples— Peter, James, and John. In the early church John was a leader in Jerusalem and later most likely at Ephesus. Apparently he was exiled to the island of Patmos for preaching at Ephesus.

John, like the other Gospel writers, chose only some of the stories of Jesus. His portrait of Jesus, however, is distinct from the picture in the other Gospels. Many experts believe that this was the last Gospel written, so perhaps John didn't include the same stories as the synoptic Gospels because he figured that people already knew them. Also, by the time that we think John wrote his Gospel several mistaken ideas about Jesus had become popular. John wanted to tell stories that would set people straight. According to John's own words, his purpose in writing was similar to the purpose of the other Gospel authors: he wanted to explain the truth about Jesus—that he was the Messiah. John wrote, "these are written that you may believe that Jesus is the Christ, the Son of God, and that by believing you may have life in his name."

"I Am"

Who is Jesus? This question is at the center of John's Gospel. In this Gospel Jesus openly declares who he is. For example, when the woman at the well mentions the promised messiah, Jesus tells her, "I who speak to you am he" (John 4:26). And when the Jews criticize Jesus for healing on the Sabbath, he claims that as God's Son he is doing what his Father did (John 5:17–18). In John's Gospel Jesus paints word pictures to help us identify him. Each statement begins with "I am . . ." These statements are all metaphors. A metaphor compares two things that aren't the same but have something in common. Our everyday conversation is full of metaphors: "She's a clown." "This room is a pigpen." "In winter the park is a fairyland." Metaphors like these are so common that we skip right past them.

But fresh metaphors make us sit up and take notice. And because metaphors suggest rather than explain, they can puzzle us. They leave us with something to think or talk about.

Miracles = Signs

Seeing is believing; at least that's what the proverb says. We tend to think along the lines of that proverb. Those who actually saw Jesus help blind people must have believed. But believed in what? In the miracle? Or in Jesus?

John included only seven miracles in his Gospel, and he called Jesus' miracles "signs." John didn't want to encourage his readers to be surprised by the miracles; he didn't want to focus on how amazing the miracles were. Rather, John wanted to emphasize the miracles' meaning.

Jesus' miracles point to the fact that he is the Son of God. The miracles show that God's kingdom has dawned and his kingly rule has broken into the world through Jesus Christ.

Eyewitness Testimony

In making his defense for Jesus as the Son of God, John called on a number of witnesses. He reported the stories of many people who were with Jesus at key events, believed in him, and were willing to tell others about what they saw.

John highlighted this theme by using the word *witness* 14 times and the word *testify* 33 times. Compare this to the other Gospel writers, who used those words a combined total of only six times. In fact, the words *witness* and *testify* occur more often in John's Gospel than anywhere else in the whole New Testament.

Jesus Gives Life

In the Gospel of John the last miracle that Jesus performs before his death is the raising of Lazarus. Of all the miracles this one most clearly shows the life-giving power of Jesus' ministry.

Raising of Lazaros by Rembrandt van Rijn, 1630.

In the hot climate of Palestine, the dead were buried almost immediately. By the time Jesus arrived in Bethany, Lazarus's body had been anointed, wrapped in strips of cloth, and laid in a cave with a low doorway. A stone blocked the cave's entrance to keep out animals. Lazarus's friends and relatives had gathered to mourn with his sisters, Martha and Mary.

Many Jews (but not all) believed in a future resurrection, so Martha's declaration that Lazarus would rise again wasn't unusual. But Jesus challenged her to believe in his power to give new life right then, for in Jesus, God's kingdom had already arrived.

In other words, the future is now. Once a person believes in Christ, he or she has new life, eternal life.

Unit 2
Jesus' Early Ministry

1 ▬ ▬ ➔ John the Baptist's Ministry

Bible Reference: Matthew 3:1–12; Mark 1:1–8; Luke 3:1–20

Time for the Messiah

The time was ripe for the messiah to come. Herod the Great, the king of Judea when Jesus was born, died while Jesus was in Egypt. A short time later Judea saw large-scale revolts against Archelaus, Herod's son and successor.

The revolts spread throughout Judea and into Galilee. The Romans bru-tally crushed these revolts. They killed thousands of Jews. In Jerusalem alone they crucified 2,000 Jews. The Romans burned Sepphoris, a town just north of Nazareth, during this time. The prophets had told of such days of judgment before the messiah would come, so some people saw the oppression as a sign that the messiah was coming soon. Then the news came that a prophet was preaching that "the kingdom of heaven is near."

Excavation of a colonnaded street in Sepphoris.

The Desert Prophet

John began preaching near the Jordan River in the desert of Judea. This was the wilderness south of Jerusalem around Jericho. Almost nothing grew in this dry area. John had no luxuries and no neighbors except for wild animals.

The Judean desert.

Matthew and Mark both tell us that John wore clothes made from camel's hair and that he ate locusts and wild honey. These were the clothes and food of a desert dweller. John fulfilled the prophesy Isaiah had made hundreds of years earlier.

The response to John's preaching was amazing. People came from far and near to hear him and to be baptized. Matthew says that people came "from Jerusalem and all Judea." Mark 1:5b tells us that "all the people of Jerusalem went out to him." Anyone who lived in Jerusalem would have to travel 15 to 20 miles to hear John preach!

People were hungry for John's message. Certainly God was at work in their hearts. But other things attracted the crowds, too. John was an attraction because it had been centuries since God had sent a prophet. Matthew gives us another reason why John attracted crowds—because he denounced the Sadducees and Pharisees, calling them the "brood of vipers."

John's Message

John's urgent message was "Repent, for the kingdom of heaven is near" (Matthew 3:2). The people needed to repent—to turn away from sin and ask God for forgiveness. John's new message also included being baptized and bearing fruit that shows a change of heart. He attacked the belief that Jews could be saved simply by being descendants of Abraham. Prior to John's coming, Gentiles had been baptized when they became believers in the Lord God of Israel, but John preached that all, including the children of Abraham, should be baptized. John burst the Jews' balloon of self-importance by saying that God could make children of Abraham from stones (Matthew 3:9).

John's message was a reminder of what the prophets had said a long time before: "Repent, for the day of the Lord is at hand!" The day of the Lord is clearly a time of judgment. The Jews had to either acknowledge Jesus as the messiah or reject him and bear the consequences.

Now the people were prepared for Jesus' ministry. But two events still had to take place in Jesus' life before he was ready.

2 ━ ━ ━ ━ ━ ━ ➤ Jesus' Baptism

**Bible Reference: Matthew 3:13–17;
Mark 1:9–11; Luke 3:21–22; John 1:29–31**

One day while John was preaching and baptizing, Jesus made an appearance. When John saw him, he knew who Jesus was. We're not positive that John and Jesus had ever met, but they probably did know each other. After all, they were relatives whose mothers had shared amazing experiences; each had become pregnant miraculously. Perhaps Mary and Elizabeth visited each other when John and Jesus were young boys.

Jesus shocked John by asking to be baptized. John protested, but Jesus insisted that it would "fulfill all righteousness." In other words, it would show that Jesus would meet all of God's righteous require-

The Baptism of Christ by Leonardo da Vinci, 1470.

ments. So John baptized Jesus. Jesus was baptized in the Jordan River, but the exact location is not known.

Preparing for Ministry

How did Jesus' baptism prepare him for ministry? First, it showed Jesus and those who witnessed his baptism that he had his Father's approval and blessing. The voice from heaven made that clear.

Second, it showed that God gave his Son the power for his work. We can compare Jesus' baptism and the descent of the Holy Spirit with the Old Testament anointing of kings. For example, when God had Samuel anoint Saul and David, he was stating that he had called them to a special task, that they were set apart from others, and that they were filled with the Holy Spirit. Jesus was also called by God, set apart, and filled with the Holy Spirit.

Finally, in his baptism Jesus identified himself with us. Even though Jesus himself had no sin that needed to be washed away, he stood in our place. He would take upon himself the sins of the whole world.

3 ▬ ▬ ▬ ▬ ➤ Jesus Battles Satan

> **Bible Reference: Deuteronomy 8:1–5;**
> **Matthew 4:1–11; Mark 1:12–13**

In Jesus' baptism we saw that God was on his side, supporting and loving him. But immediately after his baptism, Jesus underwent quite a different experience.

Matthew tells us that after Jesus was baptized, he was "led by the Spirit into the desert to be tempted by the devil." Another word for *tempted* is *tested*. No one is sure exactly where this tempting took place, but tradition places the location in the mountainous area just northwest of Jericho. In this desolate area Jesus faced Satan alone.

Matthew also tells us that Jesus did not face Satan immediately. First, he fasted for 40 days and 40 nights. Fasting was a religious exercise that showed humility, sorrow, and dependence on God. Jesus was preparing for his battle with Satan.

Why did Jesus have to be tempted? And what was the significance of 40 days? During the 40 years that Israel spent in the desert after leaving Egypt God tested Israel to see if Israel would be faithful, but Israel failed the test. The Spirit led Jesus into the desert for a similar 40-day test. Would Jesus resist Satan and show himself to be God's faithful Son?

God's Faithful Son

Each of Satan's suggestions tried to convince Jesus to be unfaithful. But by standing firm and faithful to God, Jesus showed that he was indeed God's Son.

Temptation 1
"Tell these stones to become bread."

Satan wanted Jesus to use his great power to satisfy his own needs. Jesus was hungry. He needed food. Why not use his power to get it? Because Jesus knew that there were more important things than his own hunger. Later in the Sermon on the Mount he taught, "Seek first his kingdom and his right-eousness, and all these things will be given to you" (Matthew 6:33). God's Word was a "food" more important than bread.

So in this first test, Satan encouraged two sins. First, he wanted Jesus to use his power for his own needs; second, he wanted Jesus to make his own needs more important than the kingdom of God. But Jesus showed that God's kingdom came first. He would love God above all and his neighbor as himself.

Temptation 2
"Jump from this temple and prove that God is on your side."

Satan wanted Jesus to use his power to quickly gain a large following. Angels catching Jesus in midair would be a spectacular sight. A show of power like that would make him instantly popular. But here was another, deeper temptation. By quoting Scripture, Satan made his request sound innocent. But what he actually meant was, "Let's see if God's promises are really true."

A person says, "Prove it!" when he or she doesn't trust another's word. Jesus trusted God's promises. That's why he quoted Deuteronomy 6:16: "Do not put the Lord your God to the test." Jesus knew that God would protect him and be with him. He didn't have to prove it. Jesus' response also showed that he wouldn't be a messiah who would try to win a large following through startling miracles.

Temptation 3
"All this I will give you if you will bow down and worship me."

Satan tested Jesus by trying to get Jesus to choose the easy way. He offered Jesus a deal. Jesus would become ruler of all the kingdoms of the world, but first he had to worship Satan. Why not compromise? Both Satan and Jesus would give up something, and both would gain something.

This must have been the most difficult temptation. Taking Satan's offer was a way for Jesus to avoid suffering and death on the cross. But Jesus rejected Satan's offer. He would not compromise. He would become King of Kings and Lord of Lords by dying on a cross. He would take the difficult path of an obedient son. In the desert Jesus passed the test that Israel failed.

What would have happened if Jesus had not resisted Satan? Then, of course, he couldn't be the Savior of the world. Then he himself would need someone to save him from sin. But because Jesus was without sin, he was qualified to save others from sin.

4 ━ ━ ━ ➤ Gathering His Disciples

Bible Reference: Mark 1:14–20; 2:13–17;
3:13–19; 6:7–13

Soon after his temptation, Jesus heard that Herod Antipas had imprisoned John the Baptist, who had been criticizing Herod for living with his brother's wife.

The desert temptations had not stopped Jesus from pursuing his mission and neither did this news. Jesus began to preach in Galilee, repeating John's message to repent and hinting that his kingdom was about to begin.

Jesus began by calling his disciples. He may have known some of the men he called. Simon Peter and Andrew were, for example, followers of John the Baptist and had spent time with Jesus before his call (John 1:35–42).

Jesus did surprising things

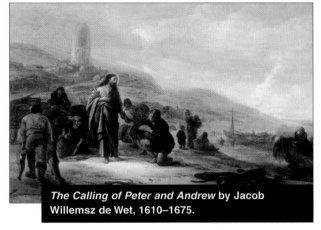

The Calling of Peter and Andrew by Jacob Willemsz de Wet, 1610–1675.

when he selected his disciples. While many rabbis had followers or disciples, the pupils usually chose their master, so the fact that Jesus called his disciples is in itself a surprise. In another radical move, Jesus did not pick disciples who would make him popular with the people in power. For example, Matthew was a tax collector. He worked for the Romans, who had conquered and abused the Jews. Tax collectors also had a reputation of charging extra to keep for themselves. Four fishermen, a tax collector, and a political extremist (Simon the Zealot) are hardly the expected choices to accompany the Son of God, the Prince of Peace.

Poor Choice?

Why did Jesus pick these people? Such a motley group attracted bad publicity for Jesus. The scribes and Pharisees certainly were not impressed by the quality of Jesus' disciples. And these disciples often failed to understand what Jesus was trying to teach them.

But his choice was deliberate. The bumbling of the disciples is our bumbling; their questions and their failure to understand Jesus' replies are our daily failures. The disciples represent everyday Christians.

Jesus made the choices that fit his calling as Messiah. The Jews would have chosen quite a different set of disciples: military experts, financial wizards, diplomats—in other words, people who would help them accomplish their goals of freedom from the Romans and peace and prosperity for the Jewish nation.

An Upside-Down Kingdom

The goals of Jesus, the Messiah, were far different. His teaching suggested a future of suffering and persecution. He praised people who were poor in spirit, who mourned, who were merciful, who made peace. He said they were blessed even when they were persecuted.

Jesus was not the kind of messiah that the people expected. He was not the kind they wanted. He believed in winning by losing, in being last, in serving, in self-sacrifice. He chose disciples who were ordinary people. This was another way God showed that his ways are higher than ours and his thoughts higher than ours.

5 — — — ➤ The First Sign at Cana

Bible Reference: John 2:1–11

▸ Wine Becomes a Sign

A wedding was the occasion for Jesus' first great sign or miracle. Jesus, his disciples, and Mary were invited to attend a wedding—one of the most joyous of Jewish social events. The entire community participated in the festivities. Although we don't know all the details of Jewish wedding ceremonies of that time, we know that the bridegroom (probably along with his family) footed the bill. Providing a wonderful feast with good food and wine was very important. A wedding feast might last for a week. Jesus and his companions were looking forward to a good time.

▸ He Revealed His Glory

In his Gospel, John always calls Jesus' wonderful works "signs" because he wants to emphasize their purpose—to point the way to salvation. Jesus' miracles aren't just some kind of marvelous magic, John says. Rather, they have meaning and significance.

At the wedding in Cana Jesus displayed power to chemically change water into wine. But he showed a lot more. Look at the story again.

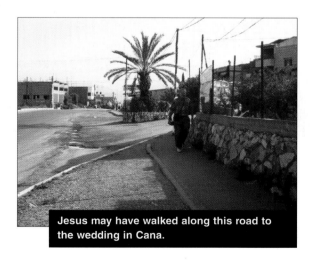

Jesus may have walked along this road to the wedding in Cana.

The setting is important. A wedding banquet was used in the Old Testament to represent the messiah's arrival. Isaiah 62:4–5 says,

"No longer will they call you Deserted,
   or name your land Desolate.
But you will be called Hephzibah,
   and your land Beulah;
for the Lord will take delight in you,
   and your land will be married.
As a young man marries a maiden,
   so will your sons marry you;
as a bridegroom rejoices over his bride,
   so will your God rejoice over you."

The Wedding at Cana by Giotto di Bondone, c. 1266–1337.

Jewish law specified many ways a person could become unclean. To cleanse themselves from some common daily activities Jews poured water over their hands. That was the purpose of the large stone jars of water that Jesus used in his miracle. When Jesus transforms their contents, he shows that the old laws must pass away.

Wine replaces the water. At the Last Supper Jesus would use wine as a symbol for his blood: "This cup is the new covenant in my blood, which is poured out for you" (Luke 22:20). The water changed to wine could be a picture of how Jesus' blood cleanses us of our sins in a way that the Old Testament rituals never could. The master of the banquet was more right than he knew when he called Jesus' wine "the best."

John notes that each water jar held 20–30 gallons, so the six jars held a lot of wine. Amos 9:13–14 also shows how this picture reveals Jesus' glory. The prophet predicted that the messiah's reign would be characterized by an abundance of wine.

When Jesus performed his first miracle at the wedding in Cana, he revealed his glory not by powerful magic but with overpowering symbols!

6 ▪ ▶ Clearing the Court of the Gentiles

Bible Reference: John 2:12–25

Passover Pilgrims

After the wedding Jesus, his family, and his disciples went to Capernaum by the Sea of Galilee for a few days. Then Jesus went down to Jerusalem for the Passover. In John's Gospel this is where the next major event of Jesus' ministry took place—the cleansing of the temple.

A pilgrimage is a journey to a holy place; the trip expresses religious belief. In Jesus' time Jewish families made a pilgrimage to Jerusalem each year. All Jewish men were required to celebrate the Passover in Jerusalem.

Making animal sacrifices at the temple was also required. Pilgrims who came from far away did not bring their sacrifices with them but bought animals for sacrifice when they arrived in Jerusalem. Local merchants, taking advantage of this opportunity, sold animals at high prices.

During their visit, Jews also were expected to pay their annual temple tax. Some kinds of coins were not acceptable. For example, if the money carried the picture of one of the Roman authorities, it could not be presented at the temple. So other vendors traded the unclean money for the appropriate change.

A Polluted Temple Court

The major entrance of Herod's remodeled temple complex was on the south. This triple entry gate was called the Huldah Gates. This entrance led

What Massive Stones!

"Do you see all these great buildings?" said Jesus. "Not one stone here will be left on another; every one will be thrown down" (Mark 13:2).

Much of the temple had been rebuilt by the exiles returning from Babylon. When Herod attacked Jerusalem, the temple was damaged. Historians suggest that Herod rebuilt the temple to please the Jews whom he now ruled.

He started with massive stones weighing 2,000 kg (2 tons) or more from the quarries in hills of Jerusalem for the outer wall. The southeast corner of the outer wall is considered the highest area and is where Satan told Jesus to jump.

The Antonia Fortress in the northwest corner may have been residence to Roman procurators who visited Jerusalem. A Roman garrison stood guard to quickly stop any disturbances.

Herod expanded the courts to accommodate as many people as possible. He trained priests to rebuild the actual temple and sacred areas. Herod wanted his temple to be more magnificent than Solomon's. Work was still going on in Jesus' time.

Jesus and his disciples may have entered Herod's temple area through the Huldah Gates into the Royal Portico. There Jesus may have driven out the buyers and sellers. (Historians are not sure if the buyers and sellers were at the Royal Portico by the Huldah Gates or Solomon's Portico by another gated entrance to the Court of the Gentiles.) Jesus and his disciples would have then entered the Court of the Gentiles, where the Gentiles were allowed to pray and worship. Covered walks lined with colonnades surrounded the Court of the Gentiles. Rabbis and their students used these areas to debate. Mary and Joseph probably found the boy Jesus talking with the teachers in one of these areas.

A second wall surrounded the temple itself. It had signs in Greek and Latin warning of death to any Gentile that entered. Only ceremonially clean Jews could enter the inner area through a gate. The Women's Court was the first area inside the wall. Wood for sacrifices and oil for lamps were available from the storage areas in the corners. Up a few steps and through another gate was the Court of Israel (for men only). The Court of the Priests surrounded the temple. There a ceremonially clean priest could make sacrifices and carry out other temple duties. The Holy of Holies could be entered only on the Day of Atonement by a high priest. A priest chosen by lot burned incense for the people on that day. In Jesus' day the Holy of Holies was empty due to the destruction of the ark when Nebuchadnezzar destroyed Solomon's temple and carried the Jews off to Babylon.

Today some of Herod's massive stones are part of the Western wall. Herod's temple was destroyed by Titus, a Roman commander. A muslin mosque, the al-Aqsa Mosque, stands in its place.

into a huge courtyard called the Court of the Gentiles. The inner courtyards were open only to ceremonially clean Jews. Each area was more restricted as to who could enter, and each was considered holier than the last.

The Court of the Gentiles was where non-Jewish "God-fearers" could pray. This was the only area in the temple where the Gentiles could gather and pray. Jews also gathered here to talk with friends or discuss the law.

South of the Huldah Gates, outside the temple complex, was the place where the vendors and moneychangers had gathered before the time of Christ. But by Jesus' time the merchants had moved their animals and money stalls into the Court of the Gentiles—the Gentiles' place of prayer.

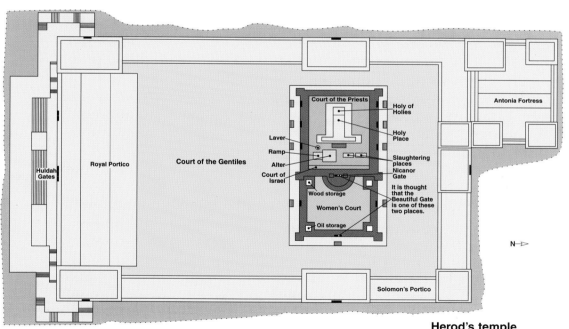

Herod's temple

7 ▬ ▬ ➡ Jesus Teaches a Pharisee

Bible Reference: John 3:1–17

Jesus' miraculous signs attracted people. One of these people was a Pharisee named Nicodemus. He was a person of importance in Jerusalem, a member of the Sanhedrin. He came to talk to Jesus.

Being Born Again

Nicodemus began by complimenting Jesus, saying that Jesus' signs showed that he came from God. Jesus answered Nicodemus with a puzzling statement, "No one can see the kingdom of God unless he is born again" (John 3:3). Nicodemus took Jesus' words literally. He wondered how in the world a person could be born again.

Jesus explained that he was talking about a spiritual rebirth. Jesus' words could also be understood as meaning "born from above." When a baby is born, he or she is a new person in the world. Jesus was telling Nicodemus that anyone who wished to see the kingdom of God must become a new person inside. The Holy Spirit makes a person new inside.

The Way to New Life

Then Nicodemus asked, "How can this be?" Remember, Nicodemus was a Pharisee, and Pharisees believed that the way to be a part of the kingdom of God was by obeying God's law. Obeying the law made people righteous. The kingdom of God was for the righteous, not for sinners.

Jesus had to teach Nicodemus a whole new way of thinking about the kingdom of God. He reminded Nicodemus of an old story that both of them had heard many times before—the story of Moses and the bronze serpent (Numbers 21:4–9). Moses lifted up a bronze serpent on a pole so the Israelites who were dying from snake bites could look at the snake and be saved.

Jesus compared himself to the bronze snake because he would be lifted up on a cross to save people from death. Just as the Israelites were saved from the snakes' poison by looking at the snake, repentant sinners are saved by putting their faith in Jesus rather than in their own works.

Finally, Jesus told Nicodemus that the way to new life was through belief in Jesus, God's one and only Son. Nicodemus could not be part of the kingdom of God through obeying laws. He had to place all his hope in Jesus!

Detail of *The Brazen Snake* by Gustave Doré.

John 3 does not record Nicodemus' response, but two later passages in the same Gospel give us a clue to the results of his talk with Jesus. Discover the role Nicodemus takes at other points in Jesus' life by reading John 7:37–52 and John 19:38–42.

Jesus left Jerusalem and headed north, back to Galilee. The Pharisees had noticed the success of Jesus' ministry. Jesus wanted to avoid confronting them at this time, so he left Judea.

8 ‑ ‑ ‑ ‑ ‑ ‑ ‑ ➔ Living Water

Bible Reference: John 4:1–42

Traveling through Samaria

This time Jesus traveled directly through Samaria. Jews regularly went around Samaria and traveled through the Jordan Valley to get to Galilee. The Jews had hated the Samaritans for centuries.

About noon Jesus and the disciples reached the town of Sychar, a small village near the town of Shechem. John notes that Jacob's well was there. A traveler could get fresh water from the well.

A Stop at Jacob's Well

It's not surprising that Jesus stopped to rest at the well. And it's not surprising that a woman came to the well for water. But after that, it's surprises all the way.

Christ and the Woman of Samaria by Anton Dorph, 1831–1914.

The first surprise is that Jesus spoke to the woman; it was rare for a Jewish rabbi to speak to a woman in public. The second surprise is that Jesus was willing to associate with a Samaritan. This showed that Jesus cares for all people, regardless of their race or gender.

But more surprises were coming. Jesus asked the Samaritan woman for a drink. She was shocked. She knew that because he was a Jew, drinking from her jar would make him "unclean." And then Jesus told her that he could give her a drink of living water.

The woman was getting a bit uneasy at the direction of the conversation, so she changed the subject. She began talking about an old argument between Jews and Samaritans—the proper location of the temple. The Samaritans claimed that Mount Gerizim was sacred; the Jews' holy place was Mount Zion in Jerusalem. The Samaritan woman wanted Jesus' opinion on this debate.

The Samaritan woman remarked that the messiah would explain everything. Jesus answered with the biggest surprise of all. He told her that he was the Messiah!

A Two-Day Preaching Mission

Jesus spent two more days with the Samaritans. Many of them became believers.

There's no evidence that Jesus performed miracles during his stay. In fact, John writes that the Samaritans became believers because of the testimony of the woman and because of Jesus' words.

Traditionally the Samaritans had thought that the messiah would be only a great teacher or prophet. At the end of his two-day stay, however, they knew that Jesus was the Savior of the world.

9 ━ ━ ━ ━ ➤ Faith in Jesus' Word

Bible Reference: John 4:43–54

After two days in Sychar with the Samaritans, Jesus traveled on to Galilee. The people there welcomed him, but not with the welcome he wanted.

Looking for a Miracle Worker

Jesus stopped in the city of Cana, the city where he had changed water into wine at the wedding feast. News of his arrival traveled fast, and soon a man came rushing up to Jesus.

The man was in a big hurry because his son was dying in Capernaum. This Gentile royal official—perhaps one of Herod's men—begged Jesus to go with him to Capernaum to heal his son.

When the official asked Jesus for a miracle, some people may have said to themselves, "All right! Now we'll get to see Jesus in action."

The Samaritans at Sychar had believed in Jesus because of his words and because of the testimony of the woman at the well. They did not demand a miraculous sign from Jesus. But in Galilee things were different. The Jews there did not welcome Jesus apart from his miracles. Jesus' comment is pointed at the Galileans—"Unless you people see miraculous signs and wonders, you will never believe."

Faith in Jesus' Word

The royal official again asked Jesus to come to his home to heal his son. Jesus replied, "You may go. Your son will live."

The Healing of the Ruler's Son by James J. Tissot, 1836–1902.

How could Jesus know the condition of the boy at that moment? The royal official didn't ask; he just "took Jesus at his word and departed." He had faith in Jesus. His faith, like the faith of the Samaritans, was based on Christ's word.

And his faith was proven right. When he was on his way home to Capernaum, his servants met him on the road with great news. His son was better! The official had shown faith in Jesus, but now he believed in Jesus as God's Son. He and his whole household believed.

The first miracle in Cana resulted in the growth of faith in Jesus' disciples. The second miracle in Cana caused faith among the Gentiles to grow.

1 - - - - → The Word Made Flesh

Bible Reference: John 1:1–5, 10–14

The Active Word

John calls Jesus something strange: the "Word." What does that name mean? Our words tell others about us and reveal who we are and what we want. Jesus is God's Word. He shows us who God is.

John used the Greek word *logos* to describe Jesus. To Greeks this word meant "the spoken word." *Logos* also was used to describe the divine mind.

$$\lambda\acute{o}\gamma o\varsigma$$

The word had another meaning for Jews; they used it to refer to God's active involvement in the world.

John says that both the Greek and Jewish meanings can be used for Christ. He is the spoken Word of God the Father, and he came to the world to save it by his actions.

The Divine Campout

John 1:14 is one of the most famous texts in the Bible. The Greek verb in this verse means "to pitch a tent, to camp." If we translated this verse literally, it would read, "The Word became flesh and camped out among us."

When we camp, we're out of our element. Our familiar home habits, the things we do at home without thinking, often don't work when we're camping. We have to stop and think about how to make coffee or cook an egg or wash our hair.

Camping has a real element of inconvenience. But there's something lovely about camping too. Waking up to the songs of the birds, seeing a blazing sunset, watching the moonlight shimmering on the water—these experiences make it all worthwhile.

Jesus' time on earth was like a camping trip. The Word was made flesh and camped out among us. Jesus was out of his element. He was inconvenienced in many ways, but there was a loveliness about it that made it all worthwhile, because the purpose of this divine camping trip was none other than salvation.

The Word of God appeared in a form quite unexpected. The eternal Son of God lived in a tent of human flesh, camped out on earth like an ordinary person. Who would have guessed it?

For those who received Jesus—for those who recognized the purpose behind this curious, divine campout—God sent his Spirit to set up camp directly in their hearts, giving them the right to be called "the children of God."

—Scott Hoezee, *When Advent Doesn't Feel Like Christmas*

2 ━ ━ ━ ━ ━ ➤ The Son of God?

Bible Reference: Selected passages from the Book of Mark

The World of Mark's Gospel

Mark wrote his Gospel for Christians in Rome. Half of Rome had burned, and a rumor was circulating that the Emperor Nero himself had ordered that the fire be set. To squash those rumors, Nero blamed the Christians.

Now the Christians were scattered and afraid. They were suffering severe persecution. What would happen to them? Why didn't Jesus return in

The burning of Rome during the reign of Nero.

power? Was it a mistake to believe in him? Was he really the Son of God?

The Central Question

Mark is what is called an "omniscient narrator." He is not a character in the stories himself; he stands above the events he describes and tells the reader things that the stories' characters don't know.

Mark took separate stories, sayings, and teachings of Jesus and combined them into one main story or narrative. He organized his story to answer this question: Who was Jesus Christ?

Right away Mark introduces the main character of his story and tells his readers who Jesus is: "The beginning of the gospel about Jesus Christ, the Son of God" (Mark 1:1). Notice how Mark's words echo the opening sentence of Genesis: "In the beginning God created the heavens and the earth." Mark is telling his readers about a new start, a new point in history.

Then Mark describes scenes that show that Jesus is the only Son of God. Jesus' coming has ushered in a new era. The kingdom of God has come. Would those who heard Jesus preach welcome him and recognize him as the Messiah, as God's Son? Would they repent and believe?

Looking at Jesus through Mark's eyes, the Roman Christians read (or heard) how Jesus was misunderstood and falsely accused and how he suffered and died at the hands of Jewish and Roman leaders. Mark's portrait of Jesus encouraged the Christians in Rome.

3 — — — — — ➡ A New Teaching

Bible Reference: Mark 1:21–45

Jesus' Amazing Authority

Jesus and his followers went to Capernaum, a city on the northwest shore of the Sea of Galilee. On the Sabbath they went to the synagogue.

A typical Sabbath day service in Jesus' day consisted of prayer, readings

The interior ruins of a synagogue at Capernaum.

from the law and the prophets, and an explanation of the readings. The teachers of the law were the authority in the synagogue. They quoted well-known rabbis when they explained the Scripture readings. But Jesus taught in a totally different way. He did not quote human authorities.

Mark begins the story by showing Jesus as a teacher. The people who heard his teaching were amazed. A man possessed by a demon called out to Jesus, who cast out the demon simply by speaking to it. His words packed such a punch that demons had to obey him. Surely his teachings must have packed the same punch!

The people who heard Jesus' teaching and saw the miracle were amazed; they sensed something great about Jesus. They recognized his authority. But they only asked, "What is this? A new teaching—and with authority!" They were unable to identify Jesus. They didn't see that he had authority in teaching and healing because he was God's Son.

Touching the Unclean

People with leprosy were social outcasts. They were forced to live in isolation, away from healthy people. When they walked in public places, they had to warn others of their approach by shouting, "Unclean!" (Leviticus 13:45–46). Although this early warning system was meant in part to protect others from getting leprosy, it had another purpose as well. Touching anyone with leprosy violated the law of Moses. Anyone who touched a person with leprosy was ceremonially unclean (impure according to the law of Moses).

Jesus showed his acceptance of the leper's faith by touching him and healing him. In order to be allowed back into the community, the man had to prove to a priest that he was healed and bring the offering ordered in Moses' law. But Jesus gave the man an additional reason to show himself to the priest: he was to be a testimony.

Finding God in Unexpected Places

Sadan lives in India. He has leprosy. His past is littered with rejection: classmates mocked him, a bus driver kicked him off the bus, employers ignored his talent and training and refused to hire him, and hospitals turned him away.

"When I got to Velore, I spent the night on the Brands' verandah, because I had nowhere else to go," said Sadan. "I can still remember when Dr. Brand took my infected, ulcerated feet in his hands. I had seen many doctors. A few had examined my hands and feet from a distance, but Dr. Brand and his wife were the first medical workers who dared to touch me. I had nearly forgotten what human touch felt like."

Dr. Brand and his wife, an ophthalmologist, performed many procedures on Sadan, including toe amputations. But despite his painful past, Sadan said, "I must say that I am now happy that I had this disease. . . . Apart from leprosy, I would have been a normal man with a normal family, chasing wealth and a higher position in society. I would never have known such wonderful people as Dr. Paul and Dr. Margaret, and I would never have known the God who lives in them."

—Philip Yancey, *Finding God in Unexpected Places*

4 ━ ━ ━ ━ ➤ On a Collision Course

Bible Reference: Mark 2–3:6

Rabbi Jesus was the biggest news to hit Palestine in hundreds of years! The people were excited about this new teacher and miracle worker. His great power and authority drew the people irresistibly to him. But this same power and authority got Jesus into trouble with the Jewish leaders. They were offended. "Who does he think he is?" they said. The following five stories show us how these leaders reacted to Jesus' ministry.

Healing the Paralytic

Jesus probably stayed at Peter's house while he was in Capernaum. The people were so excited to have Jesus back that they crowded in to hear him preach. The place was packed—standing room only!

The Palsied Man Let Down through the Roof by James J. Tissot, 1836–1902.

Some men brought their paralyzed friend so they could ask Jesus to heal him. They dug through the roof to lower their friend close to the famous miracle worker. Jesus knew that the man needed physical healing, but he saw that the man had a deeper need for spiritual healing. So Jesus said to the man, "Your sins are forgiven."

The Pharisees gasped at Jesus' statement. By saying he could forgive sins, Jesus was claiming to be God. This was blasphemy. They didn't believe that even the messiah they were waiting for would make such a claim!

Eating with Tax Collectors and Sinners

The Jewish people hated paying taxes to the pagan emperor because it constantly reminded them of their humiliating position as subjects of Rome. Some tax collectors in Jesus' day were dishonest, and Jews who were tax collectors were viewed as traitors. Levi was one of those Jewish tax collectors.

But Jesus shocked the Pharisees by eating with tax collectors and other "sinners." The word *sinners* has a special meaning here. It doesn't refer to those who broke the Ten Commandments. It applies to those who didn't follow the rules and regulations that the Pharisees had set up next to the whole law of Moses (the first five books of the Bible). In order to perfectly keep the law, the Pharisees had applied it to every detail of daily life. The Pharisees snubbed those who didn't know or keep all their rules, and they labeled these people sinners.

The Pharisees couldn't tolerate Jesus going around in such bad company. They knew how good people should behave. The Pharisees' very name meant "be separate." Jesus didn't live up to their high standards, and they let Jesus' disciples know exactly how they felt.

Defending the Disciples

John the Baptist's disciples fasted, and the Pharisees fasted twice a week. Everyone fasted—except Jesus and his disciples!

Jesus didn't answer the Pharisees directly. He simply compared himself and his disciples to a bridegroom and his guests at a wedding feast. How could they fast and be sad at such a time?

Jesus then used two more images for his questioners to think about: sewing new, unshrunk cloth onto an old garment and pouring new wine into old wineskins.

Jesus was telling the Pharisees that the old rules didn't apply anymore. His coming brought something totally new to the world scene—something so new and different that it would break the old containers, the old ways of thinking.

Breaking the Sabbath?

One Sabbath as they were walking through a field Jesus' disciples picked some heads of grain and rubbed them between their hands to separate the

Wheat field in Cappadocia.

outer shell from what was edible. Picking grain from a field like this was allowable according to the law of Moses (Deuteronomy 23:25). The Pharisees, who were always watching, were quick to criticize. The disciples had broken one of the rules they had added to the law—no harvesting on the Sabbath.

The Pharisees' attention to the law's interpretation instead of to its inner meaning is called legalism. Jesus didn't argue with their rule. Instead he reminded them of how David, a godly man, had done something forbidden. Jesus claimed that God had given the Sabbath as a day of restoration, not restriction. Then Jesus made another claim that must have shocked the Pharisees even more than his behavior. He claimed to be Lord of the Sabbath!

Healing on the Sabbath

Jesus also broke the Pharisees' Sabbath law by healing the man with the shriveled hand. The Pharisees believed that on the Sabbath only a person whose life was in danger could be helped.

Sometimes we think of Jesus as gentle and mild. But in this story Jesus was anything but meek. He was angry with the Pharisees, and he did something that made the Pharisees so furious that they wanted to kill him.

5 ━ ━ ━ ━ ━ ➤ Growing Popularity and Opposition

Bible Reference: Mark 3:7–34

Crowds by the Lake

Jesus went to the lakeside again. Mark tells us that a large crowd of people came to see him. These people came from Galilee, Judea, and the city of Jerusalem, but they also came from non-Jewish territories of Idumea and Transjordan and the cities of Tyre and Sidon.

By telling us where all these people came from, Mark illustrates Jesus' growing popularity. The broad range of people also hints at the fact that Jesus' mission is to all people.

Looking north across the Sea of Galilee.

As the crowds by the lake pressed Jesus for miracles and healing, only the evil spirits recognized who Jesus was. Jesus ordered them to be silent because it was not time for his identity to be revealed. Besides, evil spirits were hardly the proper ones to announce such important news!

The Twelve

We know very little about the 12 disciples. Mark's list hints that the members of this group were very different from one another. For example,

Simon was a Zealot. Do you recall who the Zealots were? They were a Jewish faction that believed in armed rebellion against the Roman occupation. Matthew was a former tax collector who had worked for the Romans. At first Simon and Matthew may have found it very difficult to work together or even to spend time together.

This story, like the one of the crowd by the lake, shows that Jesus draws in people from many places and backgrounds.

Two Wrong Ideas

Next Mark tells two stories: the story of how Jesus' family misunderstood him and the story of how Jesus' enemies falsely labeled him.

The teachers of the law came all the way from Jerusalem to falsely accuse Jesus. But they weren't the only ones blind to Jesus' true identity; Jesus' own family thought he was on the verge of a mental breakdown! They had probably walked about 30 miles from Nazareth to Capernaum to find Jesus and bring him home.

Then Jesus explained something about the kingdom of God, about the new era that he brought. The family of God, he said, is made up of those who obey God. Jesus' actions showed that membership in God's family is more important than membership in a human family.

6 ━ ━ ━ ━ ➤ Teaching in Parables

Bible Reference: Mark 4:1–34

People like stories. Somehow a story has the power to capture attention. People are hooked before they know it.

That's why Jesus told stories to teach about the kingdom of God. These stories were called parables. Telling parables was Jesus' favorite way of teaching the people; according to Mark, this was the only teaching method Jesus used.

Jesus' stories were about familiar things, things like farming and fishing and cooking. He used the familiar to teach about the unfamiliar, about what the kingdom of God was like. And his stories often had unexpected twists or surprise endings so his listeners went away puzzling over their meaning.

A Parable Is Not . . .

A parable is not an example. During a sermon your pastor may use one or more examples to illustrate a point. But parables are more than that. Even if your pastor includes no examples, you'll still have a sermon to listen to. But a parable is a sermon—a very short sermon—all by itself.

A parable is also not a story told in a kind of secret code so a person who figures out the code can interpret each detail. Even Bible scholars cannot agree on only one meaning for any of the parables.

A Parable Is . . .

A parable is a story that equates a scene from our familiar, everyday world with the kingdom of God: "The kingdom of God is like . . ." It says, in other words, that a situation from daily life is like one part of the kingdom of God.

The whole parable describes the kingdom of God. For example, in Mark 4:30–32 Jesus didn't just tell the people that the kingdom of God was like a mustard seed. Instead, he told them that the kingdom of God was like a mustard seed that was planted and grew to be a huge tree that shelters all kinds of birds. So it's the whole parable, the whole story, that was Jesus' point.

Jesus' parables come in all shapes and sizes. The shortest are sayings, almost like proverbs. They're called parable sayings. We read this parable saying in Mark 2:21: "No one sews a patch of unshrunk cloth on an old gar-

The Return of the Prodigal Son by Bartolomé Esteban Murillo, 1617–1682.

ment. If he does, the new piece will pull away from the old, making the tear worse." The longest parables are stories that are about more than one character and contain more than one scene, like the parable of the prodigal son.

7 - - - - - - ➤ Why So Afraid?

Bible Reference: Mark 4:35—5:43

In this section of his Gospel, Mark sketches Jesus quickly moving from one dramatic situation to the next. The boat he's in is almost swamped in a storm, he meets up with a tormented man with almost superhuman strength, he heals a woman in a crowd, and he goes to a home where a young girl has just died. And in each story the question, sometimes spoken and sometimes not, hangs in the air: Who is this?

Rebuking the Wind and Talking to the Waves

The Sea of Galilee, the setting of this story, is a freshwater inland lake. It's known for the storms that can come up and blow across it without warning.

Jesus was in the boat's seat of honor when a storm unleashed its fury.

Jesus was also asleep, his human body exhausted from the many demands of his work. The disciples woke Jesus and accused him of not caring whether or not they drowned. They didn't seem to realize how much he cared for their welfare—that he had come to die for their salvation.

When Jesus silenced the storm, the trembling disciples asked who exactly Jesus could be. They didn't comprehend that this miracle proved that Jesus was Lord of creation.

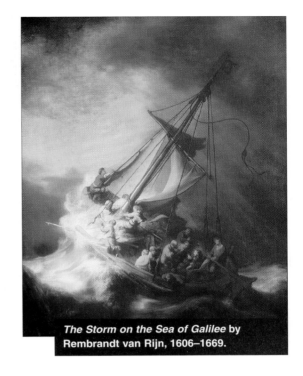

The Storm on the Sea of Galilee by Rembrandt van Rijn, 1606–1669.

Exorcising Demons

Jesus, who rules over nature, also has power over the supernatural. Mark has already recorded several of Jesus' healings of people taken over by evil spirits or demons. The teachers of the law figured that Jesus was one of them—that's why he had power. They didn't want to admit that he could be of God. Now Mark tells us about another exorcism—the act of driving out an evil spirit.

Nowadays many people don't believe that Satan or the devil really exists. These Bible stories, they say, only tell us how people long ago regarded those who were mentally ill. They didn't understand mental illness, so they called it demon possession.

Jesus had gone to war with Satan in the wilderness. His encounter with the demons was another battle scene. The demon screamed at Jesus to mind his own business. He even called on God's name for protection. Then, realizing that he would surely lose this battle, he begged Jesus not to send him away. The way the demons destroyed the pigs shows something about the demons' influence and purpose. But even a legion of evil spirits could not resist Jesus' authority.

A Man Called Legion

A dark, stormy night; a hillside graveyard; a bloody madman dragging chains and stalking about with supernatural strength—this sounds like a Hollywood horror film, but it's Jesus' encounter with a man who called himself Legion. A Roman legion was made up of 4,000–6,000 soldiers. Palestine was occupied by such Roman legions, which could be guilty

Legion's view of the town of Kursi.

of unspeakable, bloody deeds. Legion also terrorized the townspeople. Jesus, however, dramatically changed the man. What he did for him had special effects, but it was no Hollywood stunt; it was an act of love and grace.

Bothering the Teacher?

Jesus crossed over to the western side of the lake again, and a crowd immediately surrounded him. An important community leader, a ruler of the synagogue, rushed forward. Ignoring his own status and dignity, ignoring the disagreements between Jesus and the other religious leaders, Jairus pleaded for Jesus' help.

One person in the jostling crowd reached out to touch Jesus on purpose. A woman reached out to him with hope of being healed. She had no money because she'd spent all she had on doctors. Other people shunned her because according to Moses' law she was ceremonially unclean. Anyone who touched her or anything she had touched became unclean. This woman had been miserable and isolated for 12 years. She hardly dared show her face in public, but she trusted Jesus' power to make her well.

When she confessed that she was healed, Jesus told her to go in peace, in Shalom, in oneness with God and neighbor. Jesus healed her both physically and spiritually.

Meanwhile, Jairus' daughter seemed to have lost her chance to be healed. Men came from Jairus' home where they were mourning the young girl's death. According to custom, paid mourners were wailing. The grieving family would be expected to tear their clothes. Every act of mourning pointed to the finality of death. So it is no surprise that the messengers told Jairus not to bother Jesus. No wonder they laughed at Jesus when he told them that the girl was only sleeping.

The great news of this story, however, is that Jesus has power over death. He gave life back to Jairus' daughter as he would later win back eternal life for all who believe.

8 ▬ ➤ Rejection and Misunderstanding

> **Bible Reference: Mark 6**

An Evening to Remember

Act 1

Narrator 1: Jesus sent out the Twelve to go from village to village on a preaching and healing mission. When they came back to meet with Jesus again, they were excited and eager to tell everything that had happened.

James (elbowing the other disciples out of the way): Me first! Me first! Teacher, it was fantastic! It was just as you said it would be. In one town I drove out 10 demons, all by myself!

John (louder than James): My brother here is right, but I healed 16 people in that very same village.

Thomas: I doubt that you could have done as much as we did. Everywhere we went the people just crowded around, begging to hear more about your way, Jesus.

Andrew: Speaking of crowds, look at that mob coming now! How did they know we were here? I can't handle any more needy people right now.

Jesus: Come with me. We'll find a quiet place to take a break so you can get some rest.

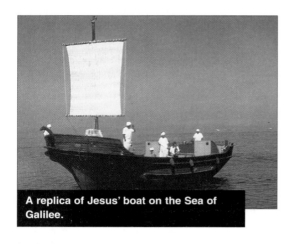

A replica of Jesus' boat on the Sea of Galilee.

Narrator 2: Jesus and his disciples got in a boat, planning to find a little peace and quiet. But they were too late. People had already seen them. While the disciples rowed, the crowd ran along the shore, reaching the landing spot ahead of the boat.

Philip: They beat us here. Now we'll never get away from them!

Peter: Don't worry, Teacher; I'll get rid of them.

Jesus: No, Peter, it's okay. Just look at them; they're like sheep without a shepherd. I love these people. I'll talk to them.

Narrator 3: So Jesus got out of the boat and taught the people until it was late in the day.

John: Teacher, this has gone on long enough. We need to send these people on their way so they can get to the village and pick up some supper on their way home.

Jesus: You give them something to eat.

Philip: What! That would cost . . . um . . . eight months of paychecks!

Matthew: By my calculations, Master, he's right. About 5,000 people are here. If you figure that the average person eats about two and a half rolls and three strips of smoked fish, and if you multiply that by the cost in denari, divide the sum by the number of work days, figuring we could earn a denari a day and factoring in days off for the holidays, of course . . . yup, eight months' wages might buy just about one bite per person. Do you really expect us to spend a fortune feeding these folks supper?

Jesus: How many loaves do you have? Go and see.

Narrator 4: The disciples quickly searched through their packs. They found a bent fish hook, Philip's crumpled sermon notes from last week, a sock that James had hidden from John, five small rolls left from yesterday's lunch, and two sardines. They shrugged their shoulders and gave Jesus the bread and the fish.

Narrator 5: Then Jesus gave the people directions. He had them all sit down in groups of hundreds and fifties, just as the Israelites had sat in camp in the desert where God fed them with the miraculous manna.

Narrator 6: Then Jesus held up the five loaves and two fishes for everyone to see. He looked up to heaven and gave thanks for the food they were about to eat.

The Feeding of the Five Thousand by Gian Paolo Cavagna, 1556–1627.

Narrator 7: Jesus broke pieces from the loaves and fishes and gave them to the disciples. The disciples brought the food to the people. And they all ate until their stomachs were full.

Narrator 8: Then the disciples gathered all the leftovers up so they wouldn't be wasted. When they were done, they had 12 baskets of bread and fish. Jesus made his disciples get into the boat and go ahead of him while he sent the crowd home.

Act 2

Narrator 9: By the time Jesus had said goodbye to everyone, it was late. The sun had set a long time ago, but the full moon was bright. Jesus had been under a lot of pressure. He wasn't ready to sleep, so he climbed up the mountainside a little way to be alone and pray.

Narrator 10: It was after three o'clock that morning when Jesus looked up from his prayers and saw what was happening on the lake. He could just make out the disciples' boat, and it looked like it was in trouble.

Bartholomew (shouting): This wind is horrible! We'll never make it!

Andrew: We're not making any headway. Pull harder!

James: Keep on rowing! Work together now! Pull! Pull! Pull!

John: Look . . . a . . . a . . . a ghost!

All the disciples: Help! Save us! A ghost!

Jesus: Take courage. It is I. Don't be afraid.

Narrator 11: Jesus said, "It is I." In Greek those words mean something more like "I am," the same words that God used to identify himself to Moses in the Old Testament. The I AM who saved Israel had come again to save his people. But in the wind and the waves, the disciples must have missed the meaning.

Narrator 12: Jesus said, "It is I." Then he climbed into the boat with the disciples, and right away the wind stopped. The night air was silent. The disciples did not know what to say. They hadn't understood about the supper, and they certainly didn't understand what was going on now. So they got busy, going through the motions of landing the boat and anchoring it.

9 ➞ Where Does Evil Come From?

Bible Reference: Mark 7:1–23

Whistle blowers are unpopular. Bucking the system is tough. Once a system is in place with people to enforce it, it's hard to change it or to convince people it's wrong.

Jesus faced the religious system of the Pharisees and teachers of the law, which had developed over a long period of time. How could a Galilean carpenter who hung out with fishermen, tax collectors, and other ordinary people dare to challenge it? Religious leaders had quizzed him before; they had labeled his healing power as being from the "other side," from Satan.

But Jesus was more popular than ever with the people, so a committee came from Jerusalem to investigate him again.

Jesus' Accusation

Jesus fired back at these dignified leaders with a blast that must have left them shaking with anger. He accused them of hypocrisy.

Jesus followed up his accusation with an example of what he was talking about. Corban was an offering made to God. In the tradition of the elders, a person could set something apart (a piece of property or perhaps a sum of money) by calling it Corban, by dedicating it to God. The person didn't have to actually give it to God, only set it aside for him. Jesus showed how the teachers of the law and the Pharisees were sticklers about enforcing the Corban law even if that meant Moses' written law was broken.

The example Jesus gave may have been a common situation. A man whose parents depended on him for help became tired of supporting them. To dodge his responsibility, he made a large part of his belongings Corban. In this way, he put his wealth out of his parents' reach. But later he was sorry that he had treated his parents badly and wanted to break his vow. He asked the teachers of the law if he could undo the Corban. They said, "Absolutely not. It's too bad about your parents, but the property is God's now."

Evil's Source

Jesus followed up his argument with the teachers of the law and the Pharisees by teaching the people that obeying rules and regulations (legalism) is not the answer to evil and sin. He zeroed in on the real source of evil—a person's heart. Getting new hearts by believing in Jesus is the only solution.

10 ▬ ▬ ▬ ➤ Faith in Unlikely Places

Bible Reference: Mark 7:24—8:26

A Syrophoenician woman, a man from the Decapolis (10 cities area), and another large crowd of hungry people. What do these people have in common? They're all non-Jews, so their stories have special meaning for those of us who are also non-Jews.

Crumbs for Dogs

Until now Jesus had limited his teaching and miracles to God's chosen people. But while Jesus was staying in the Gentile town of Tyre, a non-Jewish woman came begging him to heal her demon-possessed daughter.

Jesus knew that God's Old Testament covenant had been only with the Jews, but he also knew that God's plan had always been that all nations (including Gentiles) would be blessed through the Jews.

Jesus' answer to the Syrophoenician woman seems harsh to us. It's hard to understand exactly why Jesus spoke to her as he did. Notice that he didn't say that there wouldn't be scraps for the dogs; he merely stated that the children must be fed first. He was clearly testing her.

And he was not disappointed. She responded right away. She caught him in his own words, and because of her reply, Jesus healed her daughter.

U. N. Nepalese soldiers stand at the spot once called "Ladder of Tyre." This location provided a natural border between Palestine and Phoenicia.

Going to the Dogs

In Jesus' day people didn't have knives, forks, or napkins at the table. They ate with their hands, and then they wiped their hands on chunks of bread, which they threw to the house dogs.

When Jesus told the woman that the children needed to eat first, she replied, "I know the children are fed first, but can't I even get the scraps the children throw away?" Here was a faith that wouldn't take no for an answer. Her faith was tested, her faith was real, and her prayer was answered.

—William Barclay, *Daily Study Bible Series*

The Deaf and Mute Man Hears and Speaks

You may wonder why Jesus put his fingers into the man's ears and touched his tongue with spit. Jesus certainly didn't even need to be near someone to be able to heal him. Perhaps Jesus used these actions out of kindness.

Being deaf, the man relied on what he saw to understand what was going on. When Jesus took the man aside and touched his ears and tongue, he may have been letting the man know by his actions what he was about to do. Then Jesus looked up to heaven in a gesture that showed where his power came from.

Four Thousand Eat Bread

This story is similar to the feeding of the 5,000. The number of people, loaves, and baskets of leftovers match in these stories. But below the surface there's a big difference.

The crowd of 5,000 was made up primarily of Jews and took place in Jewish territory. This time the miracle took place in non-Jewish territory with a group that included many more Gentiles.

Just as Jesus had said to the Syrophoenician woman, the children (Jews) would eat first. And as she had suspected, plenty of crumbs were left for the "dogs."

Yeast and the Pharisees

When Jesus finally returned to Galilee, the Pharisees were waiting for him. This time they asked Jesus for a sign to prove that he was from God. They wanted hard evidence. But Jesus flatly refused.

Later, Jesus told his disciples that the Pharisees were like yeast. Yeast to the Jews symbolized evil. A tiny amount of yeast will ferment a large bowl of dough. Likewise, a little evil can do a great deal of damage. Jesus was saying that the Pharisees' legalism and skepticism would have an evil influence.

Jesus' remark sailed right past the disciples. They thought he was talking about yeast and bread because they had forgotten to bring bread with them.

Mission to the Gentiles

Mark often shows Jesus following up one of his teachings with actions that illustrate what he had been saying. After telling the Pharisees that nothing outside a man makes him "unclean," Jesus went out to meet (and touch) people who the Jews considered unclean pagans. Jesus left Galilee and went north into the Gentile area of Tyre and Sidon, then on to the Decapolis and to Bethsaida. Jesus' trip into outcast territories demonstrates that all are welcome into his kingdom through faith, not by rituals or family background.

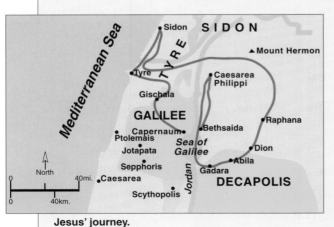

Jesus' journey.

"Be strong, do not fear;
your God will come,
    he will come with vengeance;
with divine retribution
    he will come to save you."
Then will the eyes of the blind be opened
    and the ears of the deaf unstopped.
Then will the lame leap like a deer,
    and the mute tongue shout for joy.

                              Isaiah 35:4–6a

Giving Sight

Mark ends this section of his Gospel by telling about another healing. This time Jesus restored a man's eyesight.

Mark wants to tell us about how Jesus healed the people, but he's also using these stories to point us to a deeper truth. These stories are meant to open the eyes and ears of Mark's readers—and us—to who Jesus really is. That's what Mark's Gospel is all about: being able to hear, see, and understand who Jesus truly is.

11 – – – – ➤ You Are the Christ

Bible Reference: Mark 8:27—9:1

We're at the halfway point of Mark's Gospel. Mark doesn't spend much time explaining Jesus—no family tree, nothing about Jesus' birth or childhood, and few of Jesus' teachings. Mark has been sketching a Jesus on the move. He pictures Jesus quickly doing miracles—one after the other—like someone setting off a fireworks display. And each new burst of light brings amazement. What is this? Who is this?

Now, in the very center of his account about Jesus, Mark brings us to a high point in the story. He shows us clearly where the story is leading.

Answering the Jesus Question

Jesus and his disciples left Galilee and went north to Caesarea Philippi, a city a short distance south of Mount Hermon. Here Jesus himself raised the question of his identity: "Who do people say I am?" The disciples told Jesus what the common rumors were: John the Baptist, Elijah, one of the prophets.

Part of Caesarea Philippi with a view of Mount Hermon in the background.

Then Jesus asked his disciples, "Who do you say I am?" Peter answered for all of the disciples, "You are the Christ."

Christ is the Greek word for messiah. The disciples have finally identified Jesus as the one for whom God's people have waited for centuries. They now know that Jesus is the one who will establish God's kingdom.

The Secret of the Messiah

The disciples' ideas about the messiah were no different from the ideas of most Jews at that time. Jesus, the Christ, would use his awesome power to drive out the legions of Roman soldiers and set up a government of his own. Imagine how rosy the future looked to the disciples!

But Jesus quickly and plainly told them the hard and unpleasant truth: he was going to suffer and be killed.

Even though the disciples' eyes had finally been opened to who Jesus was, they still totally misunderstood his mission.

Jesus was indeed the Messiah, but he was a messiah totally unlike the one the Jews had in mind. This messiah was not coming as a king. This messiah was going to suffer and be rejected.

The Cost of Discipleship

Jesus had more hard truth for the disciples. Being a disciple of Jesus was turning out to be tough. And Jesus' picture of the future didn't fit the disciples' fantasies. Jesus' disciples would be called to follow him—even to the cross.

The Way of the Cross

In the first half of his Gospel, Mark has been leading up to two announcements: Jesus is the Christ, and Jesus must suffer and die. All that happens from this point in Mark follows from these announcements. The conversation between Jesus and his disciples at Caesarea Philippi shows where the action is leading and why. From here on, Jesus the Christ walks the way of the cross.

But this passage of Mark also clearly announces that Jesus' death will not be the end of the story. Jesus says that he will rise and return again in glory.

12 - - - - - → Metamorphosis

Bible Reference: Mark 9:2–13

A frog and a butterfly seem to have little in common: one is earthbound and slippery, with bulging eyes; the other is airborne and elegant, with delicate wings and wafting antennae. But both have arrived where they are by the same process: metamorphosis. The frog was once a tadpole, and the butterfly was once a caterpillar.

Transfiguration

On the mountaintop Jesus' form changed dramatically. His clothes became dazzling white. He appeared before the disciples in all the glory of the Son of God. The disciples had a glimpse of Jesus as he will appear at his second coming.

Transfiguration **by Sandro Botticelli, 1444–1510.**

Elijah and Moses also appeared on the mountain. Why did these two come to speak to Jesus? Moses was the great law-giver, and Elijah was one of the greatest prophets of the Old Testament. Jesus was the fulfillment of the law and the prophets.

Suddenly a cloud surrounded them on the mountain, and a voice spoke. Earlier, at Jesus' baptism, the voice spoke to Jesus. This time the voice spoke to the three disciples, telling them, "This is my Son, whom I love."

The experience on the mountain must have convinced the three disciples that Jesus was indeed the Christ, the Messiah. But they still weren't able to understand that Jesus must suffer, die, and rise. As they were walking down the mountain, they asked Jesus about one of the things that puzzled them. The teachers of the law said that Elijah would come before the messiah. If Jesus was the Messiah, why hadn't Elijah come yet?

Jesus explained that "Elijah" had come—that is, John the Baptist, who had been beheaded.

13 — — — — ➤ Who Is the Greatest?

> **Bible Reference: Mark 9:14–50**

From Bad to Worse

Did you ever notice how people block out what they don't want to hear? "Oh, did you ask me to wash the car? I didn't hear you." "Was I supposed to be home at ten? I didn't hear you say that."

The disciples were good at blocking out the unpleasant, too. They blocked out Jesus' plain words about his coming death. They didn't want to hear it, because they were the Messiah's handpicked inner circle and thought they were headed for powerful positions.

In the next section of his Gospel, Mark describes the disciples' misguided ideas. Jesus came down from the mountaintop transfiguration experience to find his disciples sinking to new lows. Jesus tried to teach them with patient explanations and easy object lessons.

He didn't let them off the hook. He told them that they would be judged for leading others astray. Jesus' dark warnings were meant to shake up the disciples. They were thinking of themselves as part of the privileged few. Jesus told them, "If you block out my words and keep others from coming to me, you won't enter the kingdom of God. Take what I say seriously."

Notice, too, that Jesus once again told the disciples that he would be killed and would rise again in three days. The disciples were so baffled by the idea that Jesus would be sacrificed that they couldn't even find the nerve to ask what he meant.

Faith in Action

Framed by all the disciples' failures is a story about a man who wanted his son to be healed of an evil spirit. This father's faith sharply contrasts with the disciples' attitude.

The excited father cried to Jesus, "I believe; help me overcome my unbelief." These are the words of one who is leaping onto a moving train and is partly aboard. He is desperately asking for someone on the train to help him up. Jesus didn't hesitate to reach out in concern and mercy.

14 – – ➔ On the Way to Jerusalem

Bible Reference: Mark 10:13–52

The Jordan River south of the Sea of Galilee.

It was almost time for the annual Passover celebration, time for Jesus to go to Jerusalem and face his suffering and death. Jesus set out with the Twelve on their last journey together. Heading south from Capernaum into Judea, they walked along Jordan's right bank as they approached Jerusalem, probably joining the crowd of pilgrims going south on their annual Passover journey. The events of this lesson all took place on the way.

Entering the Kingdom

Jesus preached that the kingdom of God was near, and his parables taught what that kingdom was like. Mark now tells the story of the children and of the rich young man coming to Jesus. This story tells us what kind of people can be citizens of Jesus' kingdom.

Jewish mothers brought their children to be blessed by this great rabbi. While the disciples tried to shoo them away, thinking that Jesus was too important to be bothered, Jesus knew that his impending sacrifice was also for these small people. So he bounced them on his knee, smiled, and then used them to make an important point. Jesus said that anyone who does not receive the kingdom like a child will not enter it.

Then a rich young man asked Jesus how he could earn his way to eternal life. He expected that since he had always kept the law, he was already on the road to salvation. But he was not ready for Jesus' instructions to give away all his wealth and follow him. A Jewish man's first duty was to take care of his family's inheritance and stay near his family to care for them. Jesus' demands seemed unreasonable to him.

Leading the Way

Once more Jesus plainly predicted his death for his disciples. But the disciples still expected Jesus to immediately set up a kingdom here on earth, and they asked him to give them important positions in that kingdom.

Jesus asked them if they could drink from the cup he would drink from or if they could be baptized as he was. Jesus wasn't speaking about a real drinking glass or his own baptism. The cup and the baptism were metaphors. Jesus was asking his disciples if they were ready to suffer as he would.

Shouting for Mercy

The city of Jericho near the Jordan River was the last stopping place for pilgrims going to Jerusalem for Passover. Jericho was 825 feet below sea level, and Jerusalem was on a mountain 2,500 feet above sea level, so the rest of the trip would be

Jericho.

uphill. The pilgrims would sing songs as they climbed up to the Holy City.

Over all the noise and busy traffic of the pilgrims, Bartimaeus raised his voice. He desperately needed Jesus' help, and when he heard that Jesus was coming, he shouted as loudly as he could for Jesus to have mercy on him.

The rich young man was unable to give up his riches. The disciples were unable to understand Jesus' mission and to stop quibbling about positions of power. But Bartimaeus is the bright spot in this chapter. He expressed his need for Jesus. When Jesus called him and cured him, he followed without hesitating or asking for more.

Unit 4
The Suffering and the Sacrifice

1 ━ ━ ━ ━ ━ ➤ Passover Parade

Bible Reference: Mark 11:1–25

The King Enters

Jerusalem was celebrating. Jewish pilgrims from throughout the world were converging on the city to celebrate Passover, and tent cities were springing up on the surrounding hillsides. Even Pontius Pilate, the Roman governor of Judea, had left his official home in Caesarea to travel the crowded roads to the city.

Jesus was among the pilgrims walking the road that climbed to the Mount of Olives, just east of Jerusalem. In the crowd were many followers of Jesus: Galileans who had heard his parables by the Sea of Galilee, pilgrims who had seen his healing of blind Bartimaeus at Jericho, and perhaps some who had witnessed the raising of Lazarus from the dead. When they reached the little town of Bethphage, two of Jesus' disciples appeared with a donkey's colt with their cloaks thrown over it. Jesus was seated on the colt to ride it into Jerusalem like a king—the King of Israel! The crowd surged with excitement. They recalled a prophecy of Zechariah hundreds of years earlier that said the messiah would enter Jerusalem in such a way.

Shouting and praising Jesus, the crowd reached the top of the Mount of Olives and looked across the Kidron Valley to the city of Jerusalem with its shining gold and white temple. The

Christ's Entrance into Jerusalem by Bernhard Plockhorst, 1825–1907.

procession moved down the Mount of Olives toward the gates of Jerusalem. Some people ran ahead and laid their cloaks on the road, a sign of allegiance to a great king; others ran to cut branches and waved them in celebration. Could Jesus be the messiah who would establish a free and independent Israel? Would he be ready to do it now?

The Temple Mess

If the people expected Jesus to immediately proclaim himself king when the procession arrived in Jerusalem, they were disappointed. Jesus looked around the temple and the city and then returned that same evening to Bethany. After all the excitement, there was no crown, no attempt to overthrow the Romans.

On the Monday after his triumphal entry into the city Jesus returned to the temple. The temple area covered a large part of Jerusalem. The temple complex contained several courtyards. (See the diagram and Herod's temple in Unit 2, Lesson 6.) The courtyard closest to the temple's entrance was for Jewish men; the one beyond that was for Jewish women. A large open courtyard surrounding the entire temple was reserved for Gentiles who wished to worship Israel's God. Since all Gentiles were ceremonially unclean according to the law of Moses, they couldn't go beyond this courtyard. This courtyard was a place of prayer for the Gentiles; it showed that God wanted all people to worship him.

In Jesus' day, however, this court of the Gentiles had become a kind of marketplace. The high priest and his friends had rented out space in the court of the Gentiles to businessmen who sold sheep and doves for sacrifices and to bankers or moneychangers who exchanged foreign money for the proper coins for temple

The Buyers and Sellers Driven out of the Temple by Gustave Doré.

offerings. Besides, the court of the Gentiles had become a shortcut for merchants entering and leaving Jerusalem. The noise and smell of animals and the bargaining of the bankers made it impossible for the Gentiles to pray. The Jewish religious leaders didn't care that Gentiles no longer had a place where they could worship God. But Jesus cared.

Cursing the Fig Tree

Mark, as we've seen earlier, connects stories with a technique called framing. This time, too, he wants to tie two stories together—the cursing of the fig tree and the cleansing of the temple.

Jesus was not just in a bad mood when he cursed the fig tree; he cursed it because it didn't bear fruit. Jesus' clearing of the temple meant the same thing: the temple was supposed to be a place for all nations. Besides, people were abusing the temple services by acting any way they wanted and taking for granted that sacrifices would make them right with God. Jesus would take the place of the temple.

2 ▬ ▬ ➤ Confrontation in the Temple

Bible Reference: Mark 11:27—12:44

Some might think that after clearing out the temple, Jesus should have laid low for a while in Bethany. Instead, he went right back to the temple, which seems to have amazed the Jewish authorities.

The next section of Mark's Gospel tells how the representatives of the Sanhedrin confronted Jesus in the temple, called him to account, and tried to trip him up with trick questions.

The Sanhedrin was the highest Jewish authority. Among its 70 members were many teachers of the law who were mostly Pharisees, elders (heads of the rich, ruling families—like the rich young man), and Sadducees (mostly priests, including the high priest, who wanted to keep peace in Rome). The entire Sanhedrin wanted to get rid of Jesus.

By What Authority

Jesus' very first sermon and miracle recorded in the Book of Mark had amazed the people with its authority, but the teachers of the law had questioned Jesus' authority to forgive the paralytic's sins and had linked his authority to Beelzebub. Now members of the Sanhedrin were quizzing Jesus about his authority to meddle in temple affairs, to meddle with their authority. They asked, "By what authority are you doing these things?"

Jesus answered with a question of his own about the authority of John the Baptist. The chief priests and teachers of the law were supposed to be the ones who could tell whether a prophet was true or false. Not being able to answer Jesus' question must have embarrassed them.

Rejecting the Owner's Son

Jesus sidestepped the direct question about his authority, answering the question with a parable. In the parable he made clear the source of his power.

To understand the parable you need to know that in Jesus' day a landowner who owned more land than he could work by himself often allowed poor farmers to use some land to grow their crops. In exchange for using the field or vineyard, the farmers gave him some of their crops at harvest time.

The owner in Jesus' parable had done all the hard work of planting a grape vineyard, building a wall around it to keep out wild animals, digging a wine press for making wine from the grapes, and building a watchtower for guards to use in protecting it. The tenant farmers just had to maintain the vineyard, which produced good fruit because of the owner's hard work.

Centuries earlier Isaiah had told a parable in which the vineyard represented the people of Israel (Isaiah 5:1–7). Jesus' listeners would have been familiar with Isaiah's parable, so they knew Jesus' vineyard parable was also about the people of Israel.

Jesus didn't explain the story, but the Jewish leaders recognized that it was about them and their plan to kill him. "Don't forget," Jesus was telling them, "that the vineyard isn't yours. It still belongs to the owner. And he's going to give it to others who are more deserving."

Pay Taxes to Caesar?

The Sanhedrin decided to ask Jesus trick questions in front of the Passover crowds. They had carefully planned questions that couldn't be answered correctly.

The Pharisees hated the Herodians (supporters of King Herod's reign in Galilee), but they hated Jesus even more. So they teamed up with the Herodians and together asked Jesus their loaded question: Is it right to pay taxes to Caesar?

Jesus said, "Give to Caesar what is Caesar's." The coin has his image on it, so it was his. In this way he was also telling the people what they owed to God.

God of the Living

The Sadducees didn't believe in the resurrection, and they accepted only the first five books of Scripture, the Pentateuch. They didn't accept the Pharisees' oral tradition either; in fact, they bitterly opposed the Pharisees. But they joined the effort to discredit Jesus with a question of their own.

The Sadducees thought they had devised a question that made the idea of the resurrection look utterly ridiculous. Jesus answered their question by quoting a part of the Bible they believed in. In effect, he told them that their question was a wrong question.

Not Far from the Kingdom

On the whole the Jewish leaders seem to be a hardened bunch—accusing, attacking, looking for Jesus' weak spot. But Mark's account mentions a teacher of the law open to what Jesus had to say. Mark is an honest writer.

He shows the disciples, those closest to Jesus, fighting for power. And in the middle of this scene in which Jesus' enemies attack him, he shows that at least one of the "enemy" is close to the kingdom.

The Son of Whom?

No one dared ask Jesus more questions. But Jesus had another question of his own about the title "Son of David." This was a popular name for the promised messiah. An Old Testament prophecy said that the messiah would be born from David's line.

Jesus quoted a psalm (110:1) in which David called the messiah his Lord. Jesus' point was this: How can the messiah be David's Son and also be David's Lord? His statement implied that he himself was the messiah, both David's descendant and his Lord.

Be More Like This

Mark shifts our attention away from the Jewish leaders to a scene in the court of the women, where crowds of pilgrims were putting their offerings in the temple treasury.

The Widow's Mite by Gustave Doré.

Jesus called his disciples' attention to a poor widow. She was putting in the collecting box what was probably the smallest offering of the day. But Jesus said that she was giving more than anyone else because she was giving all she had.

3 ------ ➔ Watch Out!

Bible Reference: Mark 13

Knowing When

Every so often we hear a new prediction that the end of the world is near. A leader and a small band of followers gather on a mountain or beach to wait for Jesus to return. We may smile about them, but they can disturb us too. The end of the world is an uncomfortable subject.

Jesus and his disciples had a conversation about the end of the world. It was set off by a remark one of the disciples made as he left the temple: "Look, Teacher! What massive stones! What magnificent buildings!"

The Jerusalem temple was a splendid sight. Its shining white stones were huge, some of them as large as 37 feet long, 12 feet high, and 18 feet wide. (One stone might be as large as your classroom!) Parts of the temple were overlaid with gold.

Jesus answered the remark with a shocking prediction: "'Not one stone here will be left on another; every one will be thrown down.'" Jesus' prediction came true in A.D. 70 when Romans surrounded Jerusalem, starved its people, and destroyed the city to crush a rebellion among the Jewish people. Roman soldiers set fire to the temple. The gold melted into the cracks of the stones, and the greedy soldiers combined their strength to tear down the stones to reach the gold. Jerusalem's terrible destruction was a picture of how bad things would eventually be on earth before Jesus returned at the end of the age.

A model of the Jerusalem temple.

Be on Your Guard

Jesus and his disciples walked to the Mount of Olives; there they sat together overlooking Jerusalem, and Jesus talked with them about the end

Looking east from the Temple Mount at the Mount of Olives and two churches built there.

of the age. Instead of handing out timelines to the disciples, Jesus told them a short parable that emphasized what their attitude should be toward future events.

Jesus told the disciples that only the heavenly Father knows the time this would all take place. Their responsibility was to be careful of their own actions and not spend time in useless speculation.

We may feel somewhat uncomfortable at the thought of Jesus' return. We may not look forward to having our lives pass away for a new order. But we shouldn't spend our time worrying about that. Instead, we should act as the servants in the parable to take care of our assigned tasks. We should concentrate on our daily actions so that we will be ready whenever that day comes.

4 — ➜ Preparations for Jesus' Death

Bible Reference: Mark 14:1–11

Anointing the Messiah

The story of Jesus' life is rapidly drawing to a close. Mark opens this section by saying that the Sanhedrin is ready to move in for the kill—but not during the feast because they don't want any riots.

Then the scene switches to Bethany. It's dinner time at the home of Simon the Leper. Jesus is among the guests. While Jesus is still reclining at the table, a woman breaks open a flask of perfume and pours it on Jesus' head.

What she did was something like putting a whole year's salary into a suitcase and throwing it into the middle of the ocean—at least that's what the disciples thought. They considered her gift too extravagant. Jesus, however, praised her actions and said that she would always be remembered for what she did.

The woman gave without holding back. Her giving expressed what was in her heart. And her anointing of Jesus was a kind of confession. Her act recalled how kings were anointed in the Old Testament. Pouring oil on Jesus' head said that Jesus was the Messiah, the Christ. After all, the words *messiah* or *Christ* mean "anointed one."

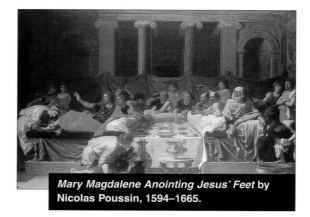

Mary Magdalene Anointing Jesus' Feet **by Nicolas Poussin, 1594–1665.**

Jesus said that her act was a preparation for his burial. According to Jewish custom, when people died their bodies were anointed with oils before burial. Jesus was predicting that he would die as a criminal; only criminals were thrown into a common grave and not anointed.

Betraying Jesus

Judas's act was the exact opposite of the woman's. He wasn't thinking about how much he could spend on Jesus; rather, he bargained for money to betray him. Judas sold out for 30 pieces of silver. How does that compare to the fortune the woman spent on the perfume? Although it's difficult to say exactly, the 30 pieces of silver probably represented about a month's salary.

5 – – → Passover and Lord's Supper

Bible Reference: Mark 14:12–26

Preparing to Celebrate

On Passover day Jerusalem was packed with crowds of pilgrims. Families were checking over their frisky year-old lambs, making sure they were perfect for sacrificing. Some families or groups of pilgrims were on their way to the temple to have the Levites kill their lambs. Others were ready to begin roasting the slaughtered lambs. The housecleaning and the preparation of special foods for the Passover meal had been completed, and soon each home would begin the celebration.

Crowds in Jerusalem during Passover week.

Passover Symbols

The eating of the Passover meal had to be done in a particular way because each part represented something special. The roast lamb reminded the people of the Passover lamb killed in Egypt. The bread was unleavened bread (bread made without yeast) because yeast symbolized sin. The bread was dipped in bitter herbs to remind the people of slavery's bitterness. The four different servings of wine—each mixed with water—had four different

Passover Checklist

TEN STEPS TO GET READY FOR A TRADITIONAL PASSOVER CELEBRATION

1. Select a lamb for sacrifice. Shop early to find one that is in perfect condition. Remember to pick one of an appropriate size. Your family must eat all the meat in one sitting—no leftovers allowed!
2. On Passover Eve, remember to make the ceremonial search for leaven. Take a candle and clean out every crumb of leaven or leavened bread. Don't sweep it under the rug; take it to the temple tomorrow morning for the priests to burn.
3. Dig an open fire pit. Collect pomegranate wood for the fire.
4. On Passover afternoon, bring your lamb for the ritual sacrifice at the temple. When you get home again, skewer the lamb whole and roast it on a spit over the fire.
5. Prepare unleavened bread to remember how our people hurried out of Egypt.
6. Prepare a bowl of salt water to remember the Israelites' salty tears during the time of slavery and the water of the Red Sea.
7. Collect bitter herbs to remember the bitterness of slavery in Egypt.
8. Prepare the Charosheth. Use your grandmother's recipe for this traditional paste of nuts, fruit, and wine. Try garnishing your Charosheth bricks with cinnamon sticks this year to represent the straw that our ancestors used for making the bricks in Egypt.
9. Prepare the four special cups of wine for the various courses in your holiday meal. Mix three parts wine with two cups water, and then heat the mixture over a low flame.
10. Be sure to collect enough water for the ritual hand-washings between the meal's courses.

meanings. When Jesus and his disciples reclined to eat their Passover meal, they knew what the order of events would be with Jesus as their host.

Two Surprises

Jesus had two surprises for them. The first surprise worried them. He announced that one of them would betray him. The shocked disciples were confused; they didn't know what Judas was up to, and they didn't trust themselves. They sadly asked, "Surely not I?"

Then Jesus surprised his disciples again by changing the Passover's meaning. Instead of looking back to the Passover lamb that was killed to deliver God's people from slavery in Egypt, he wanted this meal to remind his followers to look back to his own death as the deliverer of God's people from slavery to sin. That's why after eating the roast lamb, which was usually the very last food eaten, Jesus took some unleavened bread and announced that a new covenant had come to replace God's old covenant plan of forgiveness through animal sacrifices. The new covenant was God's plan of forgiveness through Jesus' sacrifice of himself, so Jesus said it was a new covenant in his blood.

The Last Supper by Albrecht Dürer, 1510.

6 ▬ ▬ ▬ ➤ Jesus, the Suffering Man

Bible Reference: Mark 14:27–52

A Quiet Place

How confused the disciples must have been when they left the Passover celebration in the upper room. Jesus had told them that he would die soon after one of them betrayed him. As they left the house in Jerusalem and walked down into the Kidron Valley, Jesus predicted something else: soon they would all desert him. They were headed toward the Mount of Olives, a hill east of Jerusalem where the wealthy people kept private gardens of olive trees.

An olive tree in the Garden of Gethsemane.

The garden where Jesus and his disciples were going was named Gethsemane, which means "oil press." In the garden were olive trees and a stone oil press for pressing the oil from the olives. The garden was quiet, far from the noisy Jerusalem streets. Leaving most of the disciples at the gate to the garden, Jesus asked Peter, James, and John to come and pray with him.

Jesus was overwhelmed with what lay ahead for him. He said his sorrow was so deep that he was already near death. Jesus' words show the depth of his suffering; he called God *Abba*, which means "father." It is the word a young child would call his father, like *da-da* or *daddy*. Jesus faced temptation once more; he asked his Father to consider providing salvation another way, but he forced himself to obey his Father's will.

Even at this terrible time, Jesus wasn't just concerned about himself; he also encouraged the disciples to watch and pray against their own weaknesses and temptations.

All Desert

Jesus woke up his exhausted disciples when loud noises at the garden gate announced the arrival of soldiers—not Roman soldiers, but Jewish temple guards—and a crowd of men with swords and clubs. At the front of the crowd was Judas, paid by the chief priests and Pharisees to point out Jesus, so the guards wouldn't arrest the wrong man in the dark. It was custom for students or disciples to show proper respect to their rabbi by greeting him with a kiss, and that's how Judas greeted Jesus to fulfill his bargain with the Sanhedrin.

Betrayal of Christ by Giotto de Bondone, 1266–1337.

7 ▬ ▬ ▬ ➤ Condemned by the Jews

Bible Reference: Matthew 26:57–75;
Mark 14:53–72; Luke 22:54–71;
John 18:28—19:16

Before the Sanhedrin

Jesus was led from Gethsemane to the home of the high priest, Caiaphas, where the Sanhedrin waited to deal with Jesus. The Romans had given this group of 70 men (plus their leader, the high priest) the authority to judge all cases involving disputes and criminal acts among the Jews, but they had no power to pass or carry out a death sentence. That power belonged to the Roman government.

There is some disagreement about whether or not this was a formal, legal trial before the Sanhedrin. The trial certainly didn't follow the laws that governed legal trials. For example, it was illegal for the Sanhedrin to hold a criminal trial at night; sentencing a person to death the same day he or she was found guilty was also illegal. The Sanhedrin had to meet in its own chambers on the temple ground for trials, not in the home of the chief priest. When someone was brought before the Sanhedrin for trial, people testifying for the accused person were allowed to speak first. Every accusation had to have at least two witnesses for it to be accepted as proof of guilt.

Christ before the High Priest by Gerrit van Honthorst, 1590–1656.

Why didn't Jesus' trial follow these rules? One explanation is that the Sanhedrin, eager to condemn Jesus, simply ignored the law. It acted quickly and quietly, not caring about whether or not the trial was legal.

A second explanation seems more likely. The Sanhedrin may have had no power in cases requiring capital punishment, so this was more of a preliminary hearing. When Jesus appeared before them, the Sanhedrin was trying to decide exactly what charges against Jesus they would bring to Pilate. Pilate, the highest Roman authority in Palestine, had the power to carry out a death sentence.

The Gospel writers don't give us every detail, but that's not their purpose. Their purpose is to tell us who Jesus is, to bear witness to him. In this story they all bear witness to Jesus' suffering as they tell how God's own people totally rejected and humiliated him. Instead of welcoming him as God's anointed, they abused him and condemned him to death.

"I Am . . ."

Jesus' appearance before the Sanhedrin is another climax in Mark. Up to this point Mark has stressed that Jesus' ministry was on a collision course with the Jewish leaders and that Jesus did not publicly say who he was. Now finally, in answer to the high priest's direct question, he stated that he is the Christ. As soon as Jesus revealed himself as God's Son, the Sanhedrin condemned him. Shortly afterwards, he was denied and deserted by Peter, the last of the disciples to desert. Jesus went to his death alone.

8 ▬ ▬ ➤ Condemned by the Gentiles

> Bible Reference: Matthew 27:1–31; Mark 15:1–20; Luke 23:1–25; John 18:28—19:16

Please, No Trouble

Pilate didn't want trouble. His job was to keep Judea quiet. And he'd already had more than one taste of what would happen if he crossed the Jews.

Once, for example, the Jews had rioted over an aqueduct he built to carry water to Jerusalem. They rioted after learning that he had paid for the project with money from the temple treasury. Squelching the bloody riot had not been easy.

This Jesus and Pilate float in the Passion Week parade is being carried by hooded Christians.

Besides, Pilate's good friend in Rome, Sejanus, had recently lost his place of influence at the court of Emperor Tiberius. Sejanus had been against the Jews; he had used his influence to push Tiberius toward an anti-Jewish policy. But now Tiberius had swung around to a pro-Jewish policy. Pilate knew that offending the Jews could be downright dangerous.

Flogged and Mocked

Pilate caved in under the pressure. Jesus was condemned to be crucified. Jesus was flogged, or scourged, like any other convict. In Roman scourging the convict was stripped and bound to a post. Then he was beaten with a whip of leather strips tipped with small pieces of lead or bone. Jesus must have gone through terrible pain before he died. Mark and the other Gospel writers don't spend much time on any of the details of Jesus' physical agony. The gospel, the good news, is not found in Jesus' physical suffering. They emphasize that the rejection of Jesus, the Son of God, was his true suffering.

Mark does sketch vividly the next scene of Jesus' suffering, in which the Roman soldiers mock him. The whole company of soldiers—probably about 200 to 400 soldiers—turned out for the sport. Because Jesus claimed to be king, they dressed him like one, complete with a purple robe and a crown. They also greeted him like a king. It was all a big joke to them.

9 ━ ━ ━ ━ ━ ━ ➤ The Crucifixion

Bible Reference: Matthew 27:32–66; Mark 15:21–47; Luke 23:26–49; John 19:17–37

The electric chair is a monstrous thing, an instrument of death. People on death row, condemned to die in the chair by a flick of a switch, know how dreadful it is.

The cross was Palestine's electric chair. Criminals died on crosses, fastened to them by spikes pounded through hands or wrists and both feet.

It's strange, isn't it, that anyone would want to paint a picture of a cross or wear a gold cross on a chain? But since Jesus' death on a cross on Golgotha, billions of crosses have been made. Crosses have been painted, carved, sculpted, and printed.

Jesus' death is the most famous death in history. It has held the attention of the world for centuries. But how unlikely that seemed in Palestine in A.D. 33!

Four Accounts

In the Gospels we have four records of Jesus' crucifixion and death. In all four, the basic message is the same. Still, each Gospel emphasizes something different.

In this book, the four Gospel accounts have been lined up in parallel columns to show their similarities and differences. Notice that in some cases the same material may be written in a different order. When that happens, you will see a direction like "See verse 38." Look down the same column to find the given verse for the matching information. Read the four accounts of Jesus' crucifixion and death on pages 84–89.

Crucifixion by Sandro Botticelli, 1444–1510.

Jesus' Burial

The four Gospel writers describe Jesus' burial in detail. Their record is important evidence that Jesus really died. John even includes the testimony of an eyewitness.

The burial accounts reveal another important fact as well. Not all of the Sanhedrin approved of Jesus' death sentence. Joseph of Arimathea and Nicodemus were members of the Sanhedrin, and yet they buried Jesus with love and respect.

Matthew reports that the Jewish leaders asked for the tomb to be sealed. To seal a tomb, a cord was strung across the stone and attached to the entrance with clay. The seal wasn't a lock but if the seal was broken, it would show that the stone had been moved. The Sanhedrin's request sprang from fear that Jesus' disciples would steal his body and claim that he had risen from the dead.

Matthew 27:32–40	Mark 15:21–30
[32]As they were going out, they met a man from Cyrene, named Simon, and they forced him to carry the cross.	[21]A certain man from Cyrene, Simon, the father of Alexander and Rufus, was passing by on his way in from the country, and they forced him to carry the cross.
[33]They came to a place called Golgotha (which means The Place of the Skull). [34]There they offered Jesus wine to drink, mixed with gall; but after tasting it, he refused to drink it. [35]When they had crucified him,	[22]They brought Jesus to the place called Golgotha (which means The Place of the Skull). [23]Then they offered him wine mixed with myrrh, but he did not take it. [24]And they crucified him.
(See verse 38.)	(See verse 27.)
they divided up his clothes by casting lots. [36]And sitting down, they kept watch over him there.	Dividing up his clothes, they cast lots to see what each would get.
[37]Above his head they placed the written charge against him: THIS IS JESUS, THE KING OF THE JEWS. [38]Two robbers were crucified with him, one on his right and one on his left.	[25]It was the third hour when they crucified him. [26]The written notice of the charge against him read: THE KING OF THE JEWS. [27]They crucified two robbers with him, one on his right and one on his left.
[39]Those who passed by hurled insults at him, shaking their heads [40]and saying, "You who are going to destroy the temple and build it in three days, save yourself! Come down from the cross, if you are the Son of God!"	[29]Those who passed by hurled insults at him, shaking their heads and saying, "So! You who are going to destroy the temple and build it in three days, [30]come down from the cross and save yourself!"

Luke 23:26–34	John 19:17–19

²⁶As they led him away, they seized Simon from Cyrene, who was on his way in from the country, and put the cross on him and made him carry it behind Jesus. ²⁷A large number of people followed him, including women who mourned and wailed for him. ²⁸Jesus turned and said to them, "Daughters of Jerusalem, do not weep for me; weep for yourselves and for your children. ²⁹For the time will come when you will say, 'Blessed are the barren women, the wombs that never bore and the breasts that never nursed!' ³⁰Then

"'they will say to the mountains,
   "Fall on us!"
and to the hills, "Cover us!"'

³¹For if men do these things when the tree is green, what will happen when it is dry?"

³²Two other men, both criminals, were also led out with him to be executed. ³³When they came to the place called the Skull, there they crucified him,

¹⁷Carrying his own cross, he went out to the place of the Skull (which in Aramaic is called Golgotha). ¹⁸Here they crucified him,

along with the criminals—one on his right, the other on his left. ³⁴Jesus said, "Father, forgive them, for they do not know what they are doing."

and with him two others —one on each side and Jesus in the middle.

And they divided up his clothes by casting lots.

(See verses 23–25.)

(See verse 38.)

¹⁹Pilate had a notice prepared and fastened to the cross. It read: JESUS OF NAZARETH, THE KING OF THE JEWS.

(See verses 32–33.)

(See verse 37.)

Matthew 27:41–44	Mark 15:31–32
[41]In the same way the chief priests, the teachers of the law and the elders mocked him. [42]"He saved others," they said, "but he can't save himself! He's the King of Israel! Let him come down now from the cross, and we will believe in him. [43]He trusts in God. Let God rescue him now if he wants him, for he said, 'I am the Son of God.' "	[31]In the same way the chief priests and the teachers of the law mocked him among themselves. "He saved others," they said, "but he can't save himself! [32]Let this Christ, this King of Israel, come down now from the cross, that we may see and believe."
(See verse 48.)	(See verse 36.)
(See verse 40.)	(See verse 30.)
(See verse 37.)	(See verse 26.)
[44]In the same way the robbers who were crucified with him also heaped insults on him.	Those crucified with him also heaped insults on him.

Luke 23:35–43

John 19:20–24

(Verses 20–24 are not parallel to the synoptics.)

²⁰Many of the Jews read this sign, for the place where Jesus was crucified was near the city, and the sign was written in Aramaic, Latin and Greek. ²¹The chief priests of the Jews protested to Pilate, "Do not write 'The King of the Jews,' but that this man claimed to be king of the Jews."

²²Pilate answered, "What I have written, I have written."

²³When the soldiers crucified Jesus, they took his clothes, dividing them into four shares, one for each of them, with the undergarment remaining. This garment was seamless, woven in one piece from top to bottom.

²⁴"Let's not tear it," they said to one another. "Let's decide by lot who will get it."

This happened that the scripture might be fulfilled which said,

"They divided my garments among them and cast lots for my clothing."

So this is what the soldiers did.

³⁵The people stood watching, and the rulers even sneered at him. They said, "He saved others; let him save himself if he is the Christ of God, the Chosen One."

³⁶The soldiers also came up and mocked him. They offered him wine vinegar ³⁷and said, "If you are the king of the Jews, save yourself."

³⁸There was a written notice above him, which read: THIS IS THE KING OF THE JEWS.

³⁹One of the criminals who hung there hurled insults at him: "Aren't you the Christ? Save yourself and us!"

⁴⁰But the other criminal rebuked him. "Don't you fear God," he said, "since you are under the same sentence? ⁴¹We are punished justly, for we are getting what our deeds deserve. But this man has done nothing wrong."

⁴²Then he said, "Jesus, remember me when you come into your kingdom. "

⁴³Jesus answered him, "I tell you the truth, today you will be with me in paradise."

Matthew 27:45–56	Mark 15:33–41

45From the sixth hour until the ninth hour darkness came over all the land. 46About the ninth hour Jesus cried out in a loud voice, *"Eloi, Eloi, lama sabachthani?"*—which means, "My God, my God, why have you forsaken me?"

47When some of those standing there heard this, they said, "He's calling Elijah."

48Immediately one of them ran and got a sponge. He filled it with wine vinegar, put it on a stick, and offered it to Jesus to drink. 49The rest said, "Now leave him alone. Let's see if Elijah comes to save him."

50And when Jesus had cried out again in a loud voice, he gave up his spirit.

51At that moment the curtain of the temple was torn in two from top to bottom. The earth shook and the rocks split. 52The tombs broke open and the bodies of many holy people who had died were raised to life. 53They came out of the tombs, and after Jesus' resurrection they went into the holy city and appeared to many people.

54When the centurion and those with him who were guarding Jesus saw the earthquake and all that had happened, they were terrified, and exclaimed, "Surely he was the Son of God!"

55Many women were there, watching from a distance. They had followed Jesus from Galilee to care for his needs. 56Among them were Mary Magdalene, Mary the mother of James and Joses, and the mother of Zebedee's sons.

33At the sixth hour darkness came over the whole land until the ninth hour. 34And at the ninth hour Jesus cried out in a loud voice, *"Eloi, Eloi, lama sabachthani?"*—which means, "My God, my God, why have you forsaken me?"

35When some of those standing near heard this, they said, "Listen, he's calling Elijah."

36One man ran, filled a sponge with wine vinegar, put it on a stick, and offered it to Jesus to drink. "Now leave him alone. Let's see if Elijah comes to take him down," he said.

37With a loud cry, Jesus breathed his last.

38The curtain of the temple was torn in two from top to bottom.

39And when the centurion, who stood there in front of Jesus, heard his cry and saw how he died, he said, "Surely this man was the Son of God!"

40Some women were watching from a distance. Among them were Mary Magdalene, Mary the mother of James the younger and of Joses, and Salome. 41In Galilee these women had followed him and cared for his needs. Many other women who had come up with him to Jerusalem were also there.

Luke 23:44–49	John 19:25–30
	[25]Near the cross of Jesus stood his mother, his mother's sister, Mary the wife of Clopas, and Mary Magdalene. [26]When Jesus saw his mother there, and the disciple whom he loved standing nearby, he said to his mother, "Dear woman, here is your son," [27]and to the disciple, "Here is your mother." From that time on, this disciple took her into his home.
[44]It was now about the sixth hour, and darkness came over the whole land until the ninth hour, [45]for the sun stopped shining. And the curtain of the temple was torn in two.	
(See verse 36.)	[28]Later, knowing that all was now completed, and so that the Scripture would be fulfilled, Jesus said, "I am thirsty." [29]A jar of wine vinegar was there, so they soaked a sponge in it, put the sponge on a stalk of the hyssop plant, and lifted it to Jesus' lips. [30]When he had received the drink, Jesus said, "It is finished." With that, he bowed his head and gave up his spirit.
[46]Jesus called out with a loud voice, "Father, into your hands I commit my spirit." When he had said this, he breathed his last.	
(See verse 45.)	
[47]The centurion, seeing what had happened, praised God and said, "Surely this was a righteous man." [48]When all the people who had gathered to witness this sight saw what took place, they beat their breasts and went away. [49]But all those who knew him, including the women who had followed him from Galilee, stood at a distance, watching these things.	(See verse 25.)

10 – – – – ➤ Fulfilling Prophecy

Bible Reference: Psalm 22; Isaiah 53;
Matthew 27:32–66; Mark 15:21–47;
Luke 23:26–49; John 19:16–37

Once for All

Jesus' suffering and death devastated his friends but relieved his enemies. Both his friends and his enemies had misunderstood him. Both had expected a messiah who would get rid of the Romans.

The Old Testament prophets had said that the messiah would come in glory and strength, defeating all of God's enemies. Jesus' death on the cross proved that he would not be that kind of king. But the prophets had also said that the messiah would suffer and die. The whole sacrifice system God had given his people on Mount Sinai was also a picture of the messiah's suffering and death.

Christ in Glory by Da Forli, 1481.

No one—not even Jesus' disciples—completely understood at the time what was happening when Jesus hung on the cross. But many Old Testament prophecies were coming true; God was giving his Son, Jesus the Messiah, as a sacrifice for the forgiveness of sin, just as he had promised. After Jesus' death on the cross, atonement (the restoration of friendship between God and humans through a sacrifice) was no longer based on the shedding of animal blood. Jesus' blood would be atonement.

The Apostles' Creed

I believe in God, the Father almighty,
    creator of heaven and earth.

I believe in Jesus Christ, his only Son, our Lord,
    who was conceived by the Holy Spirit
    and born of the virgin Mary.
    He suffered under Pontius Pilate,
    was crucified, died, and was buried;
    he descended to hell.
    The third day he rose again from the dead.
    He ascended to heaven
    and is seated at the right hand of God the Father almighty.
    From there he will come to judge the living and the dead.

I believe in the Holy Spirit,
    the holy catholic* church,
    the communion of saints,
    the forgiveness of sins,
    the resurrection of the body,
    and the life everlasting. Amen.

*that is, the true Christian church of all times and all places

Unit 5
Resurrection and Ascension

1 ━ ━ ━ ━ ━ ➤ The Empty Tomb

> Bible Reference: Matthew 28:1–15; Mark 16:1–20; Luke 24:1–12; John 20:1–18

Early on the First Day

It was all over. Jesus was dead. Joseph had wrapped Jesus' corpse in linen cloth and laid it in a tomb. Then he had rolled the large, flat stone in place. The Marys had followed and watched Joseph; they wanted to know where Jesus was buried.

When Jesus was laid in the tomb, the Sabbath was about to begin. The women had not been able to buy the special spices that were usually used at burials as expressions of love for the dead. They didn't have time to use them anyway before the Sabbath rest was to begin. So as soon as the Sabbath was over, they hurried to take care of this sad work.

Three Women at the Grave by Carl Julius Milde, 1803–1875.

What about Mark's Ending?

Most scholars agree that verses 9–20 were added to Mark 16 at a later date. Maybe the author didn't get to finish what he was going to write. Some people think that the book may have had another ending that was lost, but that's only a guess. Besides, ending the book at verse 8 stresses what Mark has been trying to say all along.

Almost from the beginning of his Gospel, Mark has shown the disciples' failure to understand Jesus. At the crucifixion he includes a group of women that he hasn't mentioned before. They seemed to be doing what Jesus' disciples should have been doing. They watch the crucifixion. They find out where Jesus is buried so they can anoint him. And they are the ones to hear the angel announce that Jesus has risen. But then they seem to fail too. They don't obey the angel's command. Instead, they say nothing to anyone.

This could be Mark's way of telling us that none of God's people recognized Jesus as God's Son. It could be his way of showing his readers that all believers have moments of weakness—like the young man who ran away naked from Jesus' arrest, like Peter outside of Jesus' trial, and like these women. Of course, it could just be that Mark thought all his readers would already know the rest of the story.

There is one thing, however, that Mark leaves no doubt about. Jesus had risen. And just as he had promised, he would meet his disciples again. In Galilee. In the place where he healed and taught.

Surrounded by Mystery

The events of that first Easter were so unimaginable that everyone was shaken up. In the Gospel stories people are terrified, crying, looking for Jesus, trying to figure out what has happened.

The accounts of the resurrection are packed with confusion and mystery. None of the Gospels explains how it happened, and the descriptions vary so much that it's hard to figure out the exact order of events.

But three facts are plain in all four Gospels: the tomb was empty, the women were the first to hear about Jesus' resurrection, and after his resurrection Jesus appeared to his disciples.

2 ▬ ▬ ▬ ▬ ▬ ▬ ➤ Power for Living

Bible Reference: Selected New Testament passages

What If?

It's hard to imagine what life would be like if Jesus had never risen from the dead that first Easter Sunday. Everything would be quite different. There would be no churches. If Jesus had never risen, people would think of Jesus as a good man who died for a crime that he didn't commit. But many people have been unjustly condemned to death. And even if anyone were foolish enough to believe in a dead man for salvation, he or she still wouldn't have any reason to hope that people could ever rise from the dead.

Something to Look Forward To

Jesus' resurrection is the gospel, God's good news to us. Jesus' power over death shows us that we can trust him to save us from our sins. After all, if Jesus had the power to raise himself from the dead, surely he has the power to forgive us our sins.

But that's not all. Jesus' resurrection gives all believers something to hope for. Have you ever been invited to a party or other event that you eagerly looked forward to attending? Just thinking about how much fun it was going to be was exciting. Well, that's the kind of eagerness that Christians can have for the future because Jesus rose on Easter Sunday.

3 ▬ ▬ ➤ Open Minds, Open Hearts

Bible Reference: Luke 24:13–49

Fire!

Have you ever sat in front of a fire, just watching it? You can sit there for hours, can't you? The flames leap and jump, sparking energetically, roaring into full strength and then gradually, ever so slowly, turning the wood into white-hot coals.

Fire seems to fascinate everyone. Maybe that's why God chose to reveal himself in it. Or maybe it's because God chose to reveal himself in fire that we are so fascinated by it. Think about it. God has revealed himself through fire over and over again.

Moses ran into a fiery God in the desert of Midian. Moses was just minding his own business—shepherding his father-in-law's sheep. There, off in the distance, he saw a brighter light than the usual sun reflecting off the white sand and polished rocks.

Moses and the Burning Bush by James J. Tissot, 1836–1902.

"Probably just another spontaneous combustion of a desert tumbleweed," he perhaps thought. But something was strange—even miraculous—about that fire. Tumbleweeds are bone dry. When they are ignited, they flare up fast. In a burst of flame they are over and done with. But this flame didn't die out. If anything, it became brighter as Moses watched.

He decided to take a closer look. And as he got close, the real shock came. Moses heard his name. "Moses! Moses!"

He turned one way. He turned the other. No one was there. Just the sheep. He thought it best to answer, "Here I am."

"Don't come any closer. Take off your sandals, for the place where you are standing is holy ground."

And from that burning bush, Moses received his marching orders to free God's people from slavery.

God used fire to call his servant to attention.

Later, after the Israelites were freed from bondage in Egypt, God led them through the Red Sea over dry ground toward the land of promise. But the Hebrews needed a guide, something or someone to light their way.

By day the Lord went ahead of them in a pillar of cloud, and by night —do you remember?—with a pillar of fire. God's guiding light never left them. In the darkest, loneliest of nights, there was the fire, the light of God.

God used fire to lead his people to the Promised Land.

Later, the Israelites camped at the foot of Mount Sinai. God called to Moses from the mountain. He wanted to give the people guidelines for living. When the Israelites were all cleaned up and ready to meet God, they gathered around Mount Sinai.

They saw thunder and lightning. They heard a loud trumpet blast. The mountain was covered with smoke, because the Lord descended on it in fire.

God used fire to remind the people that he is a holy God, that he had a plan for their lives.

Malachi prophesied about a messenger God would send who would be "like a refiner's fire."

And a man named Jesus came, baptizing "with the Holy Spirit and with fire."

God revealed himself many times in the pure-white light of fire!

That's why what happened on Good Friday afternoon was so terrifying. You remember what happened. It got dark. In the middle of the day, it was as dark as night. Jesus was dead. There was no light! The Light of the world hung dead on the cross.

For three long hours, right in the middle of the day, people must have wondered if God had left them.

Can you imagine what that would be like? No light. No God. No direction. No revelation. That would be hell—if God would leave us.

But he didn't, did he? Three days after Jesus was buried, some women came to the garden. The stone was rolled away; the body was gone. And an angel—bright as fire—told them, "He is not here. He is risen, just as he said."

And later that day, two believers were walking from Jerusalem to Emmaus. A man joined them. They didn't know it, but it was Jesus. They talked with him. He showed them from Scripture how God had planned everything that had happened that week to turn out just like it did. They ate supper with him. Then suddenly, it all made sense.

And do you know what they said to each other? They said, "Were not our hearts burning within us while he talked with us on the road and opened the Scriptures to us?"

The fire hasn't gone out. God is still with us. The only change is that now the fire is inside of us.

Burning Hearts

Cleopas and his friend felt a burning in their hearts when they realized who the Messiah really was and what he had come to do. The fire they felt within sent them racing to tell others about this good news.

Now the flame has been passed to us. Jesus asks us to bring his fiery light into the world by sharing his love with each other and anyone else who will listen.

The Supper at Emmaus by Catena, 1520.

Someday Jesus is going to come again. He will invite everyone who believes in him to join him in a new heaven and a new earth. That new world will have no night, no darkness, and no loneliness.

We won't need the light of a lamp or the light of the sun because, the Book of Revelation tells us, the Lord God will be all the Light we need.

4 ━ ━ ━ ━ ━ ➤ Doubt and Faith

Bible Reference: John 20:24–31

Jesus' resurrection sometimes seems almost too good to be true. The early disciples who witnessed all the events felt that way. Matthew described the women when they saw the empty tomb as being "afraid yet filled with joy." Maybe their fears were the natural reaction to seeing a supernatural being—the angel. But perhaps they were also afraid because in one corner of their minds they doubted if the amazing news could really be true. Even the disciples had questions when the women ran to tell them how they had seen a risen Jesus in the garden.

Dealing with Doubts and Questions

What doubts do you have about Jesus?

Almost every Christian has doubts at one time or another. Struggling through our doubts is an important way to grow as Christians. But when we have doubts, we should talk about them rather than keeping them to ourselves. We'll often find that other people have had the same doubts. Sometimes we can learn from how they resolved their questions or how they learned to accept Jesus' Word by faith in spite of their doubts.

Sometimes, though, the only way to get through doubting is to struggle through it by ourselves. But we should remember that we're not really alone. Just as Jesus loved Thomas, he also loves us as we are—even with our doubts and questions. In all our challenges and struggles, he won't leave us.

5 — — — ➤ Resurrection Appearance in Galilee

> **Bible Reference: John 21;**
> **1 Corinthians 15:5–7**

What Next?

The risen Jesus wasn't with the disciples all the time, at least not in the same way that he had been before. Most likely the disciples wondered about what would happen next. When would God's kingdom come? Why wasn't Jesus appearing to the entire nation of Israel and setting up a throne in Jerusalem? Why didn't Jesus pay a visit to the Sanhedrin?

Ordinary Appearances

Christian author Frederick Buechner has pointed out that whenever Jesus appeared to his followers, he came to them during their ordinary

Jesus appearing to his disciples (19th century engraving).

activities. He came while they were fishing, eating, or walking on the road. He came without fanfare. Mary Magdalene, crying at the tomb, heard a voice—and there was Jesus. The disciples were hiding in fear—and then Jesus was standing in the room with them. Jesus joined the two walking on the road to Emmaus and struck up a conversation with them. And when the disciples were tired and perhaps angry because they'd been fishing all night without catching anything, Jesus stood on the beach and asked how things were going.

Breakfast on the Beach

Narrator: Jesus died; and then he was alive again. The disciples saw him; and then they didn't. What would happen next? The disciples didn't know. What should they do now? They didn't have a clue.

Thomas: Well, we can't stay locked in this room forever—that's for sure. We've all seen him now. We know he's alive. But the big shots at the temple will never believe us. Maybe they'll just think we're crazy. All I know is that if I stay hiding in this room forever, I *will* go crazy.

Nathanael: I'm with you, Thomas. But what should we do? Where will we go?

Peter: I've still got that fishing boat. I'm going fishing.

James: Good idea. At least then we won't starve.

John son of Zebedee: Fishing's a good enough line of work. We're obviously getting nowhere with this kingdom thing. Let's go back to the sea!

Narrator: So they went fishing, but that night they didn't catch anything.

Thomas: I knew it—empty nets! Aren't there any fish in this lake?

Peter: Quit grumbling and cast out that net.

James: Cast it out yourself!

John the son of Zebedee: Yeah, Peter. We've been fishing as many years as you, but you act like we don't know what we're doing.

John the beloved disciple: Be quiet! I think I hear someone calling from the shore.

Jesus: Friends, haven't you any fish?

All of the disciples: No!

Jesus: Throw your net on the right side of the boat and you'll find some.

Thomas: What does this guy think we've been doing all night? I haven't even seen a single fish.

Nathanael: He called us "friends." I didn't think we had any friends left.

James: Let's give it a try. What have we got to lose?

Narrator: So they cast out the nets again.

John the son of Zebedee: Hey! Hang on everybody! This net is going to burst!

Thomas: Where did all of these fish come from?

Miraculous Draught of Fishes by Raphael, 1483–1520.

Nathanael: There must be every kind of fish in the sea here!

Narrator: The disciples were unable to haul the net in because of the large number of fish.

John the beloved disciple: Peter, I know who that guy on the beach is. It's Jesus. It's the Lord!

Narrator: Peter knew that John was right. He immediately jumped out of the boat and splashed toward the shore. The other disciples followed in the boat, dragging the net full of fish behind them. When they landed, they saw that Jesus had made a fire and was cooking something.

Jesus: Bring some of the fish you've just caught. Come and have breakfast.

Narrator: As they ate, Peter gazed into the fire, feeling its warmth and remembering another fire that had chased away the chill. He would never forget the fire outside the chief priest's house where he had sat while Jesus was on trial. He could never forgive himself for saying that he didn't know Jesus—not once, but three times. Then he noticed that Jesus was looking at him, and he remembered how Jesus had looked at him that night.

Jesus: Simon Peter, do you truly love me more than these?

Peter: You know I'll be your friend forever.

Jesus: Feed my lambs.

Narrator: Again Jesus asked Peter if he truly loved him.

Peter: Lord, you know I do.

Jesus: Take care of my sheep.

Narrator: Then Jesus asked Peter again—one question for each time Peter had denied him—"Do you love me, Peter?"

Peter: Lord, you know everything . . . everything. You know I love you.

Jesus: Feed my sheep.

Narrator: Now Peter saw something different in Jesus' eyes. It had probably been there all along, but he hadn't noticed. Peter saw forgiveness and acceptance. Jesus still would trust him. Jesus still wanted him!

Peter: Then Jesus told me one more thing.

Jesus: Follow me!

Peter: And ever since that breakfast at the beach, I have.

6 — — — — — ➤ Mission Possible

Bible Reference: Matthew 28:16–20

On the Mountain

Matthew, like John, ends his Gospel in Galilee. But Matthew's closing scene is on a mountain. The word *mountain* should make us sit up and take notice. In the Old Testament a mountain was one of the special places where God revealed himself. Jesus taught about the law of the kingdom on a mountain (Sermon on the Mount), and it was on a high mountain that Jesus was transfigured. Once more, this time as the risen Lord, Jesus met his disciples on a mountain.

Special Commissioning

Because Jesus had been obedient and finished the salvation work that he and his Father had agreed he would do, Jesus had authority over everything. And he gave his disciples a big mission.

Jesus said that anyone who calls himself or herself a disciple must go into the world to make disciples, teaching about salvation and baptizing new believers.

Jesus ended his commission with a promise. He promised to be with his followers always, to the end of the age. The end of the age will come only when Jesus returns as Lord. Then he will show himself to everyone as the King.

7 ▬ ▬ ➤ Going Away to Come Closer

Bible Reference: Luke 24:50–53; Acts 1:1–11

Eyes on the Skies

Have you ever just lain on your back, watching the sky? With the clouds drifting into mesmerizing shapes, the universe seems to stretch out forever. With your shoulders pressed against the ground and your hands behind your head, you can feel very small but also very much a part of all creation. Imagine David doing the same thing all those years ago when he wrote, "For great is your love, higher than the heavens; your faithfulness reaches to the skies. Be exalted, O God, above the heavens, and let your glory be over all the earth" (Psalm 108:4–5).

When Jesus made his last appearance to the disciples, they met on the Mount of Olives with a clear view of the open skies. The disciples were convinced now that Jesus had risen from the dead and that everything that had happened fulfilled the Scriptures. He had promised the disciples a special gift. But before their gift would come, one more event needed to take place.

The Ascension by Gustave Doré.

Going Up?

Is heaven really somewhere up among the clouds in the skies? We don't know. Luke writes that Jesus was "taken up into heaven." But can we really agree with popular images of heaven as a cloudy space in the sky?

We don't where heaven is or exactly

what the disciples saw that day. But the word *up* is probably a good choice to describe the event anyway. It does describe how Jesus was exalted—lifted up—to his new position.

Jesus Reigns

Jesus' journey on earth was finally over. He had come to do his Father's will by living a perfect life, dying in the place of his people, and showing his power over death through his resurrection. Now he is reigning at his Father's right hand.

Keeping the Faith

From the beginning, various creeds were designed as a norm or rule of faith. Like a carpenter's square, creeds help people measure what is right and true and what is crooked and untrue.

Some of the first creed-like statements can be traced all the way back to the earliest days of the Christian church. The simplest and most powerful of these is, "Jesus is Lord!" This is the same realization that brought the disciples such great joy as they returned to Jerusalem after seeing Jesus ascend.

The early church also tried to capture the essentials of the faith in other phrases that believers could remember and pass along to others. In a day when having one's own copy of the Scripture or any printed material was unheard of, believers needed small chunks of the gospel to carry with them. They needed something longer than "Jesus is Lord" and shorter than the entire Bible.

Turn to page 91 in this book to read the Apostles' Creed.

Unit 6
The Birth of the Church

1 ➡ The Church's Birthday

Bible Reference: Acts 1–2; Leviticus 23:15–21

An Old Testament Festival

Jerusalem still swarmed with Passover pilgrims from the areas around the Mediterranean Sea. They were staying in Jerusalem to celebrate the Feast of Weeks, which came 50 days after Passover (it was also known as Pentecost, which means "fiftieth"). Pentecost was a joyous harvest festival, much like our Thanksgiving Day. Jewish families were required to celebrate the feast in Jerusalem if they could. No one was allowed to work on that day. In the morning the people gathered to watch the high priest make a special offering of two freshly baked loaves of bread made from the newly harvested wheat. Then the men danced and celebrated God's goodness in the temple courtyard, singing songs of praise to God for providing good crops. During the rest of the day families would bring their own bread to the temple for an offering and then enjoy a wonderful meal together.

A New Testament Festival

On Pentecost morning 10 days after Jesus had ascended, Jesus' followers were gathered together to wait for the Holy Spirit. They were probably meeting in the large upstairs room where some of them had been staying (Acts 1:13). One hundred twenty people were there. The group included the apostles, the women who had helped support Jesus' ministry, Jesus' mother and half-brothers (or relatives), and perhaps Cleopas and the 70 disciples whom Jesus had sent out as missionaries from Galilee.

The holiday crowds outside were probably already walking through the streets toward the temple with their loaves of bread and their sacrificial lambs, talking in their many different languages. The disciples inside were most likely praying.

Peter's Sermon

The Jerusalem crowd suspected something strange was happening when

The Descent of the Spirit by **Gustave Doré.**

they heard the jumble of sounds coming from Jesus' followers. But they didn't know what it was. Peter heard some of the crowd joking that the disciples had been drinking too much wine. So he stood up in front of everyone and in a loud voice started explaining what was going on. He said that it was too early to be drunk—it was only nine o'clock in the morning. No, this was the Holy Spirit's work, the work that the prophet Joel had prophesied to the Jewish people hundreds of years earlier. What the people saw happening was exactly what God had been planning for centuries.

The Birthday of the Church

The church of Jesus, the Messiah, had come at last! No one called it a church, and believers hadn't yet begun calling themselves Christians, but with the Holy Spirit's coming, the church was born. Even on its first day, the church had leaders (the apostles, especially Peter and John) and members (over 3,000); and these leaders and members had the power of God's Holy Spirit living in them!

Though the Holy Spirit had been active during Old Testament times and during Jesus' earthly ministry, never before had the Spirit come to live inside God's people, as the prophet Joel had promised. And the good news was that because of Jesus' death and resurrection, all believers would receive the Holy Spirit to dwell inside them—not just Jerusalem Jews and not just men, but also Gentiles and women and families.

That didn't mean that these believers wouldn't sin anymore, but it did mean that they would have power to say no to sin and to tell others about God's love in Jesus. And that's exactly what the members of that early church did. They told everyone about God revealing himself in his Son and about how salvation was available to all who believed. The visitors to Jerusalem who became believers in Jesus went back to their homes throughout the world and told others about the gospel and about God the Father who loved them, Jesus the Son who died for them, and the Holy Spirit who was living inside of them!

2 ----➔ Courageous Christians

Bible Reference: Acts 3:1—4:31

Staying in Jerusalem

After Pentecost the apostles didn't return home to Galilee. They stayed in Jerusalem because Jesus had told them to begin their witness there. Jesus had said, "'You will receive power when the Holy Spirit comes on you; and you will be my witnesses in Jerusalem, and in all Judea and Samaria, and to the ends of the earth'" (Acts 1:8). By staying as a group in Jerusalem, they also were learning about life in Jesus' kingdom and about how to live with one another in love and unity. In fact, Jesus' followers spent two years after Pentecost (from A.D. 33–35) living and preaching in Jerusalem before starting out for Samaria and the ends of the earth.

An Unexpected Gift

Three o'clock in the afternoon was one of the three special hours of prayer set aside each day. Of course, a person could pray anywhere, but people believed prayer was more effective if offered in the temple. Even after becoming Christians, Peter and John continued their custom of going to the temple to pray during the special hours.

Gates leading into the temple courts.

The temple gate called Beautiful was the most popular of the gates leading into the temple court. Maybe that's why beggars often sat by that gate, waiting for worshipers going into the temple to drop coins into their outstretched hands. One day a beggar sitting at the gate asked Peter and John for money as they entered the temple to pray.

A Daring Prayer

On the night before Jesus was arrested he had told his disciples what to expect after his death and resurrection. He had said, "'If the world hates you, keep in mind that it hated me first. . . . If they persecuted me, they will persecute you also. . . . They will treat you this way because of my name, for they do not know the One who sent me'" (John 15:18–21). Jesus' prediction was coming true. Peter and John's arrest and imprisonment by the Sanhedrin was the first evidence of the Jewish leaders' hatred for Christ's followers.

3 ━ ━ ━ ━ ━ ➤ One in the Spirit

Bible Reference: Acts 2:42–47; 4:32—6:7

Life in the Early Church

When the Holy Spirit enters a believer's heart, love overcomes selfishness and forgiveness replaces hatred. The Holy Spirit draws Christians together in a special kind of unity so that caring about each other is natural. The Christians in Jerusalem had that kind of unity.

The brand-new church in Jerusalem was excited about Jesus. Those who hadn't heard much about him wanted to learn more. In the temple courtyard and in homes the apostles preached the gospel and taught what they had learned from Jesus. New converts joined the church every day.

Sharing Possessions in Love

Some people think the description of the way that the early Christians lived reflects Communist beliefs. But that's not what Luke meant when he said that the believers "had everything in common." He meant that church members cared enough about each other so that those who had plenty shared with those who needed help.

Luke tells about one man in particular, a man named Joseph. He was so generous and wanted to help others so much that the apostles gave him a new name, Barnabas, which means "Son of Encouragement."

Luke also tells us about a couple who had a different kind of attitude. The husband's name was Ananias and the wife's name was

Death of Ananias by Gustave Doré.

"Lying to God is like sawing the branch you're sitting on. The better you do it, the harder you fall."

—Frederick Buechner

Sapphira. Together they created a scheme that allowed them to receive praise for being generous while keeping their money.

Sharing Work in the Church

After a while, the Jerusalem church became so large that taking care of the poor, especially the widows, was a large task. Some problems also cropped up concerning how the job was being done. Two kinds of Jews had joined the Church: Grecian Jews (who spoke Greek and followed Greek customs) and Hebraic Jews (who spoke Hebrew and followed Jewish customs). Apparently the Hebraic widows were getting more food and money than the Grecian widows. The Grecian Jews complained about this to the apostles. The apostles were busy preaching, and they knew that it wouldn't be right for them to quit preaching in order to distribute food and money. So they called the believers together to solve the problem.

4 ⇥ Sharing Jesus' Suffering

Bible Reference: Acts 5:17–42; 6:8–15:7

Attack and Counterattack

The apostles were busy witnessing for Jesus in Jerusalem, even preaching in the temple right under the noses of Jesus' enemies, the members of the

Sanhedrin. Just inside the temple's eastern wall was Solomon's Colonnade, a long covered porch lined with elegant columns. Almost every day the apostles stood in this area to teach groups of Christians about Jesus. Jews who hadn't heard about Jesus were often part of the crowd. To them the apostles announced that Jesus of Nazareth was the "Christ" (the Greek word for messiah), that God's kingdom had come through Jesus, and that Jesus could be present in their hearts through the Holy Spirit. Many people—even some of the priests—repented and believed.

So Jesus' name was back in the news in Jerusalem. The authorities who thought that they had gotten rid of Jesus were even more outraged and jealous because the apostles also healed the sick and exorcised evil spirits. The healings that Jesus had performed had provoked the teachers of the law and the Pharisees. The healings that the apostles performed in Jesus' name incited the same reaction from the authorities—just as Jesus had warned his disciples.

As long as the followers of Jesus hid behind locked doors, the Sanhedrin left them alone. But as soon as the Holy Spirit breathed life into Jesus' followers and they began to act with God's power, the opposition began. When God attacked, Satan counterattacked.

The First Christian Martyr

Stephen was one of the seven church leaders appointed to the ministry of taking care of the poor. Luke describes Stephen as "full of God's grace and power." It wasn't long before Stephen was in trouble with synagogue authorities for his views.

Stephen's enemies falsely accused him and brought him to trial before the Sanhedrin. Stephen gave a long speech to the Sanhedrin in which he told the history of God's people,

St. Stephen's Gate, possibly the site where Stephen was martyred.

The stoning of Stephen (19th century engraving).

beginning with Abraham. It was an unflattering picture of the Jews. He told the Sanhedrin that the Jews had always resisted and disobeyed God, worshiping idols and mistreating prophets.

Stephen's speech made the members of the Sanhedrin and the crowd furious. Screaming in hatred, the crowd dragged him out of the city and then pelted him with rocks. They kept throwing rocks until Stephen was dead.

Stephen was the first Christian martyr—a person who sacrifices his or her life rather than deny faith in God. He loved his Lord more than he loved his life, and for that he was stoned to death.

5 — — — ➡ The Gospel for Samaria

Bible Reference: Acts 8:4–40

Philip's Ministry

The heat of persecution in Jerusalem drove Christians to leave for safer places to live. So after two years of growing together in love and unity, the church members were scattered. This began a long period of witnessing in Judea and Samaria. The apostles themselves, however, continued to live in Jerusalem and provide leadership for the scattered churches.

What Are You Looking For?

Acts 8 tells us about two people who met Philip. Each one was looking for something special. Simon was amazed by the miracles he had seen, and he hoped to add these supernatural powers to his bag of magic tricks. The Ethiopian, on the other hand, was looking for answers. He had read the Scriptures and wanted to know who the Suffering Servant was.

Simon thought Christianity was something he could buy his way into. The Ethiopian understood that Jesus Christ had bought his salvation for him. Simon, in the end, found bitterness and fear. The Ethiopian found joy. What are you looking for? What will you find?

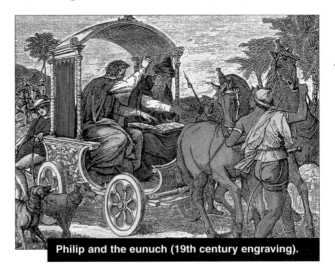
Philip and the eunuch (19th century engraving).

6 ▬ ▬ ▬ ▬ ▬ ▬ ➤ Switching Ideas

Bible Reference: Acts 9:1–31

Jesus Speaks to Saul

It was becoming increasingly obvious that God intended that Gentiles as well as Jews would be included in his kingdom. In fact, God had already chosen the person who would be his great missionary to the Gentiles. The Jerusalem Christians would have been shocked to know who that person was—their worst enemy, Saul. He hated Christians because he was convinced that they were traitors and blasphemers. He was a leader of the persecution. He put all of his energy into tossing Christian men and women into prison. He even got the Jerusalem priests to give him permission to travel to other cities to hunt down the Christians who had run away from Jerusalem. While Saul was on a "hunting" trip to Damascus (a city in Syria about a six-day trip from Jerusalem), God interrupted Saul's plans.

Converted on the Road

Narrator: Travelers were walking on the road. A light flashed around Saul, and he heard a voice.

Lord: Saul, Saul, why do you persecute me?

Saul (falling to the ground): Who are you, Lord?

Jesus: I am Jesus, whom you are persecuting. Get up, go into the city, and you will be told what to do.

Saul's fellow travelers: What's that sound? What's going on?

Narrator: Saul got up quietly.

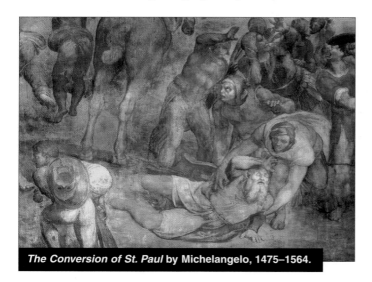

The Conversion of St. Paul by Michelangelo, 1475–1564.

Fellow travelers: What happened? What's the matter?

Saul: What have I done? I thought I was serving God when I persecuted Jesus' followers.

A fellow traveler: What are you talking about? We sure didn't see anything. Let's be on our way.

Saul: The light blinded me. I can't see.

Another traveler: We're almost there. Here, take my hand. I'll lead you the rest of the way.

Narrator: Meanwhile at a house in Damascus, the Lord was speaking to a disciple in a vision.

Lord: Ananias.

Ananias: Yes, Lord.

Lord: Go to the house of Judas on Straight Street and ask for a man from Tarsus named Saul, for he is

The house of Ananias.

praying. In a vision he has seen a man named Ananias come and place his hands on him to restore his sight.

Ananias: Lord, I've heard what this Saul is up to. Because of him many Christians in Jerusalem have suffered harm. And he's come here to do the same thing—arrest Christians. He'll probably arrest me!

Lord: Go! I've chosen this man to carry my message to the Gentiles and their kings and to the people of Israel. Now he'll have to suffer for my name.

Narrator: So Ananias went to Damascus.

Ananias (knocking on the door): Is Saul of Tarsus here?

Judas: Yes, but he's not well. He hasn't had anything to eat or drink since he arrived. I'll show you to his room.

Ananias (putting his hands on Saul): Brother Saul, the Lord Jesus, the one you saw on the road, has sent me here so that you may see again and be filled with the Holy Spirit.

Saul: Ananias, you've given me my sight back. As you put your hands on me it was as though scales fell from my eyes. I have been blind. I couldn't see that Jesus was the Messiah. How wrong I was. I have sinned against the Lord.

Ananias: Saul, I didn't want to come to you, but the Lord appeared and commanded me. He said you were going to carry his message to the Gentiles.

Narrator: Then Saul got up and was baptized, and after taking some food, he regained his strength. The next few days he spent with the disciples in Damascus. At once he began preaching in the synagogues that Jesus is the Son of God.

7 ━ ━ ━ ━ ➤ Transforming Dreams

Bible Reference: Acts 9:32—11:18

After reading Luke's account of Saul's conversion, you might think that Saul went right to work as God's missionary to the Gentiles. That's not quite how it happened. According to Galatians 1:13–21, Saul first spent many years studying the Scriptures and preaching in various small towns.

Meanwhile, God was gradually preparing the other Jewish apostles and Christians to welcome believing Gentiles into the church. Philip's ministry to the Samaritans was an in-between step. The Samaritans were not fully Jewish, but they weren't fully Gentile either, and Peter and John saw them receive the Holy Spirit just like the Jews. The Ethiopian eunuch's conversion was another step; his conversion started the church among the people of Africa. But the Jewish Christians still didn't fully understand the direction that the church must take in the future. In this lesson we'll see how God opened the early Christians' eyes to his will for the Gentiles.

Peter's vision on the housetop (19th century engraving).

8 ▬ ▬ ▬ ▬ ▶ First Called Christians

Bible Reference: Acts 11:19—12:25

The Church Spreads to Syrian Antioch

After Stephen's death some of the believers who had escaped Jerusalem went to Phoenicia, Cyprus, and Antioch (the capital city of Syria). The group of believers in Antioch had an experience similar to Peter's. When some of these believers told not only Jews but also Greeks the good news about Jesus, surprising things happened.

An altar in the front of St. Peter's church in Antioch.

Government Persecution

After Saul's conversion the persecution of the Christians stopped for a time. But soon another wave of persecution broke out. Most likely it was sparked by the report about Peter's activities in Caesarea. Until now, the new movement had carefully obeyed the law of Moses. But to eat with Gentiles and baptize them without circumcising them was too much!

This time, however, the Sanhedrin wasn't the persecutor. King Agrippa, the new ruler, headed up the attack. Political problems had forced Pontius Pilate to return to Rome. The Roman emperor had put King Herod Agrippa in power in Palestine, and Herod Agrippa was partly Jewish.

When the story begins, Herod is in Jerusalem for the Passover celebrations about ten years after Jesus' death and resurrection.

9 — ➤ Letter to the Scattered Church

> ## Bible Reference: The Book of James

Mail Call

In our age of instant communication and comfortable transportation, it's hard to imagine how lonely the scattered Christians probably felt. Believers in cities distant from the home church in Jerusalem didn't hear any news from church leaders for many months at a time, and sometimes these new believers developed wrong ideas about what Jesus wanted them to do in their new Christian lives. Because they were suffering persecution, perhaps some of them even wondered if God had deserted them. Some may have thought that since God had saved them by grace they didn't have to obey any laws and could live as they wanted. The new churches always had problems because the churches were made up of sinful people, who often quarreled or became critical or forgot to love each other.

The church leaders in Jerusalem knew that the scattered Christians faced these kinds of problems. Because they couldn't easily visit the churches, they sent letters (also called epistles) teaching the new Christians what to believe and how to behave. Some of these epistles were later recognized as special enough to be part of the Bible. One of the first of these letters sent to the scattered churches—the Book of James in our New Testament—was probably written around A.D. 50 (although some scholars think it might have been written later than that).

Fitting Together Faith and Good Works

James is very down-to-earth. He gives clear advice on how Christians should live. Some scholars think that the Book of James emphasizes doing good works too much. They say that James was teaching that salvation is not by faith in what Jesus did but by faith in what Christians themselves do. But James doesn't say that a person is saved by good works. Jesus himself said, "If you love me, you will obey what I command" (John 14:15).

Unit 7
Expanding the Church

1 — — — ➤ A New Stage in Mission

> **Bible Reference: Acts 13:1–4**

Did You See? Hear? Touch?

You never saw Jesus.
You never heard him.
You never touched him.
But there were those who did.
There were those who saw him with their eyes
      and heard him with their ears
      and touched him with their hands.
   And they told others,
     who told others,
     who told still others,
       and so on . . .
     until someone told you.

That's how you came to Jesus. Through people. Through parents, grandparents, a teacher, a pastor, or a friend. Others introduced you to Jesus, and you came to see him, to hear his voice, and to touch him.

People have been telling about Jesus for about 2,000 years. Those who first gathered around him found that they had to speak about him. They were full of hope and amazed at what God had done in Christ Jesus. They *had* to tell about Jesus' death and resurrection. Looking back across all those years and reading the accounts in Acts, we can recognize that we are a living part of that story.

This open-ended story continues in your church today. Your part of the story is just beginning. What do you think your part will be in the future?

The Acts of the Spirit

Some have suggested that this second book by Luke should have been called the Acts of the Spirit rather than the Acts of the Apostles. The Spirit is the main actor in Luke's story of the expanding church. The Spirit is the dynamic power driving the church to proclaim the good news in the face of great difficulties. Through the Spirit, Jesus' followers continue his work.

The first step of changing those followers into missionaries was taken in Jerusalem—when the Holy Spirit came upon the disciples and empowered them to speak. Then people who believed their preaching also received the Spirit and "spoke the word of God boldly." The Spirit continued to lead, sometimes directing missionaries to go to specific places to preach. Then the Spirit brought the church to a major turning point: Peter, following the Spirit's instructions, baptized the first Gentiles. Now in Acts 13 the Spirit is leading the church to begin a new outreach.

As you continue to read the story in Acts of how the church witnesses the gospel of Jesus Christ, notice how the Spirit guides every crucial point.

Bridging Two Worlds

In Acts 13 the Spirit acts to "set apart" Saul and Barnabas for a new stage in mission. The two are commissioned to carry Christ's name to the Gentiles. This challenging mission required extraordinary gifts.

The gospel message, after all, was wrapped in a Jewish package. Jesus was born a Jew; he was the Messiah promised first of all to the Jewish people; promises and prophecies about Jesus were in the Jewish Scriptures.

The ruins of the temple built in Antioch for Caesar Augustus by Herod.

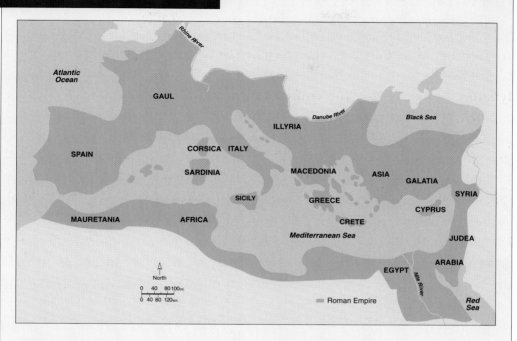

By the time the church began at Pentecost, God had already been at work for centuries preparing the world for the gospel message. By choosing a people as his own he had prepared the way for Jesus, the Messiah. But God had also been preparing the wider Gentile world.

The Roman Empire dominated the world into which the church was born. The empire surrounded the Mediterranean Sea, stretching as far north as Britain and covering most of the known world. The emperor and Roman Senate ruled this vast area through appointed kings and governors. Soldiers were stationed in every conquered territory to uphold Rome's rule. To transport their soldiers easily, the Romans built an excellent system of roads, established sea routes, and kept the roads and the seas safe for travel and trade. This strong Roman government led people to respect Roman law. Consequently, the Mediterranean world enjoyed remarkable peace.

During this time one language, Greek, was the common language of the Roman Empire. Before the Romans, the Greeks had ruled much of the world, and they had widely spread their language and culture. Some Greek rulers had even forced their subjects to learn the language. So in the first century Greek was understood almost everywhere.

Barnabas

Barnabas was a Levite from the island of Cyprus. His name was Joseph, but the disciples had renamed him Barnabas, meaning "son of encouragement." He was a generous man, active in the church from the beginning (Acts 4:36–37) and "full of the Holy Spirit and faith" (Acts 11:24).

Reaching Gentiles required bridging the gap between the Jewish and Gentile worlds.

God had prepared Saul to do exactly that, and Barnabas had been sharp enough to recognize Saul's exceptional abilities. Saul was at home in both the Jewish and Gentile worlds. He was the bridge the church needed.

Following the Spirit's leading, Saul set out from Antioch on a series of preaching missions that spread Christianity all the way to Rome. In fact, the rest of Acts is the story of Saul's tireless efforts to bring the gospel to the Gentiles.

2 — — — ➤ Launching Out in Faith

Bible Reference: Acts 13:4–52

Sailing, Sailing

Barnabas, Saul, and John Mark, a cousin of Barnabas, began their journey with the blessings and farewells of the Christians in Antioch still ringing in their ears. Leaving the city, they headed for Seleucia, a town about 16 miles west of Antioch. Situated on the Orontes River only five miles from the Mediterranean, Seleucia was the seaport of Antioch. This was the place to catch an outbound ship.

Imagine the sights and sounds that the travelers met in Seleucia: sailing ships and fishing boats on the river, workers unloading ships, merchants delivering and picking up shipments, ships being repaired, fishermen bringing in their catches, and Roman soldiers overseeing port activities.

Crusader castle at the ancient port of Seleucia.

The three men were looking for a ship sailing to Cyprus. They had traveled the Mediterranean before and knew that this wouldn't be a leisurely cruise with roomy cabins and gourmet food. The main task of these ships was to transport cargo, not passengers. Still, Barnabas, Saul, and John were eager to be off, confident of their mission and the Spirit's presence.

A Matter of Strategy and Theology

Paul and Barnabas targeted the big cities for their preaching mission. This was a good strategy. The empire's main roads ran through the cities, and travelers who heard the good news would in turn tell it to others along their route. Farmers and merchants who came to the cities to sell goods would bring the gospel back to their villages.

But another more important reason, a theological reason, supported this strategy. Most of the larger cities around the Mediterranean had Jewish synagogues where both Jews and God-fearing Gentiles met every Sabbath for worship. As you follow Paul and Barnabas on their journey, you will notice that in every city they visited they went first to the synagogue to preach the message of salvation in Christ.

Why? First of all, because Paul firmly believed that salvation should first be offered to the Jews, God's chosen people. What other strategic reasons do you think Paul might have had?

And speaking of strategies, in Acts 13 Luke for the first time identifies Saul by his Roman name, Paul. Why at this point? Probably because here Paul is talking with a Roman official, and using Paul's Roman name is not only courteous but also good strategy.

Traveling Light and Far

When Paul and Barnabas left Antioch, they may not have realized that they were leaving on a two-year trip—two years of traveling down unknown roads, on foot most of the time, separated from family, getting by with odd jobs and handouts from believers.

Trace the travels of this extraordinary team on the map. Notice that after leaving Cyprus they sailed to Asia Minor (modern Turkey), landing at Attalia, the chief port of the coastal province of Pamphylia, and staying briefly at Perga, a few miles inland. Here John Mark abruptly left the team and sailed back home.

Paul and Barnabas pressed into the interior, eager to get to a new field for their work. Reaching their goal of Pisidian Antioch required a long, tough journey through wild mountainous country. There were no paved roads or tourist stops here, but the view must have been spectacular. As

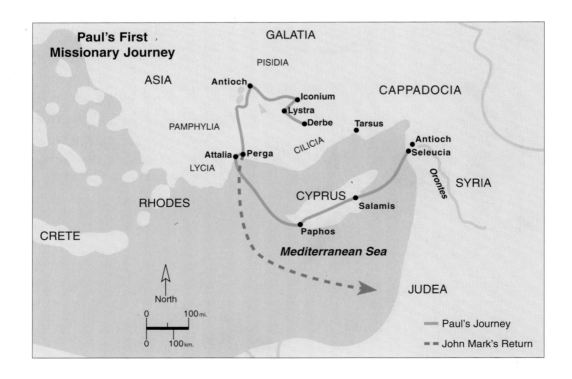

they neared Antioch, the two men must have walked along the shores of Lake Egridir, one of the most beautiful lakes in the region.

Trace the rest of their journey on the map. What other cities did they reach on this preaching mission?

The Island of Cyprus

Cyprus, an island in the Mediterranean, was a province under the rule of the Roman Senate. About 150 miles long and 60 miles wide at its widest point, it has two mountain ranges, one along the north coast and one in the southwest. The island was known for its copper mines. The Jewish historian Josephus reports that Caesar Augustus gave Herod the Great a present of half the copper mines and made him supervisor of the other half. Many Jews came to Cyprus to work in the mines, and, as a result, the island

The Troodos Mountains on Cyprus.

had several synagogues. Also Barnabas was from Cyprus and may have had contacts there. Acts 11:19 says that Christians who were scattered by the persecution had already been "telling the message" in Cyprus.

Acts 13 mentions two cities on Cyprus, Salamis and Paphos. Salamis was a prosperous seaport on the east coast, near the modern resort city of Famagusta. The Jewish community in Salamis was large enough to support more than one synagogue. Paphos, on the other end of the island, was the seat of the Roman government and the most important city on the island.

Pisidian Antioch was a beautiful city about 3,600 feet above sea level. Situated on the east-west highway from Ephesus to Syria in the Roman province of Galatia, Antioch was a Roman colony. Retired Roman soldiers were settled in colonies there and given free land. These colonies were planted at important points on main roads to protect Rome's interests. Antioch was a cosmopolitan city made up of people with different ethnic and national backgrounds.

A colonnaded street in Pisidian Antioch.

3 ━ ━ ━ ━ ━ ➤ Penetrating Galatia

Bible Reference: Acts 14

The Gospel Comes to Iconium

Narrator 1: Leaving Antioch, Paul and Barnabas took the main road out of town toward the east. They traveled on to Iconium, a distance of about 100 miles.

Narrator 2: Once they got their bearings in the city and found a place to stay, they went, as they always did, to the synagogue.

Narrator 3: When they had the opportunity, they presented the message they had come to bring. They spoke so effectively that many Jews and non-Jews believed!

Narrator 1: But some of the Jews who would not accept their message started stirring up trouble. They did their best to turn the authorities and people against Paul and Barnabas.

Narrator 2: But the apostles didn't scare easily. They stayed in Iconium for a long time—for weeks, maybe months—and continued to speak freely of what God had done in Jesus Christ.

Narrator 3: The apostles also did many miracles and signs that showed they were filled with God's word and power.

Narrator 1: As Paul and Barnabas continued preaching and teaching the good news, the citizens began taking sides. Some sided with the Jewish unbelievers and some with the apostles.

Narrator 2: Learning that a mob of Jews and non-Jews were hatching a plot to beat and stone them, Paul and Barnabas slipped out of the city and fled for their lives.

Narrator 3: They took the road leading to Lystra, about a two-day walk.

Narrator 1: But they left behind in Iconium a group of believers who continued to meet and worship the risen Christ.

In Lystra and Derbe

Narrator 1: In Lystra Paul was speaking to a gathered crowd when he noticed that one man was listening closely to him.

Narrator 2: The Bible says, "There sat a man crippled in his feet, who was lame from birth and had never walked." Paul saw that the man had faith to be healed.

Paul: Stand on your feet!

Narrator 3: The man obeyed, jumped to his feet, and began to walk.

Crowd: Look! Publius is walking. How can this be?

Voice 1 from the crowd: This is the first time he has ever walked. I should know. I've lived next door to him my whole life.

Crowd: These men are gods!

Voice 2 from the crowd: The gods have once more come down to us. The quiet one must be Zeus. The other must be Hermes; he does most of the talking.

Voice 3: Remember the stories of the old ones! Show respect for the gods or things will not go well for us.

Crowd: Zeus has again come to Lystra. Prepare the sacrifices!

Narrator 1: The priests of the temple of Zeus, which was near the city gates,

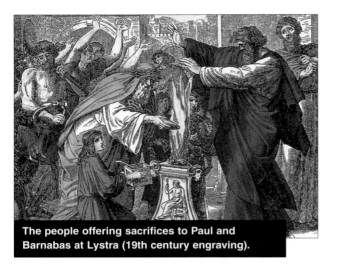

The people offering sacrifices to Paul and Barnabas at Lystra (19th century engraving).

quickly brought sacrifices fitting for the gods: oxen decorated with garlands.

Narrator 2: At first the apostles didn't understand what was going on. The people were using a dialect unfamiliar to them.

Narrator 3: But when the truth dawned on them, Paul and Barnabas were horrified. They rushed into the crowd.

Paul: Why are you doing this? We're not gods, only men like you. Your gods are false gods. Turn to the living God.

The living God made the whole world—the skies, the earth, the seas, and everything in them. It's the living God who sends you rain and gives you crops, who gives you a full stomach and a glad heart.

Narrator 1: Paul talked hard and fast, trying to convince the crowd to give up the idea of sacrificing to them.

Narrator 2: Paul was making some progress when Jewish troublemakers from Antioch and Iconium showed up. Quickly they whipped up the crowd against Paul and Barnabas.

Voice 1: He's not Hermes any more than the other one is Zeus. Why should we listen to him?

Voice 2: They're just rabble-rousers. Imagine, saying our gods are false!

Voice 3: What impostors, claiming to know about the living God!

Crowd: Don't let that big-mouth get away with it!

Narrator 1: Paul suddenly became the mob's chief target. They came at him from all directions.

Narrator 2: They pelted Paul with stones. Cut and bleeding, he was finally knocked unconscious.

Narrator 3: Thinking he was dead, the crowd dragged Paul out of the city and dumped him.

Narrator 1: The disciples found him and gathered around. And wonder of wonders, Paul got up!

Narrator 2: Undaunted, the next day Paul and Barnabas went to Derbe, where they preached and founded another church.

Retracing Steps

Narrator 1: Paul and Barnabas retraced their steps, visiting the young churches they had established in Lystra, Iconium, and Antioch.

Narrator 2: In each church they urged believers to stick with the Christian faith.

Narrator 3: In each church they picked leaders. They prayed and fasted and committed the new leaders to the Lord.

Narrator 1: Then, crossing the mountains one more time, they made their way south to the coast.

A Visit from the "Gods"

Behind the events at Lystra is a Greek myth recorded by the writer Ovid. One day, the myth says, two Greek gods decided to visit the earth. Zeus, the chief god, and Hermes, his messenger, traveled through the area around Lystra. On their visit everyone they met mistreated or ignored them—everyone except one old couple, Baucis and Philemon. This open-hearted couple welcomed the gods, and the gods handsomely rewarded them.

No wonder the people in Lystra wanted to please Paul and Barnabas. When the people of Lystra saw the healing miracle, they thought that the gods had again come down to visit them. The Lystrans didn't want to repeat their ancestors' mistake. This time the gods would be welcomed and treated royally.

Zeus.

Hermes.

Iconium, Lystra, and Derbe

Like Antioch, Iconium (modern Konya) was founded as a Roman colony to help establish Roman authority in Galatia. A flourishing center of commerce and agriculture, the city was also on the east-west trade route between Syria and Ephesus. Iconium was known for its wool and textile industries.

Lystra, another Roman colony, was 20 miles south-southwest of Iconium. The city may not have had a Jewish community large enough to support a synagogue, for here Paul began his mission by preaching to the Gentiles.

Derbe, about 60 miles to the east of Lystra, was near the Galatian border. At Derbe Paul had reached the edge of the province of Galatia, and he made this his last stop. Archaeological discoveries, consisting of two inscriptions and a tombstone, point to modern Kerti Huyuk as the site of the ancient city of Derbe.

Shepherds near the location of Derbe.

Narrator 2: After stopping to preach in Perga, they went on to the port of Attalia, where they boarded a ship for the return trip to Antioch.

Narrator 3: The mission, launched with the Spirit's leading, had been completed. It was a solid, satisfying piece of work.

Narrator 1: When they arrived in Antioch, Paul and Barnabas reported to the church, telling how God had used them to open the door of faith to the Gentiles.

Narrator 2: Then the two apostles settled down, happy to be part of the Antioch church again.

4 ▬ ▬ ▬ ▬ ▬ ➤ Trouble in Galatia

Bible Reference: Galatians 1–2

Another Gospel?

After Paul and Barnabas had returned to Syrian Antioch, news reached them that Jewish Christians from Jerusalem had been disturbing the Galatian churches. These Jewish Christians, called Judaizers, had evidently followed on Paul's heels in Galatia. They were visiting the new churches because they didn't approve of Paul or of the gospel that he preached. They accused Paul of being a false apostle, claiming that he didn't speak with God's authority. They said that he had received his message from the original apostles and then watered it down to make it more acceptable to Gentiles. These Jewish Christians insisted that Paul's message of salvation by faith in Christ alone was misleading: Gentiles had to adopt Jewish practices to be saved.

The new Christians in Galatia didn't understand everything about their new faith, and the ideas of the Judaizers confused them. In fact, the Galatians began to question everything Paul had told them.

Have you ever built a terrific sandcastle—complete with moats, drawbridges, and towers—only to have someone level it with a well-aimed kick? Or maybe you've worked hard on a school project only to have someone carelessly ruin it. If so, you have some idea of how Paul felt when he found out what was happening in the churches that he and Barnabas had helped to start in Galatia.

Paul was hopping mad. The Judaizers were lying about God.

They were undermining not his work but the Spirit's. The Spirit had led Paul and Barnabas to strike out in a new direction and begin a mission to Gentiles. But these Jewish Christians were afraid of the wind of the Spirit. They were trying to turn back the clock. They wanted to control the way the church would develop. More was at stake here than a human project.

Also, Paul was concerned about the young Christians in Galatia. He knew that they were right with God because they trusted in Jesus Christ; they did not have to obey all of the Jewish laws. So Paul wrote a letter to the Galatian churches showing the Christians the danger of believing the Judaizers' teaching.

A True Apostle—No Other Gospel

Paul begins his letter by dealing with the challenge to his authority as an apostle. The challenge was serious, because if the Galatians didn't think Paul was a true apostle, they would doubt his teaching and their own salvation. So Paul forcefully defends himself, giving proof that he was commissioned to be an apostle just as those in Jesus' original circle had been. You can find Paul's defense in Galatians 1:11–2:21. Paul's ringing words in Galatians 2:15–21 are some of the best known in the Bible.

In his letter to the Galatians Paul takes on the Judaizers and their ideas. Not only are they wrong, he says; they are also in danger of eternal condemnation. Strong words! He charges them with preaching a "different gospel—which is really no gospel at all" (Galatians 1:6b–7a). In Galatians Paul proclaims a gospel that breaks down walls and leads believers from a closed prison into Christ's freedom, where there is "neither Jew nor Greek, slave nor free, male nor female" (Galatians 3:28). All believers are united, for all are one in Christ.

5 — — — — — ➤ Freedom in Christ

Bible Reference: Galatians 3–6

Choose Freedom

Paul urges the Galatians to choose freedom in Christ. What Paul says in Galatians is not, of course, original with him. Listen to these words of Jesus: "Are you tired? Worn out? Burned out on religion? Come to me. Get away with me and you'll recover your life. I'll show you how to take a real rest. Walk with me and work with me—watch how I do it. Learn the unforced rhythms of grace. I won't lay anything ill-fitting on you. Keep company with me and you'll learn to live freely and lightly." (Matthew 11:28–30, *The Message*)

Jesus invites us to step into the freedom that comes with believing in him. Faith isn't a list of endless do's and don'ts. Your faith isn't a load you carry. No, Jesus carries you. You can come to Jesus with your disappointments, your jealousies, your fears, your loneliness. Jesus is the only place you will find rest and freedom.

Creative Reading—Galatians 5

Reader 1: Christ has set me free! I don't have to obey rules to earn God's approval. I don't have to earn salvation.

Reader 2: In Christ I'm justified.

Reader 3: Made right with God.

Reader 1: Great! Now I can do anything I feel like doing.

Reader 2: Whoa! Watch out! That way you'll destroy yourself!

Reader 3: Whoa! Watch out! That way you'll bite and destroy others!

Reader 2: Doing what you feel like doing all the time leads to a pile of garbage.

All: Loveless sex, falling for magic religions, hatred, competition and one-upmanship, fits of temper, nasty cliques, mindless partying . . .

Reader 1: Enough! I get the picture. Doing anything I feel like doing will lead me right out of God's kingdom. But then what can I do with my freedom? What's it for?

All: To serve others in love. Live by the Spirit! Walk with the Spirit!

Reader 1: What difference will that make?

Reader 2: You'll be surprised.

Reader 3: You and your life will change.

Reader 2: You'll find new qualities springing up in you . . .

Reader 3: something like fruit growing on a tree.

All: For the fruit of the Spirit is
        love, joy, peace,
        patience, kindness, goodness,
        faithfulness, gentleness, and self-control.

Reader 1: But that's beyond me!

Reader 2: You're right. It is.

Reader 3: But it's not beyond the Spirit.

Reader 1: Thank God, Christ has set me free!

All: We belong to Christ, and Christ has made us new creatures. Let's walk with the Spirit. Let's stop comparing ourselves to others! Each one of us has the freedom to develop as the Spirit leads. Thanks be to God.

6 — — — ➡ The Jerusalem Council

Bible Reference: Acts 15:1–35

Debate in Jerusalem

In Acts 15 the Judaizers are stirring up trouble again, this time in the church in Syrian Antioch. "Unless you're circumcised," the Judaizers bluntly told the Gentile Christians, "you can't be saved. The church is basically a Jewish organization—although you're welcome to join after you're circumcised. And here's a list of dos and don'ts: baths for purifying, foods you're not allowed to eat, special ways to prepare food . . ."

Imagine how the Gentiles felt. After joyfully believing in Christ, being baptized, and receiving the Spirit, hearing these new "requirements" for salvation must have given them quite a jolt. Paul and Barnabas were outraged. (Remember your study of Galatians?)

The church leaders in Antioch saw that this issue had to be settled—and quickly. So they sent a delegation to Jerusalem to talk with the apostles and elders there. The group included Paul, Barnabas, and other believers from Antioch.

The Party of the Pharisees

Acts 15 identifies "believers who belonged to the party of the Pharisees" as those who stood up in the Jerusalem meeting and demanded that Gentile believers must be circumcised and required to obey the law of Moses. The "party of the Pharisees" is also known by the name Judaizers. This faction evidently was led by some Pharisees who had become Christians but were still convinced that Gentiles had to be routed through Judaism to be eligible for God's grace in Christ.

The church in Jerusalem warmly welcomed the group. The believers were eager to hear how God was working through Paul and Barnabas to bring Gentiles to Christ. But the Judaizers soon broke up their fellowship and unity, renewing their demand that Gentiles must observe the requirements of the law of Moses.

Then the apostles and elders sat down to thrash things out.

The Name James

The name James must have been popular in New Testament times. James pops up so often in the New Testament that sometimes it's downright confusing. The name comes from the Hebrew name Jacob. There are at least four different men named James in the Bible:

- James—apostle of Jesus, son of Zebedee, and older brother of John. He was in the circle of Jesus' closest disciples. His mother was probably Salome, Jesus' mother's sister, making him Jesus' cousin. Herod executed James about 10 years after Jesus' resurrection (Acts 12:2). In church tradition this James has become known as James the Great.
- James—apostle of Jesus and son of Alphaeus. He is called James the Less. Although his name appears on lists of disciples in the Gospels (see Matthew 10:3), little else is known about him.
- James—father of one of the 12 disciples, Judas (not Judas Iscariot; see Luke 6:16; Acts 1:13).
- James—brother of Jesus (Mark 6:3). At first James did not believe that Jesus was the Christ (John 7:5), but later he became a leader in the Jerusalem church. He came to be known as James the Just because he was a wise and godly man. He wrote the epistle of James. This James is the one the account of the Jerusalem Council refers to in Acts 15:13. He was martyred around the year A.D. 62.

7 ━━➤ The Gentile Mission Continues

Bible Reference: Acts 15:36—16:40

What's Freedom?

Paul's second missionary journey covered more than 2,000 miles and took two to three years. Luke's account of the journey takes only three or four pages in your Bible. So what we know about the trip is a fraction of what actually happened. That's true of what we know about events in Philippi too. Paul, Silas, Timothy, and perhaps Luke made quite a few converts in Philippi—enough to start a church. But Luke tells about only three new Christians: Lydia, the slave girl, and the jailer.

We meet Lydia first. She's a rich businesswoman who is a worshiper of God. The Lord opens her heart, and she believes Paul's gospel message. She opens her home, urging Paul and the others to stay with her.

The story of Lydia shows barriers disappearing. First, Lydia was a Gentile, but a barrier came down when Paul, a Jew, accepted her hospitality. Second, she was a woman. In the first century women occupied a low rung on the social ladder, but Paul and Silas talked to her in public and associated with her. Besides, Lydia seems to have been a leader in the early church. So another barrier tumbled down. The way the early church treated women was not society's way. In Christ Lydia was free to welcome Paul and Silas into her home, and they were free to accept her as an equal in Christ.

The slave girl is the second new Christian we meet. The young woman has a "spirit" and makes a lot of money for her owners by telling fortunes. In the name of Christ Paul commands the evil spirit to come out her, and she is free. Her owners are furious. They ought to be celebrating with her, but to them she's a piece of property that has just lost its value. To get even, they trump up charges against Paul and Silas. "These men are Jews" sets up racial barriers. "Advocating customs unlawful for us Romans" appeals to more barriers, those between nations and traditions.

The bringers of freedom are thrown in prison. Midnight finds Paul and Silas—their backs bleeding and their feet locked in stocks—singing hymns and praying. Then an earthquake rocks the building, the prison doors fly open, and the chains fall from the prisoners.

Now we meet the third convert, the jailer. The quake wakes him. When he sees the open prison doors, he knows he's in trouble and draws his sword; it seems better to kill himself now than face the authorities. The jailer's ring of keys doesn't make him free.

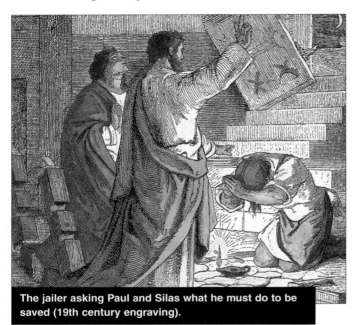

The jailer asking Paul and Silas what he must do to be saved (19th century engraving).

Seeing the jailer, Paul shouts, "Don't harm yourself! We are all here."

The jailer calls for lights and rushes in. Amazed, he escapes his own prison. He is baptized and believes—and is free. He welcomes Paul and Silas into his home, just as Lydia did.

By now you may have figured out why Luke chose just these three converts to write about. Lydia, the slave girl, and the jailer are very different from one another; but they—along with Paul, Silas, and Timothy—are one in Christ. Christ breaks down barriers and divisions.

Luke is saying that this is what being in Christ is like. In Christ all are one, "for there is neither Jew nor Greek, slave nor free, male nor female." And remember, he adds, things aren't always what they seem. Who in the story appears to be free? Who appears to be tied in bonds? Who really is free?

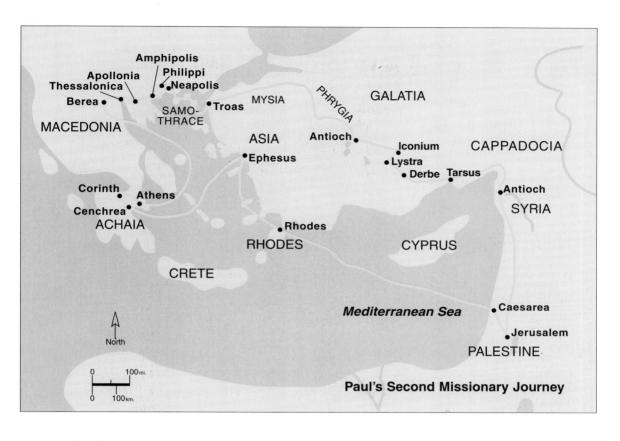

Paul's Second Missionary Journey

Look at the map and trace the route that Paul and Silas followed. Check out the names of the cities where the two brought the gospel. Also notice how much farther north Paul penetrated on this trip.

Lictors

Chief magistrates in Rome and other Roman cities were attended by officials called lictors. Lictors carried bundles of rods called a fasces, sometimes with an ax in the center, as a sign that magistrates had the right to order physical punishment—even death. In Philippi lictors stripped Paul and Silas and then beat them with rods. (In 2 Corinthians 11:25 Paul says that he was beaten with rods three times.)

Fasces

Troas, Samothrace, Neapolis, and Philippi

The city of Troas, founded at the end of the 4th century B.C., became a Roman colony in the time of Emperor Augustus. Troas was 15 miles south of the site of the famous ancient city of Troy. Strategically positioned on the Aegean sea, the port was a regular stop for

The harbor at Troas.

ships traveling between Asia and Macedonia during Roman times.

The mountainous island of Samothrace rose from the Aegean sea to a height of 5,000 feet. Most likely the missionaries broke their voyage from Troas to Neapolis with a night's stay on this island.

Paul and his companions disembarked at Neapolis, the port of Philippi. From there they walked along one of the great Roman roads, the Egnatian Way, which started in Neapolis and continued to Rome. Philippi was only 10 miles to the north, although the road cut through a range of rocky mountains. Today the modern port of Kavalla stands where Neapolis once stood. Near Kavalla archaeologists have uncovered ruins of a village and a temple dating from the time of Greek rule.

Philippi sits on a plain circled by mountains, right on the Egnatian Way. Philippi was prosperous: there was gold in the nearby mountains. It seems that not many Jews lived in Philippi, which had no synagogue. (A synagogue required a group of at least 10 Jewish men.) The few Jews living there met each Sabbath outside the city walls on the banks of the Gangites River. The city of Philippi existed until the late Middle Ages. If you travel to Greece, you can see extensive ruins of this ancient city. Near Philippi you can still see some of the huge, worn paving stones of the Egnatian Way.

8 ━ ━ ━ ━ ➤ The Spirit Leads On

Bible Reference: Acts 17:1—18:22

When Paul, Silas, and Timothy left Philippi, they followed the road along the coast to Thessalonica, a large and important city. A number of Jews lived in Thessalonica, so Paul began teaching and preaching in the synagogue. Some of the Jews and many of the God-fearing Gentiles believed. But then some of the people in the Jewish community became jealous of Paul's success, and—you guessed it—caused a riot. Paul and the others had to be sneaked out of the city during the night.

The evangelists went on to Berea, where the synagogue put out the welcome mat. Here the Jews were so open and eager that Paul went to the synagogue every day to talk and teach. But Jews from Thessalonica arrived on the scene, and believers escorted Paul out of the city and on to Athens. Silas and Timothy stayed in Berea for a time.

Athens—a cultured, beautiful city—was filled with idols. Paul was revolt-

Thessalonica and Berea

Thessalonica, the modern Salonika, was a large city with a population of 200,000; it was the capital of the Roman province of Macedonia. A center of trade, it enjoyed easy land access along the Egnatian Way and by sea across the Aegean Sea. At Thessalonica, archaeologists have uncovered a Roman forum, a synagogue, and other buildings dating from the first century or earlier.

Berea (sometimes spelled Beroea) was 65 miles southwest of Thessalonica in a beautiful hilly region. The city itself sat right at the foot of Mount Bernius. The city of Verria stands on that site today. In Paul's day the city was known for its community of artisans and stonecutters. If you visit Verria today, you can see the old Jewish quarter of the city.

Athens and Corinth

Athens was one of the most famous centers of culture and learning in the ancient world. When the city fell to the Romans in 86 B.C., the Romans, respecting its great reputation, made it a free city.

A hill called the Acropolis was in the center of Athens. Here stood many temples, among them the Parthenon, the famous temple to Athena. To the northwest of the Acropolis was the Areopagus (Mars Hill), the place where Paul addressed the philosophers. Farther to the northwest was the marketplace, the open area where Athenians gathered to discuss current issues and conduct business. In Athens the marketplace was surrounded by colonnades and temples as well as by official buildings and bazaars. Archaeologists have been working in Athens for many years, uncovering many of its ancient buildings and recovering thousands of coins, art objects, and other artifacts.

The Parthenon on the Acropolis.

Corinth was one of Greece's chief cities. Rebuilt by Julius Caesar in 44 B.C., the city was proud of its culture. Every other year Corinth hosted the Isthmian games, famous in the ancient world (more famous, some say, than the ones in Athens that inspired our modern Olympics).

Corinth was a center for international east-west trade. Just south of a narrow isthmus connecting the mainland Greece with its southern peninsula, the city had two harbors. Six miles to the east on the Saronic Gulf was Cenchrae; a mile and a half to the west on the Corinthian Gulf was Lechaion.

The marble podium where Paul addressed the Corinthians.

Cargo was transported across the isthmus on a road built for that purpose. Small ships complete with their goods moved on the road; goods from the larger ships were loaded into wagons and hauled across the isthmus. In this way traders from the west, from Italy and Spain, came past Corinth; so did traders from from Egypt, Phoenicia, and other points east.

ed by what he saw. He went to the synagogue and to the marketplace, the center of public life, to argue and discuss. When he was invited to address a meeting of philosophers on the famous Mars Hill, his starting point was the altar he had seen to "an unknown god." Then with bold brushstrokes Paul painted the picture

Paul preaching at Athens (19th century engraving).

of the one God who created, sustains, and judges the world. Again, resurrection was the controversial topic.

From Athens Paul moved on to Corinth, a more promising city. Paul, who knew the tentmaker trade, stayed with two Jewish tentmakers he met there. The three of them supported themselves with the business. Paul stayed in Corinth a year and a half. God was with him, and he was able to work without much interference. When Paul finally moved on, he left behind a lively church.

Going down to Cenchrae, Paul caught a ship for Ephesus. After a brief stay, he traveled by ship to Caesarea and then home.

Paul went from place to place sowing the seed of the kingdom of God. Some heard and dismissed the message. What Paul and his companions were doing seemed unimportant to them.

Perhaps at times the evangelists themselves may have wondered about their mission. Troubles, disputes, riots, beatings, midnight escapes . . . and the task was incredibly huge. But maybe they pondered what Jesus had said about the kingdom of God—that it's like a mustard seed, a seed the size of a period on this page. The sower sows the seed, and a plant appears. It grows, slowly and quietly, into a tree. The power is in the seed—that's the secret of the kingdom of God.

9 ➡ Letters to Thessalonica

Bible Reference: The Books of 1 and 2 Thessalonians

During Paul's year and a half in Corinth he often thought about the churches he had planted in Macedonia and Achaia and wondered how they were doing. In Thessalonica a mob of angry Jews had come after Paul and later followed him to Berea, so Paul must have wondered about the young church in Thessalonica. Finally, Paul sent Timothy to check up on the Thessalonians.

St. Paul Preaching to the Thessalonians by Gustave Doré.

Timothy brought back a good report: the believers in Thessalonica were holding to the faith and telling others about Jesus. But Timothy also told Paul that the new believers were confused about Christ's return. Expecting Christ to return any day, some of them didn't think going to work was worthwhile. Others were concerned about believers who died before Christ returned. Would those who died miss out?

So Paul wrote a letter to the Thessalonians. After greeting the Christians (1 Thessalonians 1:1), he gives thanks for their faith and witness (1:2–10). Next, he tells them what has happened to him and how much he would like to see them (2:1–3:10). He ends this personal section of the letter with a moving prayer of blessing (3:11–13).

Then Paul turns to the new Christians' needs. First he urges them to live as God's children, mentioning specific practices they should avoid (4:1–12). Then he clears up some of their misunderstandings about Christ's return (4:13–5:11). Paul closes the letter with instructions to the church, and then

Writing in Paul's Day

Writing in Paul's day wasn't easy, with no typewriters and no computers and printers. He wrote on parchment, using a pointed reed and ink made of carbon. Parchment was expensive. It took time to make: the skins of sheep or goats were placed in a lime solution, the hair taken off, and then the skins stretched and made smooth with pumice.

Not everyone in Paul's day knew how to read and write. That's one reason why Paul's letters were read aloud in church when they were received. Often the letters were copied and circulated to several churches in the region.

adds his blessing and closing greetings.

That's Paul's first letter to the Thessalonians in a nutshell.

Here's a question for you to think about as you read the letter. It was written for the Thessalonians about 2,000 years ago, so what does it have to say to you?

2 Thessalonians

Paul wrote a second letter to the Thessalonians about six months after the first. The purpose of the two letters was similar: to encourage the new believers, to urge them to hang onto their faith, and to correct their misunderstandings about the Lord's return.

10 - - - - - ➤ Paul in Ephesus

Bible Reference: Acts 18:18—19:22

Wonder-Working Power

In Ephesus God did mighty things through Paul. The Spirit of God showed that he was with Paul through many signs and wonders. In fact, in Ephesus people were healed of diseases by touching material that had touched Paul. Imagine: remnants of Paul's work clothes—pieces from aprons that he tied around his waist or sweatbands that he tied around his head—had enough power to heal!

Those who practiced the occult took notice. They were worried that Paul would put them out of business. Among these magicians were seven brothers, Jewish exorcists, who tried to imitate Paul and tap into the power of Jesus' name. But when they used Jesus' name to command a demon, the demon didn't recognize their right to use the power. Their exorcism backfired. The demon-possessed man—with sudden abnormal power—reacted violently and the seven brothers ran out on the street naked and bleeding.

Saint Paul Preaching in Ephesus by Eustache le Sueur, 1616–1655.

What does this incident tell you about taking God's name in vain? And what does it say about Paul and his message?

Magicians and sorcerers in Ephesus certainly got the message: Jesus' name was nothing to trifle with. The bungled exorcism terrified the magicians. Luke says, "And the name of the Lord Jesus was held in high honor."

Ephesian Scripts

First-century Ephesus, with a population of about 200,000, was the fourth largest city in the world. A seaport in the province of Asia under Roman rule, the city was an important commercial center. Today a village called Ayasoluk stands over the site of the old city of Ephesus.

The incident Luke tells of the exorcism and the magicians in Acts 19 fits in with what historians tell us about Ephesus. Ephesus had a reputation in the ancient world as a center for practicing magic. In fact, scrolls of magical spells were sometimes called "Ephesian scripts." Archaeologists have found a number of scrolls such as those burned in Ephesus. Some of them can be seen among collections in Europe. The spells in these scrolls are gibberish, a mixture of words and names, sometimes arranged in patterns.

A number of magicians who became believers "confessed their evil deeds." Many of them publicly burned the scrolls of their magic spells.

Wonder-Working Power Again

Although Paul's healings and exorcisms grab our attention, they're only part of the story. In Ephesus God also did mighty things through Paul's preaching and teaching. Despite his bad track record in synagogues, when Paul arrived in the city, he went boldly to the synagogue and spoke about the kingdom of God. After three months he ran into a brick wall of stubborn unbelief, so he took his disciples and relocated his center of operations to a lecture hall. Paul discussed and taught here for two years until, Luke says, "All the Jews and Greeks who lived in the province of Asia heard the word of the Lord."

Where's the Devil Today?

In our culture we no longer like to call the Devil by his name. We don't like to use words like *evil* or *sin* either.

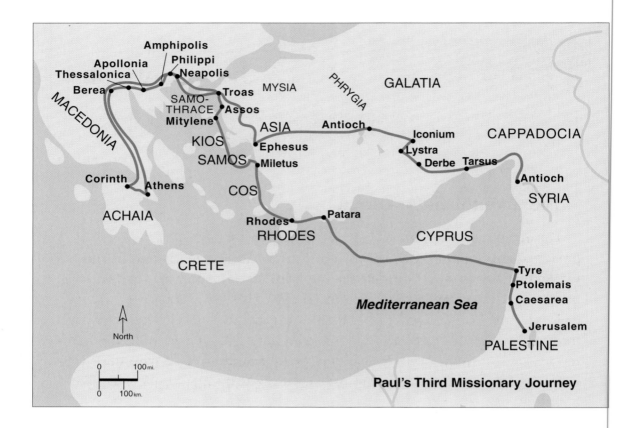

Paul's Third Missionary Journey

Our books and movies and television programs show how things have changed. In one children's book, *The Devil's Other Storybook*, the Devil is a friendly fellow who reads novels and drinks cider. In the movie *The Devil's Advocate* the Devil has become a sharp operator heading a law firm that specializes in things such as getting rich murderers off the hook. These days being wicked is made to appear more interesting than being good.

Several writers have pointed out that the very qualities that used to be considered evil are qualities we now think of as traits a person needs to get ahead: pride, selfishness, ambition. TV and movies have made wickedness seem so common and so accepted—and even so funny—that the Devil doesn't even shock us anymore.

It sounds like this is beyond a local bonfire.

11 ➡ A Letter to the Corinthians

> **Bible Reference: 1 Corinthians 3:1–9; 5–6;
> 10:1–17**

The Corinthians Ask for It

During his three years in Ephesus Paul worked with great energy. He preached and taught daily in Tyrannus's hall and also worked at his tent-making trade to support himself. He must also have taken time to supervise others who preached throughout the province of Asia; churches such as Colossae and Hierapolis were founded in this time. Paul felt responsibility for the churches he had started in Macedonia and Achaia as well. So when reports came to him about these churches, he communicated with them by letter. Paul wrote his first letter to the Corinthians from Ephesus, most likely around the year A.D. 55.

Two things prompted Paul to write to the Corinthians. First, visitors arriving in Ephesus from Corinth brought Paul disturbing news. Second, the Corinthians themselves sent a letter full of questions for Paul: Should Christians eat meat that's been used in pagan worship? What's the Christian view of sex, marriage, and divorce? How should we think about the gifts of the Holy Spirit? Are some gifts more important than others? How can the dead be raised to life?

Paul's letter begins with straight talk about what was going on in the Corinthian church. Paul minces no words. He tells the believers to change their ways. Then, starting with chapter 7, he deals with their questions.

In this and the next few lessons we will look at what Paul wrote to the Corinthians. We share many of their problems and questions.

Culture Zone

The Christians in Corinth lived in an anti-Christian culture. Living a

Roman Corinth

When Julius Caesar refounded the city of Corinth as a Roman colony, it prospered almost immediately. The city had not only Rome's support but also a good water supply from springs and a natural defense at its back in the towering Acrocorinth with an elevation of about 1,800 feet. Add to these things its two harbors and location for trade, and you can understand why the city mushroomed in size. At the time of Paul Corinth's population was about 650,000; of this number about 400,000 were slaves.

Vice and religion mushroomed too. Old Corinth had many gods and sacred places. One writer describes 26 sacred places (not all temples). Among them were temples to Apollo, to Asclepius (the god of healing), and to Aphrodite (the goddess of love).

Corinth had a reputation as a city of evil and immorality. Someone even coined the verb *Corinthianize*, meaning "practice sexual immorality." The practices at the temple of Aphrodite, which stood on the flat top of the Acrocorinth, promoted immorality.

The temple of Apollo in Corinth.

According to the historian Strabo, the temple had more than 1,000 female priests who practiced prostitution in the city.

Archaeologists have mapped out the location of many of Roman Corinth's important buildings. Included in their findings is a piece of white marble bearing the inscription "Synagogue of the Hebrews." The marble had most likely been above the doorway to the synagogue.

Christian life was hard. We're in much the same situation, facing the same basic problems as the Corinthians: How can we live as Christians in a secular and often anti-Christian culture? How can we live by biblical values when the values around us ignore or contradict them?

Knowing biblical values and clearly identifying our culture's values is one way to begin to get a handle on the situation. Sex, for example, is one area that our culture has twisted out of biblical shape. According to the media, nothing is absolutely right or wrong. Anything that "feels right" is right, including adultery and premarital sex. How does this measure up to biblical standards?

Take a critical look at what society is trying to sell you. Be aware that most movies and television programs are based on values that are the opposite of biblical values. A recent poll shows that most people working in the media are hostile to religion. The majority don't believe in the God of the Bible, and nine out of ten don't go to church. What they produce in the media reflects their own values.

So root yourself in Christian values. Don't blindly conform to your culture and its values.

God washed you—and your sexual behavior.

The Holy Spirit lives in you—in your body.

You belong to Christ; you are not your own.

So honor God with your body.

12 ▬ ▬ ▬ ➤ What's Most Important?

Bible Reference: 1 Corinthians 12–13

Racket in Corinth

Many conflicts plagued the church in Corinth, one of which was about gifts of the Spirit. Some young Christians in Corinth were wondering how they could be sure that the Holy Spirit lived within them. Other church members thought they knew the answer. You have

The site of Corinth.

Fearfully and Wonderfully

"When I listen to music, I can detect sound frequencies that flutter the eardrum as faintly as one billionth of a centimeter. That is only one-tenth the diameter of a hydrogen atom. This vibration is transmitted into my inner ear by three bones known as the hammer, anvil, and stirrup. When the middle C note is stuck on a piano, the piston of bones in my inner ear vibrates 256 times per second. Further in are individual cilia, like the rods and cones of the eye, that transmit specific messages of sound to the brain. Whenever anything goes wrong with any part of the ear—with the hammer or the anvil or the stirrup or the cilia—hearing is distorted or destroyed. Even the smallest parts of the body are important to the body's total well-being."

—Dr. Paul Brand, *Fearfully and Wonderfully Made*

the Holy Spirit, they said, "when you have one or more spiritual gifts. For example, you might have the gift of healing or teaching or organizing. Speaking in tongues, though, is the gift to have. The Spirit takes direct control of you and speaks through you. If you speak in tongues, you can be sure you have the Holy Spirit.

You're wrong, Paul tells them. "Any gift, no matter how great it seems, means nothing in itself. It means something only when you use it for the common good. And remember, gifts are not rated first- or second-class. Every single gift—and the Spirit gives every believer a gift—is necessary for the well-being of the whole, just like even the smallest parts of the body are important to the body as a whole."

God doesn't care which gifts we have. But he does care how we use our gifts. That's why chapter 13, which is about love, follows chapter 12, which is about gifts. If we lack love, even speaking in tongues is just making a lot of noise, like the racket of crashing cymbals or noisy gongs.

"The Greatest of These"

Once upon a time a man who could really turn on an audience filled assembly halls and churches wherever he went. People sat on hardwood benches and stared at him, entranced. When the speech was over, many went out crying, claiming that their lives were changed forever. The man was a phenomenon. Thousands obeyed him; those who didn't, he despised.

Once upon a time a writer spent years studying the world she lived in; then she wrote a shelf full of books about how things were and how they might be. Thousands read her books and later her newspaper columns because she seemed to have a crystal ball. If she said there would be war or peace, there was. She lived alone in a mountain cabin and refused to see any guests.

Once upon a time a scientist worked his entire lifetime to find a cure for a crippling disease. He was so devoted to his task that he cared very little for his wife, and his children never knew him. When the man was almost 60, he found the cure that had eluded him for so long. His story appeared in all the leading magazines. Soon an inoculation was developed; the disease he fought against was conquered. He received a medal of honor.

Once upon a time a preacher who read the Bible very carefully decided to start his own church, convinced that all other preachers were dead wrong about their doctrine. Often, right in the middle of worship services, he would thunder against those who didn't believe exactly what he preached. Sometimes he would weep, right up on the pulpit. Everywhere he looked he found enemies. All of them, he claimed, were children of Satan.

Every single one of these "once-upon-a-time" people were headliners. Every one of them was really gifted with talent and power. Every one did great things. But every one fell short.

Love, Paul says, is "the greatest of these." Big talk, big money, big brains, big zeal—are all second fiddle to the kindness, the humility, the sweet honesty of selfless love.

The Pharisee and the high priest saw a beaten man in the ditch. They thought about helping him, but they were busy—they had big things to do. The Samaritan never thought—not even for a moment; he just acted—out of love.

Faith is important, hope is necessary, but love is something else altogether, Paul says. Love—loving others as Christ has loved us—is "the greatest of these."

13 ━ ━ ━ ━ ━ ━ ➜ To Live Again

Bible Reference: 1 Corinthians 15

Resurrection Guaranteed

"For what I received I passed on to you as of first importance: that Christ died for our sins according to the Scriptures, that he was buried, that he was raised on the third day according to the Scriptures, and that he appeared to Peter, and then to the Twelve" (1 Corinthians 15:3–5a).

Resurrected Christ by Fra Bartolommeo, 1516.

This testimony to Jesus' resurrection is our earliest Christian creed. Paul didn't claim to compose the testimony. Rather, he says, he is passing on a testimony from early Christian tradition. You see, from the very beginning the church believed in the resurrection. That's how the church got started. And the church stands or falls with the belief in Jesus' resurrection. So Paul tells the people in Corinth to hold firmly to this gospel or

Firstfruits

Paul calls Jesus "the firstfruits of those who have fallen asleep" (1 Corinthians 15:20). Firstfruits was the first sheaf of the first barley harvest that was offered to the Lord as sign that all the harvest was the Lord's (Leviticus 23:9–11, 17, 20). Here Paul uses the metaphor to mean that Jesus' resurrection is the first of the harvest, serving as God's guarantee for the full harvest, the resurrection of all the believing dead.

they won't have anything to cling to.

But some members of the Corinthian church in Corinth had already let go of the resurrection. The whole idea was too hard to swallow. There was no resurrection of the body, they said.

Paul tells them to stop and think about what they are claiming. If what they said is true, then the whole Christian faith falls in like a house of cards. It's all a complete waste of time and an outright lie.

Paul continues, "But Christ has indeed been raised from the dead, the firstfruits of those who have fallen asleep" (1 Corinthians 15:20). Christ has nailed down the coffin of death. Our resurrection is guaranteed.

Like a Grain of Wheat

Have you ever wondered about what life will be like in the new creation? What age will we be? Will babies be forever babies? Will the aged stay that way for all eternity? Will we recognize people we know?

The Christians of Corinth had questions, too. They asked Paul what kind of a body the resurrected would have.

Paul has no easy answer. He's trying to explain something beyond his experience—like an unhatched chick trying to explain to other unhatched chicks what life is like outside the shell. The best Paul can do is describe the world outside the shell in terms of the world inside the shell.

So Paul advises the Corinthians to look around them. Look, for example, at a grain of wheat. A bare seed goes into the ground, and the plant that

Resurrection Clothes

A skeptic asked second-century Rabbi Meir: "When the dead rise, will they rise naked or in their clothes?"

The rabbi told the questioner to look at a grain of wheat. "If the grain of wheat is put into the earth naked and grows up in who knows how many garments, how much more should you expect appropriate clothing for the raised righteous ones who are buried in their clothes?"

comes up is wheat; but the plant has a different "body" than the seed. It has continuity, but it also changes.

In creation, Paul points out, God is continuously transforming one body into another. So what makes you think that God can't change your present body into an entirely new kind of body? Giving you a resurrection body is no more incredible than what God has been doing since the creation.

One thing is sure, Paul says. The present body bears the likeness of the "man of dust," but the new body will bear the likeness of the "man from heaven." In other words, God will transform our bodies to be like Jesus' body.

In spite of Paul's help, it's hard to imagine what our resurrection body will be like; but we know that it will be buried weak but rise up powerful.

So, along with the believers in Corinth, continue believing in the resurrection, confident that nothing you do for the Lord is a waste of time.

14 — — ➤ A Riot and Another Letter

> **Bible Reference: Acts 19:23—20:1; selected passages from 2 Corinthians**

A Riot in Ephesus

Narrator 1: Paul had been teaching and preaching in Ephesus for almost three years. Through the power of the Spirit many believed and turned from worshiping idols.

Narrator 2: Those who served the goddess Artemis also began hearing about the Way. And those who made silver shrines to Artemis began noticing that sales were down. Demetrius, one of the silversmiths, traced the problem to Paul's preaching.

Demetrius (to other silversmiths): How were your sales today? Business getting any better?

Darius: Well, sales are down. But the weather's been bad all month.

Zenas: Be honest, Darius. It's not the weather we're fighting here. It's that rabble-rouser Paul. He goes around telling people to get rid of their idols. Why, just yesterday when I offered an Artemis shrine to a woman passing by my stall, she refused. Then she quoted Paul to me. My statues, she said, are worthless.

Demetrius: Worthless! If she keeps talking that way, they soon will be.

Darius: Calm down, Demetrius. Don't forget that our temple to Artemis is one of the wonders of the world. Pilgrims come from all over to worship here. What damage can one man like Paul do?

Zenas: It's okay for you to take the long view, Darius. You've been in business for years and probably have a stash of gold under your mattress. But I've got to sell enough shrines each month to buy materials to make the next month's batch.

Demetrius: You're right, Zenas. Taking the long view is no good. If the Way becomes more popular, business can only get worse. We should nip this thing in the bud.

Demetrius inciting the Ephesians against Paul (19th century engraving).

Narrator 3: So Demetrius gathered the silversmiths and other temple traders and addressed them.

Demetrius: Men, you know that we have a good income from our businesses. But now this man Paul is going around saying that gods made with human hands are not gods at all. And he's getting lots of people to go along with him—in Ephesus and also throughout the whole province of Asia!

Our trade is losing its good name. But even worse, if Paul's allowed to keep talking down Artemis, her name will be tarnished. The great goddess Artemis, who is worshiped throughout the province of Asia and the world, will be robbed of her divine majesty.

Narrator 1: When the crowd heard this, they were furious and began shouting:

Crowd: Great is Artemis of the Ephesians! Great is Artemis!

Narrator 2: The crowd spilled into the city streets, all the while chanting in praise to Artemis.

Crowd: Great is Artemis! Great is Artemis of the Ephesians!

Narrator 3: Soon the whole city was in a huge uproar. People were rushing into the streets and asking each other what was going on.

Narrator 1: By now the crowd was an ugly mob looking for trouble.

Voice in the mob: Hey, look over there! There's two of the Way. Grab them!

Narrator 1: Seizing Gaius and Aristarchus, companions of Paul, the crowd surged down the road and into the theater.

Narrator 2: News of the trouble reached Paul.

Paul (to friends): The mob has Gaius and Aristarchus and there's no telling what the mob will do. Get my cloak. Pray for me.

Disciple 1: No, it's madness for you to wade into that mob. They're so angry, they'll tear you limb from limb.

Disciple 2: We won't let you do this. Wait, here's a messenger from your friends in the province council. They'll know what's going on.

Messenger: My masters beg you not to go near the theater. The mob is out of control. An official is on the way to try to quiet things down. Can I tell them that you accept their advice?

Paul (grudgingly): All right. Tell them I accept their advice. I'll stay away from the theater and lie low for a while.

Narrator 3: Meanwhile, the scene in the theater was mass confusion; some people were yelling one thing, some another. Most didn't even know why they were there. Some Jews pushed forward one of their group, Alexander. But he never got a chance to talk. As soon as the mob realized he was a Jew, they started shouting the same refrain.

Crowd: Great is Artemis of the Ephesians! Great is Artemis of the Ephesians!

Narrator 1: They chanted for two hours. Then the city clerk pushed his way through the mob and stood where everyone could see him. He motioned for quiet.

City clerk: Men of Ephesus, doesn't all the world know that the city of Ephesus is the guardian of the temple of the great Artemis and of her image, which fell from heaven? These facts are undeniable, so be quiet and don't do anything rash! You have brought these men here, though they have neither robbed temples nor blasphemed our goddess. If Demetrius and the other artisans have a complaint against anybody, they can press charges in court. Bring any other problems to the town meeting to be settled. Don't you realize you're putting our city in danger? There's no way to reasonably explain what went on today. Rome won't put up with rioting. Now go back to work or go home.

Narrator 2: When the uproar was over and life returned to normal, Paul sent for the disciples, said goodbye, and set out for Macedonia.

One of the Seven Wonders

Ephesus was one of the most sacred sites and one of the seven wonders of the ancient world, mostly because of the temple to Artemis. Artemis was known as the bountiful earth mother, the goddess of fertility and household protector. In the temple was a magnificent statue of Artemis made from a meteorite. People in Ephesus thought the statue showed a supernatural hand because it had fallen from the sky.

A statue of Artemis recovered in Ephesus.

Pilgrims from around the world flocked to the temple to worship. In Ephesus the pilgrims bought miniature silver shrines of Artemis to carry into the temple with them and later use as shrines in their homes. The temple was good business for Ephesus.

Today the village of Ayasoluk stands near the site of old Ephesus. Archaeologists have uncovered much of the ancient city. One visitor wrote that Ephesus has "the most impressive ruins in Asia Minor." Looking at the excavations, it's easy to picture the scene of the riot in Ephesus.

When the angry craftsmen went running into the street, they probably took the Arcadian Way, the main street of Ephesus. Eleven meters wide, the street was paved with marble and lined on both sides with colonnades. This street led straight from the harbor to a large open theater set against the foot of Mount Pion. The mob took Gaius and Aristarchus to this theater. This theater is well-preserved and seats at least 24,000 people.

Good News, Bad News

After he left Ephesus, Paul anxiously waited in Troas for Titus, who was bringing news from Corinth. But Titus never showed up, so Paul went on to Macedonia. When Titus arrived, he had both good and bad news for Paul. The good news was that the Corinthians had received Paul's letter with love and godly sorrow. The bad news was that some in the church were attacking Paul, questioning whether he deserved to be called an apostle.

Paul answered the charges in the Book of 2 Corinthians. He calls his critics "super-apostles" because they claimed to be better apostles than Paul.

Paul also told what he had suffered for Jesus' sake as an apostle to the Gentiles. Paul has a list of things to "boast" about: five floggings of forty lashes minus one, three beatings with rods, one stoning, three shipwrecks, and hunger. That's not even the whole list.

Paul's second letter to the Corinthians gives us more details about his life than any other New Testament book. As you read parts of this letter, try to imagine what Paul's life was life. If you could talk with Paul, what questions would you like to ask him?

15 — — — ➤ Letter to the Romans

Bible Reference: Romans 1–5

A Theme for a Letter and for a Life

The letter Paul wrote to the church in Rome didn't make a splash—not even a ripple—when it arrived in the city. In *The Message*, Eugene Peterson says that there was much to read in Rome—much of it world-class. "And yet in no time, as such things go, this letter left all those other writings in the dust. Paul's letter to the Romans has had a far larger impact on its readers than the volumes of all those Roman writers put together."

In this letter to the Christians in Rome Paul is working out the implications of Jesus' death and resurrection. He is thinking through the effects of this event on the world and on each person in the world. Most Christians find following Paul's thinking a challenge, but those who make the effort discover new ways of looking at troubling issues.

One key to understanding the letter is identifying Paul's main theme. Paul states the theme in Romans 1:16–17:

I am not ashamed of the gospel, because it is the power of God
for the salvation of everyone who believes: first for the Jew,
then for the Gentile. For in the gospel a righteousness from God
is revealed, a righteousness that is by faith from first to last,
just as it is written: "The righteous will live by faith."

Although Paul brings in many subthemes, he always relates them to the major theme: that the gospel is the power of God for salvation.

Being ashamed of the gospel is easy, because accepting the gospel means admitting that we need to be made righteous, admitting that no matter how "good" we are we can't make it on our own. What a blow to our self-esteem! No wonder most people say, Thanks, but no thanks. What do we have to be saved from?

Paul answers, Look around you. The world is not the way it's supposed

The City of Rome

Rome, the capital of the Roman Empire, was at the peak of its growth in the first century. Located on foothills near the Tiber River and about 18 miles from the Mediterranean, the city was the pulse of the empire. Magnificent buildings made up the heart of the city: temples to various gods, theaters, baths, and complexes of public buildings. The Romans were proud of their city's wealth and culture.

But Rome reflected not only the best but also the worst of the empire's culture. With people converging on the city from all over the world, it teemed with life—like Tokyo, Amsterdam, or New York do today. But it also suffered the same problems of today's large cities. More than a million of its citizens were poor and lived in blocks of tenements while not far away the rich lived in great style. The social problems were overwhelming.

The Roman wall still surrounds some parts of the city.

to be. You're not the way you're supposed to be either. And the only way out of this mess is through faith in Jesus Christ. "I am not ashamed of the gospel," he says, "because it is the power of God for salvation for everyone who believes" (Romans 1:16).

Believers across the centuries have stated the theme in many different ways. George Herbert, for example, wrote a ten-line poem in which he hid words that spelled the theme of his life. One word in each line connected diagonally with a word in the next line to read: "My life is hid in him who is my treasure."

How would you spell out the basic theme of your life?

The Church in Rome

❯ **Who started it?** No one knows, but people have guessed that it was either the visitors from Rome in Jerusalem who heard Peter preach on Pentecost (see Acts 2:10–11) or Christians traveling to Rome on business on pleasure.

❯ **When was the church founded?** We don't know, but by the time Paul wrote his letter around the year 57, the church had been there for some time. Perhaps a better word to use is churches. Evidently several groups of Christians were meeting in homes in different parts of Rome. We know that one group met in the home of Priscilla and Aquila, who had returned to Rome after working with Paul in Corinth and Ephesus (Romans 16:3–5).

❯ **Was the church made up of Jews or Gentiles?** Both. Although Claudius had exiled Jews from Rome in the year 49 because of disturbances among them, after he died in 54 many moved back. Priscilla and Aquila were among the returning exiles.

Early Christians in Rome listening to a reading of the epistle of Paul (19th century engraving).

16 ▬ ▬ ▬ ▬ ▬ ➤ More on Romans

Bible Reference: Selected passages from Romans 6–16

New in Christ

In the March, 1994 issue of *Christianity Today* Philip Yancey tells the story of Larry, who was converted by the hymns "Just as I Am" and "Amazing Grace." When the words of those hymns sank in, Larry finally realized how amazing God's grace was. Since then, Larry has been trying to follow God in his own way. But, says Yancey, "Larry admits he has not experienced the 'victorious Christian life.' He overeats, chain-smokes, and sex continues to be a problem. And since he never manages to get up in time for church, he misses out on worship and Christian community. Once, Larry stated his dilemma this way: 'I'm stuck somewhere between "Just as I am" and "Just as God wants me to be."'"

Paul is talking about this basic dilemma in Romans 6–7. He starts chapter 6 with a question: "Shall we go on sinning so that grace may increase?" Why bother to be good if we know that God is going to forgive our sins? In fact, if the more we sin the more grace God gives, why not give God the opportunity to give even more grace?

"By no means!" Paul thunders back. Grace does more than defeat sin's power. It also gives power to become new persons in Christ, as though our sinful nature died with Christ on the cross and a new person came to life with Christ's resurrection. We can't go on sinning like we did before.

Then Paul goes on to show what it means to be a new person in Christ—and what it doesn't mean. It doesn't mean, he says, that struggles with sin are over. Telling about his own struggles, Paul bursts out, "I do not understand what I do. For what I want to do I do not do, but what I hate I do" (Romans 8:15). And every Christian hearing Paul's outburst knows instantly what Paul is talking about. Paul's talking about me, we think.

A Song of Hope, a Shout of Victory

But in chapter 8 Paul breaks out in a kind of song. The Spirit's life-giving power is renewing and recreating us and all of creation. For creation is also waiting to be set free, groaning in birth pains as the new creation is being born.

We're also suffering as we wait for that new creation. Our faith in its coming, along with the knowledge that the Spirit is groaning within us, sustains us. When we're weak, afraid, or over our heads in trouble, we know that the Spirit will pray for us.

Suddenly at the end of the chapter Paul switches gears. His song of hope becomes a shout of victory:

If God is for us, who can be against us?

Who will separate us from the love of Christ?

Shall trouble or hardship or persecution or famine or nakedness
or danger or sword?
No, in all these things we are more than conquerors through
him who loved us."

Romans 8:31b, 35, 37

Christians have found these words to be stronger than the stake, stronger than the A-bomb, stronger than cancer.

God works in *everything* for our good: he works in our trouble to make us rely on him, he works in persecution to make us loyal to Christ, he works in hunger to make us thankful for our daily bread. Being conquerors doesn't mean that we won't know fear or pain or loss or depression. It means that nothing in all of creation can separate us from the love of God in Christ Jesus our Lord.

Reflect on what these words mean to you. We don't face some of the hardships that Paul lists. In North America we don't know gnawing hunger or hiding out from terrorists or the sound of gunfire or bombs or being thrown in jail because we're Christians. But our part of the world is still a mess. What kind of trouble do we see around us in our part of the world?

We know that these troubles, along with others that may lie ahead, can't separate us from the love of God in Christ Jesus. The power of the risen and ascended Jesus will bring about a new world where big troubles and little troubles are banished. Romans 8:28–39 is worth memorizing. It's something to carry you through your entire life and beyond.

17 ▬ ▬ ▬ ➤ The Road to Jerusalem

> **Bible Reference: Acts 20–21:20**

Photo Album of a Journey

Wouldn't it be fascinating to look through a photo album of Paul's mission travels? One of the best things about the album would be the pictures of Christians we read about in Acts. Seeing pictures of Paul and of some of his traveling companions—Luke, Silas, Timothy, Barnabas, or John Mark—would make the events of Acts more real to us.

From Luke's report of Paul's trip to Jerusalem, one picture we could expect to see in the album is a group photo of Paul's traveling companions: Sopater, Aristarchus, Secundus, Gaius, Timothy, Tychicus, Trophimus, and Luke himself. The caption would tell us that these men were from churches in different provinces: three from Macedonia, two from Galatia, and two from Asia. These delegates of the churches went along with Paul to bring a gift of money for poor Christians in Jerusalem. Paul had arranged for the group to meet him at Troas so that they could make the trip to Jerusalem together.

Another photo might be of Eutychus, a young member of the church at Troas. Eutychus was in church on the Sunday evening Paul preached. Paul's heart was so full of things he wanted to say to the Christians that at midnight he was still going strong. But the room was warm, and Eutychus nodded off. That wouldn't have mattered had he not been perched on the sill of a third-floor window. He toppled over and fell to the ground below. Paul ran downstairs, briefly stretched himself over the young man, and then said, "He's alive!" And then, as though falling out of third-story windows and living to talk about it was the most normal thing in the world, Eutychus got up, went upstairs, and had something to eat. The miracle in Troas energized the Christians. They continued their meeting, breaking bread together, talking and encouraging one another until daylight.

Breaking Bread

A cts 20:7 shows the Christians in Troas meeting on the first day of the week to break bread. This statement in Acts is the first clear evidence that early Christians regularly gathered on that day for worship. The breaking of bread probably means that Christians ate a fellowship meal together. During that meal they celebrated the Lord's Supper.

A third photo might be of Paul and the elders of Ephesus saying goodbye. When Paul's ship stopped in Miletus, the elders of the church in Ephesus came to meet Paul. But Paul had a sense of foreboding about this trip to Jerusalem. His instructions to the elders have the ring of a last will and testament. Every face in the picture would reflect the pain of this parting.

A fourth photo might be a group of men, women, and children kneeling on a beach. Christians from Tyre brought Paul to his ship after his seven-day stay with them. Through the Spirit they knew that trouble lay ahead for Paul, so this was no "see you soon" goodbye either. A camera equipped with a zoom lens would have captured the tears on the faces.

A fifth photo might be of a man scrunched up with both hands and feet tied up with a long belt. That man would be Agabus, a prophet who had a message from the Holy Spirit. Agabus made a special trip to see Paul in Caesarea, and his roleplay gave Paul a clear idea of what was going to happen to Paul in Jerusalem.

The last picture in the album might surprise us—everyone's smiling. The caption could read, "Arrived in Jerusalem just before Pentecost. We turned over the offering. Warmly welcomed. Especially good to see James."

Although we don't have actual photos, Luke does flash some powerful pictures on our mind's screen of this critical journey. One picture that gradually takes shape and fills the screen is the picture of Paul taking up his cross, following his Lord, and setting his face toward Jerusalem.

Unit 8
Strengthening the Church

1 – – – – → The Gathering Storm

Bible Reference: Acts 21:17—23:11

Squelching Rumors

Before Christ turned him around on the highway to Damascus, Paul had been a Pharisee with all his heart and mind. Each day he had started his morning prayers, as did all Jewish men, by giving thanks to God "who has not made me a Gentile . . . who has not made me a slave . . . who has not made me a woman."

That was the "before" Paul. But the "after" Paul knew that in Christ the walls between Jews and Gentiles, women and men, slaves and free people had crumbled. Jesus' death had shattered those divisions. God's revolution of grace was undoing what sin had done.

For Paul, returning to Jerusalem must have been something of a shock. For more than a decade, he had been teaching and preaching this gospel of grace. He had lived and worked among Gentiles. Now as soon as he was back in Jerusalem, Jewish Christian leaders politely asked him to show his dedication to his Jewish roots by purifying himself at the temple.

Why did James make this request of Paul? Both Paul and James believed that salvation was through Christ and not through the law. Both believed that Gentile converts did not have to obey the whole Jewish law code (remember the Jerusalem Council?). Both also agreed that all of God's people—Jews and Gentiles—must live a God-pleasing life. So why the request?

According to Jerusalem gossip, Paul had been telling Jewish believers not to observe Jewish practices. The gossip was untrue. As proof, James wanted Paul to join four other Jewish Christians who were going through a purification rite at the temple. Because Paul had been away from Jerusalem among Gentiles for a long time, according to Jewish ideas he was

Fortress Antonia

Fortress Antonia, built by Herod the Great, stood at the northwest corner of the temple. Built on a rocky outcropping, it was the high point in Jerusalem and the ideal place for Roman military headquarters.

The historian Josephus describes it as a magnificent fortress, worthy to stand next to the temple. It looked like a large tower, but inside "the entire complex was like a palace: spacious, with all sorts of palatial accommodations and even military facilities; it was adorned with many porticoes, its own baths, and wide courtyards for the troops."

A model of Herod's temple with the Antonia Fortress in the center back and the Court of the Gentiles in the foreground.

The fortress was surrounded by four other towers. One of these overlooked the temple grounds. "This tower had stairs on both sides; one set led to the temple area, and the other into the Antonia Fortress. When the Roman procurators governed Palestine from A.D. 6, a cohort of about 1,000 Roman soldiers was permanently stationed in Antonia, and a brigade of between 120 and 200 men was positioned on this southeastern tower." During the Jewish festivals when thousands of pilgrims came to Jerusalem and thronged the temple courts, soldiers took up positions on the roofs of the fortress to keep an eye on the crowds.

Paul was held in the Fortress Antonia. It was possibly on the stairs leading from the fortress to the temple complex that Paul made his speech to the people.

—Richard M. Mackowski, S.J., *Jerusalem: City of Jesus*

"unclean." Going to the temple and making sacrifices would put the gossip and rumors to rest.

In a way it's surprising that Paul agreed to go along with what James asked. Paul knew that Jesus' sacrifice had taken the place of these temple sacrifices. But Paul had a generous and sensitive spirit. He was willing to do this to keep peace in the church.

Following Jesus in Jerusalem

Luke's story of the early church describes the strong opposition of most Jews to the gospel of Jesus' death and resurrection. From almost the beginning of Acts we read stories of Jewish leaders mistreating the apostles, putting them in prison, and forbidding them to preach or teach. Imagine how the conversion of Paul, once one of the Sanhedrin's most enthusiastic supporters, must have especially rankled. In the following years the Jerusalem authorities must have heard reports of Paul popping up in synagogues from Syria to Achaia and preaching not only that Jesus was the resurrected Son of God but also that Gentiles and Jews were equal in God's sight. Paul was a marked man. One wrong step and the authorities would pounce.

Ironically, the wrong step happened while Paul was trying to make things right with a visit to the temple. And it wasn't Paul's wrong step. Jews from Asia recognized Paul. Thinking that he had defiled the temple by taking an uncircumcised Gentile into the inner court, they jumped him and dragged him out of the temple. The whole thing could be called a misunderstanding or, more accurately, a rush to judgment by Paul's enemies.

When Paul had the chance to address the issue, he didn't defend himself by setting the record straight. He didn't say, "Listen, this is all a big mistake. I didn't bring a Gentile into the Court of Israel." Instead, he defended every-

St. Paul Rescued from the Multitude by Gustave Doré.

thing he stood for. He spoke to his enemies' unspoken accusations. All went well until Paul claimed that the Lord God of Israel had sent him to the Gentiles. Then the crowd erupted in pure rage. How could Paul dare to claim that Gentiles and Jews were equal before God?

As Luke tells this story of Paul in Jerusalem, he draws parallels to Jesus in Jerusalem. Both Jesus and Paul were arrested unjustly, accused by false witnesses, and put in prison. Both were condemned by angry crowds yelling, "Crucify him! He is not fit to live!" What are some other similarities? What is at least one basic difference between Jesus' suffering and Paul's?

Innocent before Roman Law

Luke has also showed all along how Roman authorities defended Christians' rights and found them innocent of any criminal charges. In Corinth Gallio had dismissed the Jews' charges against Paul. In Ephesus the city clerk had told the mob that the Christians were innocent. Instead, he said, the silversmiths and the crowd could be charged with causing a riot for no good cause. Now in Jerusalem the Roman tribune, Claudius Lysias, protected Paul from the crowd. And later in a letter to the governor, the tri-

Nazarite Vows

Four members of the Jerusalem church had decided to dedicate and purify themselves through a Nazarite vow. Keeping their Nazarite vow meant abstaining from eating or drinking any products of the vine, from touching dead bodies, and from cutting their hair. At the end of their vow period, they also had to make certain special animal, grain, and drink offerings to the priests, plus an offering of the hair they had grown during the period of the vow. For more information about Nazarite vows, read Numbers 6:1–8, 13–21.

To publicly show Jewish believers that he was not opposed to Jewish customs, Paul sponsored the four men and paid their expenses. The gesture was costly because he had to buy the animals to be sacrificed. The expensive offerings were meant to show total commitment to the Lord.

Warning Signs

The temple complex consisted of a series of courts designed as worship areas for different groups. The outer court, the largest, was the only place where Gentiles could worship. The next court, the Court of Women, was set aside for Jewish women. Closer to the Holy Place was the Court of Israelites where Jewish men worshiped.

Any Gentile entering an inner court committed a capital offense. To ensure that no Gentile just happened to wander into forbidden areas, warning signs in Greek and Latin were posted at the steps leading to the inner courts. Archaeologists have found two of these signs. They read, "No foreigner may enter within the barricade which surrounds the temple and enclosure. Anyone who is caught doing so will have himself to blame for his ensuing death."

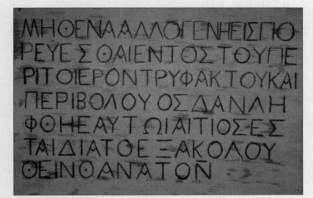

A "keep out" sign written in Greek and posted in the Court of Gentiles.

bune wrote that no charge against Paul was worthy of death or imprisonment (Acts 23:26). In the chapters ahead Luke continues to develop this theme, stressing again that Paul has done nothing against Roman law.

Why is this so important to Luke? One of Luke's purposes in writing Acts was to make absolutely clear that the Christian faith was legal. The trials—not only Paul's but also Jesus'—were clear evidence that the accusations of treason brought against Christians in the first century were unfounded. Believers were law-abiding citizens of the empire.

What's your take on this topic? When might a Christian have to stop being a law-abiding citizen? How should a Christian's confession that Christ is King affect obedience to Caesar?

Ananias was the high priest of the Sanhedrin at this time. According to the historian Josephus, this Ananias was a disgrace to his office. He took for himself the tithes meant for the ordinary priests, he assassinated any opponents, and he collaborated with Rome.

His pro-Roman policy finally did him in. During the Jewish revolt in the year 66, freedom fighters went looking for Ananias, a traitor to his people. They found Ananias hiding in an aqueduct, dragged him out, and executed him.

2 ————————➤ Paul on Trial

Bible Reference: Acts 23:12—25:12

Paul and Felix

In today's passage Paul and Felix are the two main characters. Paul is on trial, and Felix is doing the trying. Paul is under house arrest, and Felix has the keys in his pocket.

But overall Felix doesn't seem like a bad sort of guy, does he? At least he's friendly to Paul and to the Christian faith. Paul is allowed a certain amount of freedom. Felix tells the guards to let Paul's friends visit and bring care packages. And—this is a surprise—Felix asks Paul to tell him more about Jesus Christ. Felix is not a brute, not compared to someone like Herod, anyway.

Felix, though, is playing Trivial Pursuit. Maybe you've played it. It's a game of questions and answers about facts. If it's your turn, you can keep moving around the board as long as you keep giving the right answers.

The questions are mostly about nonessential things: How many fingers did Anne Boleyn have? Which baseball team won the 1936 World Series? What was Hitler's favorite movie?

The game may be a relaxing way to pass a few hours with friends, but Felix is spending a whole life on trivia. Rather than uncovering the truth and giving an honest verdict in Paul's case, Felix keeps Paul in custody for two years. It's easier to keep Paul under wraps and to let things slide than to make a decision and risk angering the Jews.

And then there's Felix's pursuit of money. He's interested enough in Paul to talk with him often, but Felix is really after a bribe. He hopes that eventually Paul will slip some money under the table. For money he would risk angering the Jews.

Compared to Paul, Felix—despite his position and power—seems weak. Paul, even as a young man, had never been sidetracked by trivia. He had made God's kingdom his top priority. Of course, he had it all wrong when he persecuted the Christians, but once Jesus appeared to him, Paul threw his all into following Christ.

Who's the free one in this story? Who is under lock and key?

Paul knew the secret of a free life. In spite of being under arrest, Paul was as free as the birds of the air or the flowers of the field. Paul's future didn't seem like much, but it was much brighter than Felix's.

In this Bible passage we're allowed one glimpse of Felix coming face to face with his real self. Felix and Drusilla had sent for Paul to find out more about the Christian faith. They listened with interest as Paul told them about faith in Christ Jesus. But as soon as Paul began talking about what the faith had to do with Felix's life, Felix became uncomfortable. When

Antonius Felix

Antonius Felix ruled as governor of Judea for seven or eight years. Emperor Claudius had made him governor around A.D. 52, and he owed his appointment to his brother Pallas, who was a favorite of Claudius. Nero recalled Felix to Rome around the year 60 to answer for improperly handling disturbances in the province.

Felix allowed the case against Paul to drag on for two years—all the while keeping Paul in custody, hoping that the pressure would generate a bribe.

Paul spelled out why people had to be made righteous, Felix became uneasy. And then when Paul described the coming judgment, Felix was downright afraid. The mirror that Paul held up gave Felix a brief, unnerving look at who he was. "That's enough for now!" he said.

In two years of conversations with Paul, Felix never found it convenient to be saved from his sins.

Who's the one on trial here—Paul or Felix?

3 ▬ ▬ ▬ ➡ Defense before Agrippa

Bible Reference: Acts 25:13—26:32

Carrying Jesus' Name to a King and a Governor

Paul had been commissioned on the Damascus road to carry Jesus' name "before the Gentiles and their kings and before the people of Israel." Jesus told his disciples: "They will lay their hands on you and persecute you.

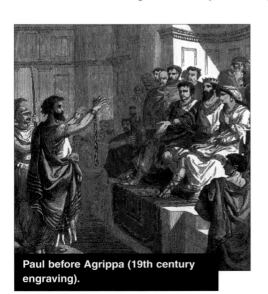

Paul before Agrippa (19th century engraving).

They will deliver you to synagogues and prisons, and you will be brought before kings and governors, and all on account of my name" (Luke 21:12). In Acts 26 a part of Paul's commission and Jesus' prophecies are being fulfilled as Paul testifies before Festus, a governor, and Agrippa, a king.

Agrippa makes a get-acquainted visit to Festus, his high-ranking new neighbor. Festus must present Paul's case in a letter to Caesar, and he is eager for Agrippa's input, so he arranges a grand hearing. At

Herod Agrippa II

Agrippa's full name was Herod Agrippa II. He was the fourth of the infamous Herodian dynasty. The others:

- Herod the Great, who tried to kill the baby Jesus, founded the dynasty.
- Antipas, Herod's son, was the king who beheaded John the Baptist.
- Agrippa I, Herod's grandson, was responsible for beheading James, the brother of the apostle John.

Because Agrippa II was only 17 when his father died, Claudius had appointed a procurator to rule Judea. But in the year 48 Agrippa was given a small kingdom to the north, which he exchanged for a larger one in 53. More importantly, Claudius had given Agrippa the power to appoint the Jewish high priest.

the appointed time the Roman governor, King Agrippa, Bernice (Agrippa's sister), leaders of the Jews and the Roman government, and top Roman officers enter the hall and are seated.

Standing before this high and mighty audience, Paul must once again defend what he stands for. Paul simply tells what has happened to him. He describes his personal experience with the risen Jesus. And he ends with a direct appeal to Agrippa: "I pray God that not only you but all who are listening to me today may become what I am, except for these chains."

It would be great if everyone in the hall had believed and gotten baptized, but that's not what happened. Even so, all agreed that Paul was not guilty.

Ready with Your Own Defense?

Both Paul's example and Peter's words nudge us to think about how to defend what we believe. What do we say when people ask about our faith?

Here are some suggestions made by Peter Kreeft in *Your Questions, God's Answers*:

- You will get nowhere unless both you and the other person are committed to truth and honesty. The only honest reason anyone should ever believe anything is because it is true. If one party believes in truth and the other party does not, no real dialogue can take place.

- If you cannot reason with your neighbors in a spirit of love, it is better not to reason with them at all . . . "I win, you lose" arguments are doomed, for even when you win them, you lose your neighbor. You want to win your neighbor, not the argument, first of all.

- People only listen to a listener. Let your neighbor give his reasons for his beliefs. Listen, sincerely. Ask him questions. Be his student, let him be your teacher, at first. Then find the weakness in what he believes and ask questions about that. Be interested in his beliefs and he may be interested in yours. . . .

- Your reasons for your faith need not be scientific proofs. When we're talking about people, and reasons for trusting people, we don't expect scientific proofs, just good reasons, good clues. . . .

- Don't rely on your own cleverness, but on God. . . . We cannot convert anyone, only God can. But we can sow seeds for God to give growth to.

- Don't be afraid to reason with an unbeliever, no matter how much smarter you may think he is. You have something unconquerable on your side: truth. . . . There can never be a real contradiction between faith and reason, or faith and science, or faith and logic. All truth is God's truth, and God cannot contradict himself.

- Remember that people are moved by their hearts more than by their heads. Show them the God of love, and they will want to believe in him. People disbelieve mainly because they misunderstand and fear; they may think that God is a kind of celestial bank manager, or bookkeeper, or policeman. The world was converted by twelve peasants who showed them God.

What do you think of these ideas? Do you have suggestions of your own to add to this list?

4 ━ ━ ━ ━ ➤ Voyage and Shipwreck

> **Bible Reference: Acts 27–28:16**

Breaking News

"Early this morning a sailing vessel ran aground off Malta. People on shore watched with horror as the ship broke up in the pounding surf. Amazingly, every single person from the ship made it to shore. The ship, carrying grain and some 276 passengers, was on its way to Rome. Included among the passengers were a centurion, his soldiers, and a number of prisoners. The centurion was taking the prisoners to Rome for trial.

"So far I've talked to just two people. A crew member told me, 'We were tossed around in a storm for 14 days. Had to dump just about everything overboard. Never did see anything like it in all my 20 years at sea. Sure never thought I'd see my home again. Don't want to brag, but the crew really came through. We did all we could, and luckily that was enough.'

"But the other person, a passenger who refused to be identified, credited one of the prisoners with the incredible escape.

"We'll be giving you more details of the shipwreck as they become available."

A news report of Paul's shipwreck might have gone something like that. But the report would have missed the most important part of the story—the story behind the story.

Of course, news reports have their place. Sometimes they cover events that end up in our history books: wars, famines, revolutions, medical breakthroughs, election results, and so on. But the news story of the shipwreck is not the whole story—or even the true story.

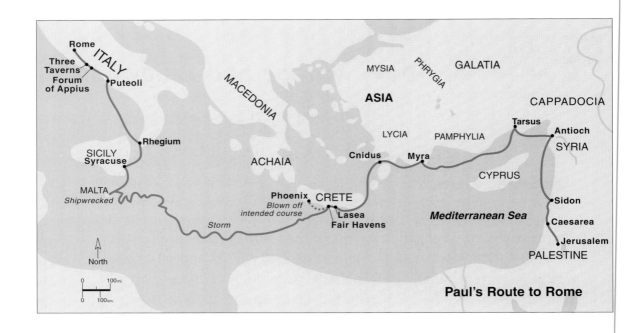

Paul's Route to Rome

St. Paul Shipwrecked by Gustave Doré.

As far as the news report is concerned, the ship was on an ordinary trading voyage. But as far as God was concerned, this voyage was his mission. Its main purpose was to bring Paul to Rome to carry Jesus' name before Caesar. That purpose decided what happened to Paul, the other passengers, and the ship's cargo.

The news, you see, is the news about the progress of the kingdom of God in the world. That's the history behind the history. That's salvation history. And that's the history you're reading in your Bible as you read about the shipwreck off Malta.

Rough Sailing

Sailing on the Mediterranean was possible but treacherous from mid-September to mid-November. After the middle of November venturing into the open sea was impossible until winter was over.

Paul's voyage to Rome came late in the sailing season. Sudden wind changes from south to north are common on these seas. During the short 40-mile sail from Fair Havens to Phoenix, the wind changed, and Paul's ship was caught in gale-force winds blowing down from the mountains of Crete. The ship was swept south, away from the island and into the dangerous open sea.

After about 20 miles the ship sailed along the leeward side of the island of Cauda (modern Gavdho). The crew made good use of this short breathing space to prepare the ship to ride out the storm. Working furiously, they pulled on board the lifeboat, or dinghy, that they had been towing; they "undergirded" the ship by wrapping cables around the hull transversely to brace it and keep its timbers together; and they lowered the sea anchor to serve as a drag. This last safety measure, they hoped, would keep the ship from running onto the quicksand off the African coast.

Once back out in the open sea, the ship was turned with its right side to the wind. The next day the crew dumped some of the cargo overboard. On the third day the ship's tackle and any nonessential equipment went.

The ship drifted in the storm for 11 more days and nights, probably leaking badly. The only way out was to run the ship aground, but no land was in sight.

About midnight of the fourteenth day, the crew heard the sound of breakers. Breakers meant rocks. Unable to see where the rocks were, the sailors dropped four anchors from the stern. Thus the ship was kept away from the rocks, but it faced the shore, ready to land.

When daylight broke, they spotted a sandy beach. Leaving the anchors behind, they unleashed the steering paddles (used as rudders), hoisted a small foresail to guide the ship's course, and made for the beach. But because the bay they were entering (now called St. Paul's Bay) was a point "where two seas met," they hit a bar of sand or mud. The ship's bow stuck fast in the bar while the surf pounded the stern to pieces.

But Paul's word from the Lord was true. Everyone reached the shore safely.

—From James Smith's *The Voyage and Shipwreck of St. Paul*,
written in 1848 and quoted in F. F. Bruce, *The Book of the Acts.*

5 ------- ➔ Rome at Last

> **Bible Reference: Acts 28:17–31**

From Jerusalem to Rome

The ending of Acts doesn't satisfy our curiosity about what happened to Paul. Paul lived in Rome in his own rented house for two years—and then what? Was Paul tried, convicted, and then executed? Or was he tried, found innocent, and freed?

Luke doesn't say. The dark predictions earlier in Acts suggest that Luke knew what happened to Paul. Also the angel's statement "You must stand before Caesar" tells us that Paul must have stood trial in Caesar's court. Luke, an able writer, probably deliberately ended his account to Theophilus at this point.

Remember that the story of Acts is, first of all, the story of the Holy Spirit and not the story of Paul. The Holy Spirit empowered believers to contin-

The Appian Way

Paul walked into Rome along the Appian Way. One of the oldest Roman highways, the Appian Way was built by Appius Claudius in 312 B.C. The original section of the road linked Rome with Capua. Later the road ran east, crossing Italy and ending in Brundisium on the Adriatic coast, a distance of 333 miles. The road connecting the two coasts not only promoted trade with countries to the east but also helped unify the country.

Basil

Basil, a twentieth-century Russian Christian, preached the gospel without fear. In 1962 he used his own money to begin a small publishing company, where he printed Christian pamphlets. He managed to distribute 700,000 of these before the KGB (the Soviet Union's harsh security agency) commanded him to stop. Because he refused to stop, he was arrested and sent to a labor camp.

Basil didn't understand why God had allowed him to be punished for serving him—what good could he do in a labor camp? Then one morning he saw that God had given him a new opportunity to serve. Early each morning the camp's prisoners gathered in the dark for roll call. The camp guards and commanders were seldom punctual, so Basil saw his opportunity and grabbed it. He preached to this captive audience.

Basil usually had about two minutes before the guards showed up, once in a while he had as long as five minutes. Because he had such a short time each day, it took him about two weeks to preach a single sermon, and he had to shout so that the thousands of prisoners could hear him. He preached like this for ten years, at the top of his voice and at breakneck speed, and afterwards could not break the habit of speaking this way.

When Basil was released in 1972, he built an unregistered church in his village. Occasionally he visited the church in the labor camp, where even today a community of 100 believers still worships.

—Philip Yancey in "Russia's Untold Story," *Finding God in Unexpected Places*

ue to speak about Jesus' death and resurrection and the kingdom of God. The Holy Spirit made sure that the kingdom included people from all nations and races. By the power of the Spirit a small handful of obscure people became a church with 3,000 converts on Pentecost in Jerusalem and in about 30 years grew to many thousands.

Now Paul was in Rome, the capital of the world, free to preach the kingdom of God and to teach about the Lord Jesus Christ. "Boldly and without hindrance he preached the kingdom of God and taught about the Lord Jesus Christ," says the last verse of Acts. That verse is a mini-summary of the whole book. Acts tells the story of the advance of God's kingdom from Jerusalem to Rome. The Spirit overcame every obstacle. And the book ends with Paul still preaching and teaching. We know that as long as Paul had breath he would continue.

The Unfinished Story

Acts closes in hope and confidence that the story of the acts of the Spirit are ongoing. We know that's true, because we today are living in that ongoing story. Paul is long gone, but the Spirit is still alive, still energizing people to spread the good news of God's kingdom.

Before Jesus ascended he told his disciples, "But you will receive power when the Holy Spirit comes upon you; and you will be my witnesses in Jerusalem, and in all Judea and Samaria, and to the ends of the earth."

That command of Jesus is still in effect today. And the Spirit's power comes to everyone who confesses Jesus as Lord. That's why the gospel of Jesus Christ has been preached for 2,000 years and will continue to be preached until the end of the earth. Nothing can hinder that.

The question left hanging in the air is this: How will the kingdom move forward through you? What will your part be in the ongoing story?

6 ▬ ▬ ▬ ➤ Four Letters from Prison

Bible Reference: The Books of Ephesians, Philippians, Colossians, and Philemon

Spilling Out All over the Place

These four letters Paul wrote to Christian believers from Rome show amazing confidence and strong spirit. In fact, his hopeful spirit seems unreal, given the facts. Paul was under house arrest; he was constantly forced to defend his beliefs, and false teachings and believers' squabbling constantly undermined his work in the churches.

But the strong spirit that shines through in the letters is real. Paul is not putting on a show. He has been set free from within. He lives a free life in Christ. When we read Paul's letters carefully, his hope and energy carry us along. His spirit is catching.

That's what happens when we experience Christ's life from within. Eugene Peterson puts it this way: the life of Christ spills out "into the lives of those who receive him, and then continues to spill out all over the place."

That strong "spilling out" fills Paul's letters. Paul quotes hymns, argues, encourages, teaches, blesses, praises God. Read his letters in the spirit in which he wrote them. You'll be surprised at what will spill out into your life.

Letter Carrier

Tychicus is not a household name. It's not even one of the New Testament names we have stashed in memory. Still, Tychicus deserves special mention. He often traveled as Paul's representative, and he was Paul's letter carrier. Tychicus carried two of Paul's letters to Colosse—one for the church and one for Philemon.

Do you think that this was an insignificant job? How many copies of the letters do you think Paul had? They weren't stored on a computer disks. There were no carbon copies. So remember Tychicus, Paul's letter carrier—actually, God's letter carrier.

See Acts 20:4; Ephesians 6:21, Colossians 4:7, 2 Timothy 4:12, and Titus 3:12. You can find out a little more about Tychicus from these references in the New Testament.

First-Century Letters

Paul's letters, inspired as they are by the Spirit, are more than ordinary letters. But their form follows that of ancient ordinary letters.

Hundreds of letters written by ordinary people in the ancient world have been found. Written on papyrus, the letters were well preserved (at least as long as they were dry). Scholars have collected and translated many of them. These letters not only give us a picture of life in ancient times but also show us that letters followed a pattern.

Here's an example from *Selections from the Greek Papyri* by G. Milligan:

> *Apion to Epimachus his father and lord heartiest greetings. First of all I pray that you are in health and continually prosper and fare well with my sister and her daughter and my brother. I thank the lord Serapis [Apion's god] that when I was in danger at sea he saved me. Straightway when I entered Misenum I received my traveling money from Caesar, three gold pieces. And I am well. I beg you, therefore, my lord father, write me a few lines, first regarding your health, secondly regarding that of my brother and sister, thirdly that I may kiss your hand, because you have brought me up well, and on this account I hope to be quickly promoted, if the gods will. Give my greetings to Capito, and to my brother and sister, and to Serenilla, and my friends. I send you a little portrait of myself done by Euctemon. And my military name is Antonius Maximus. I pray for your good health.*
>
> *Serenus the son of Agathos Daimon greets you and Turbo the son of Gallonius.*

This letter shows the typical four-part pattern of ordinary letters: a greeting, a prayer and thanksgiving, the main reason for the letter or special content, and the closing greetings. Although in ancient times people often didn't write their own letters, at the end they usually signed their name or made some mark to show that the letter was genuine.

As you read Paul's letters, check their form. How are they similar to this letter? How are they different?

7 — ➤ Another Missionary Journey?

Bible Reference: 1 and 2 Timothy; Titus; selected New Testament passages

Maybe One More

Reconstructing Paul's last years is impossible. Did he die shortly after two years of house arrest in Rome? Or was he released after two years, and later arrested again, tried, and put to death? No one knows.

Pieces of information about these last years of Paul's life come from different places in the Bible. Trying to fit them together is like trying to put a jigsaw puzzle together when some of the pieces are missing.

These are the main pieces we have:

- In Romans 15:24 and 28 Paul mentions a plan to go to Spain. Clement, who lived in the second century, states that Paul did take the gospel as far as Spain.
- At the time Paul wrote his first letter to Timothy and his letter to Titus, he was freely traveling from one place to another. But when he wrote his second letter to Timothy, Paul was in a prison (not house arrest) in Rome. Paul's movements in these letters don't fit into the sequence of Paul's movements in Acts. That's why some scholars have said that the events in these letters must have taken place after Acts. This would mean that 2 Timothy was written during Paul's second imprisonment in Rome.
- Early Christian tradition gives some support to a second imprisonment.

These puzzle pieces don't fill in the complete picture. It's tantalizing to try to build a whole fourth journey out of the pieces we have, but that's just a guessing game. We have to accept that the Bible doesn't tell us exactly what happened to Paul. Instead of telling all the facts of his life, the Bible gives us his testimonies to the amazing grace in Jesus Christ.

The Pastoral Letters

Three letters—1 and 2 Timothy and Titus—are grouped together in the Bible. These three are called the pastoral letters because they instruct about pastoral care in the churches. The first two letters were sent to Ephesus, where Paul had left Timothy in charge of the church. The other letter went to Titus, who was working in the church at Crete.

Paul was profoundly aware of the challenges the two churches faced. These weren't churches in carpeted buildings with annual budgets and full-

The Island of Crete

About 150 miles long, the island of Crete lies in the Mediterranean between Sicily and Cyprus. The Old Testament mentions the island as the native territory of the Philistines (Amos 9:7), and the New Testament identifies it as the home of some Jews who were in Jerusalem at the time of Pentecost (Acts 2:11).

Mykenos Harbor on Crete.

Crete's claim to fame was its role in Minoan civilization around 1500–3000 B.C.

time pastors and youth ministries. These were house churches, groups of believers meeting in homes. Paul knew that it would take work for these fledgling churches to survive and thrive. It would also take solid spiritual leadership.

In the pastoral letters Paul sets guidelines for his younger coworkers, Timothy and Titus, to follow in both their work and their personal behavior. He urges them to sustain the pattern of sound teaching they have learned from him. He spells out how to deal with issues in the church and what kind of people should be appointed as church leaders. More than that, Paul's letters show that he is living along with Timothy and Titus in their work and vitally interested in everything that goes on in the churches.

You'll find that these letters have a lot to say to Christians today. We still deal with the issues Paul addressed. And, again, Paul's strong and hopeful spirit shines through these short letters.

8 ➤ Building up the Church

Bible Reference: 1 Timothy; Titus

True or False

As soon as he gets past the opening words in his letter to Timothy, Paul attacks false teachings in the church in Ephesus. He waits a few sentences longer in his letter to Titus before doing the same thing. In fact, in all three pastoral letters Paul distinguishes between false and true teaching, false and true teachers.

Paul takes aim because false teachers were stirring up trouble in the churches, distorting the gospel in various ways. Some converts, for example, were setting themselves up as part of a spiritual elite, but they were teaching their own blend of gospel and mystical ideas. They were mixing up Christian teachings with various "secret" meanings in the Old Testament genealogies or with Jewish myths. Others were teaching unbiblical ideas about the importance of strictly avoiding certain foods—and even marriage. Still others were swinging to the other extreme and practicing an "anything goes" outlook. They claimed to know God, but they would tell lies to make money (1 Timothy 6:5; Titus 1:11).

Paul also zeroes in on people who were arguing about speculative matters along the lines of, What if Adam and Eve had not sinned? Would Christ still have come into the world? Before sin entered the world, were animals meat eaters?

These arguments were ruining the spirit in the church, creating hard feelings. And for what purpose? Pride, Paul says, leads to this arguing over useless subjects.

Paul doesn't spend a lot of time talking about these false teachers. Rather, he moves on quickly and offers the antidote. He tells Timothy and Titus to teach sound doctrine, to build a solid foundation. If the foundation is good, communicating Jesus Christ, then those other things will fall away. Concentrate on Christ; that's the answer to false teachings and teachers.

True or False Today

You may think that these ancient letters addressed to Timothy and Titus don't speak to us today. Well, think again. In these letters God warns us to look out for false teachers and to build on Christ alone. Besides, some types of false teaching circulating today look a lot like the first-century variety.

Many religious groups today, for example, mix various other teachings with the gospel. They take a little bit from here and a little bit from there and also use the name of Jesus Christ.

One of these groups is the New Age religious community founded around 1978 by Rev. Carol Parrish-Harra. Set in the hills of northeastern Oklahoma, the Sparrow Hawk Village has more than 100 residents. The community has about 50 houses that are built around a church, a design "supposedly inspired by ancient Egyptian and Mayan models—communities built around temples," writes Vance Muse in an article in *The New York Times* magazine. "The chapel is fragrant and a little foggy with incense. A variegated cast of divinities crowds the altar and sideboards: portraits of Jesus and Mary, statues of Buddha, Shiva and Vishnu, busts of Mother Teresa and John F. Kennedy, a Star of David. . . . Parrish-Harra accepts Jesus as the Son of God, but is more interested in Christ as holy consciousness. The light that filled Jesus, she teaches, has filled other incarnations of God on earth, and it can fill each of us."

Empty talk is another example of first-century false teaching that is still with us today. One kind of empty talk is jargon that doesn't build up believers. Listen to the religious jargon on TV today. Some of this talk has spilled into the church, and it has a deadening effect. This is gangrene talk, says Paul. The faster these empty phrases roll off our tongues, the farther we move away from Christ. Like gangrene, the empty talk spreads from cell to cell, poisoning the body. What are examples of empty talk that harms the Christian community?

In these letters to Timothy and Titus God also tells us the antidote to false teachings and teachers in our day. We are called to "fight the good fight of the faith" and to "turn away from godless chatter and the opposing ideas of what is falsely called knowledge" (1 Timothy 6:12, 20b).

9 ━ ━ ━ ➤ God-Breathed Scripture

Bible Reference: 2 Timothy 1–3

Letters to Me from Myself

Reading all these letters in the Bible is pretty tough on me. For once, I'd like to read letters from someone who sympathizes with me. Someone like me.

Come to think of it, I guess I do. I write letters to myself all the time. And not having to mail them sure saves a lot on postage.

I wrote a letter to myself in my journal just yesterday. Here it is:

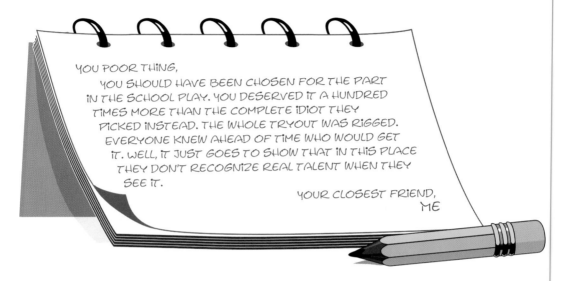

YOU POOR THING,
YOU SHOULD HAVE BEEN CHOSEN FOR THE PART IN THE SCHOOL PLAY. YOU DESERVED IT A HUNDRED TIMES MORE THAN THE COMPLETE IDIOT THEY PICKED INSTEAD. THE WHOLE TRYOUT WAS RIGGED. EVERYONE KNEW AHEAD OF TIME WHO WOULD GET IT. WELL, IT JUST GOES TO SHOW THAT IN THIS PLACE THEY DON'T RECOGNIZE REAL TALENT WHEN THEY SEE IT.
YOUR CLOSEST FRIEND,
ME

I've been my own pen pal for quite a while. It's especially helpful when I'm trying to get to sleep after a trying day. Like a soothing word whispered in my ear.

Here's another to me from myself:

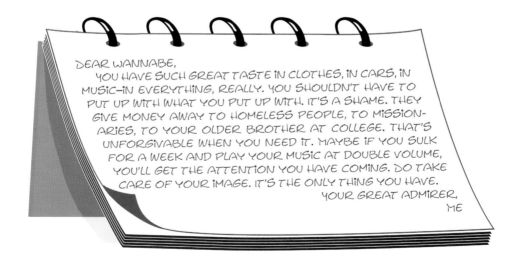

DEAR WANNABE,
YOU HAVE SUCH GREAT TASTE IN CLOTHES, IN CARS, IN MUSIC—IN EVERYTHING, REALLY. YOU SHOULDN'T HAVE TO PUT UP WITH WHAT YOU PUT UP WITH. IT'S A SHAME. THEY GIVE MONEY AWAY TO HOMELESS PEOPLE, TO MISSION-ARIES, TO YOUR OLDER BROTHER AT COLLEGE. THAT'S UNFORGIVABLE WHEN YOU NEED IT. MAYBE IF YOU SULK FOR A WEEK AND PLAY YOUR MUSIC AT DOUBLE VOLUME, YOU'LL GET THE ATTENTION YOU HAVE COMING. DO TAKE CARE OF YOUR IMAGE. IT'S THE ONLY THING YOU HAVE.
YOUR GREAT ADMIRER,
ME

You see, I understand myself so well. And I like myself so much. Still, after reading 2 Timothy 3, I was moved to try a different kind of letter.

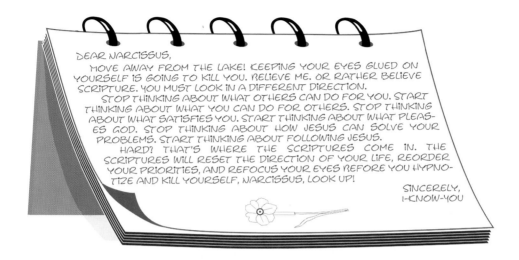

DEAR NARCISSUS,
    MOVE AWAY FROM THE LAKE! KEEPING YOUR EYES GLUED ON YOURSELF IS GOING TO KILL YOU. BELIEVE ME. OR RATHER BELIEVE SCRIPTURE. YOU MUST LOOK IN A DIFFERENT DIRECTION.
    STOP THINKING ABOUT WHAT OTHERS CAN DO FOR YOU. START THINKING ABOUT WHAT YOU CAN DO FOR OTHERS. STOP THINKING ABOUT WHAT SATISFIES YOU. START THINKING ABOUT WHAT PLEASES GOD. STOP THINKING ABOUT HOW JESUS CAN SOLVE YOUR PROBLEMS. START THINKING ABOUT FOLLOWING JESUS.
    HARD? THAT'S WHERE THE SCRIPTURES COME IN. THE SCRIPTURES WILL RESET THE DIRECTION OF YOUR LIFE, REORDER YOUR PRIORITIES, AND REFOCUS YOUR EYES BEFORE YOU HYPNOTIZE AND KILL YOURSELF, NARCISSUS, LOOK UP!

SINCERELY,
I-KNOW-YOU

God-Breathed

Voice 1: Your Word tells us that Christ Jesus has destroyed death and has brought life and immortality to light through the gospel (2 Timothy 1:10).

Voice 2: Your Word tells us about Christ raised from the dead, descended from David (2 Timothy 2:8).

Voice 3: Your Word tells us that God's solid foundation stands firm, sealed with this inscription: "The Lord knows those who are his" (2 Timothy 2:19).

Various voices: Mark this: In the last days people will be

      lovers of themselves

      lovers of money

      boastful

      proud

      abusive

      disobedient to their parents

      unholy

without love

unforgiving

slanderous

without self-control

brutal

not lovers of the good

treacherous

rash

conceited

lovers of pleasure rather than lovers of God—having the
form of godliness but denying its power.

Voice 4: But you, in the middle of all this, continue in what you have learned. Continue in the holy Scriptures which are able to make you wise for salvation through faith in Christ Jesus (2 Timothy 3:14–15).

Voice 5: For all Scripture is God-breathed.

Group (slowly): God-breathed, all Scripture is useful for teaching, rebuking, correcting and training in righteousness . . .

Voice 1: God-breathed, all Scripture is useful for thoroughly equipping God's people for every good work (2 Timothy 3:16–17).

Voice 2: The Scriptures are our perfect guide through these last days.

Voice 3: The Scriptures help us to refocus our eyes, to shift the center of our lives away from ourselves, to make Jesus Christ the center.

Voice 4: The word of God is living and active—sharper than any doubled-edged sword (Hebrews 4:12).

Voice 5: It cuts through our masquerading.

It sees the thoughts of the heart.

Nothing is hidden.

Voice 1: Your word, O Lord, is eternal;

it stands firm in the heavens (Psalm 119:89).

Voice 2: Your word is not a wandering star.

It's a fixed point for navigation.

It's always there to guide us.

Voice 3: Your word is a lamp to my feet and a light for my path (Psalm 119:105).

Voice 4: It is a light in the darkness.

If it were not for that lamp, for that light,

I would stumble and fall.

I would lose the way.

Voice 5: I have hidden your word in my heart (Psalm 119:11a).

Group (gradually fading): All Scripture is God-breathed . . . Scripture is God-breathed . . . God-breathed . . . God-breathed . . .

10 - - - - - - - → Final Words

Bible Reference: 2 Timothy 4

Time to Go

Although we have no definite information about where and when Paul was killed and buried, he was probably executed under Nero, either for disturbing the peace or for allegedly having a part in setting the great fire of 64 in Rome. According to tradition, Paul was taken to a place outside the city, the Ostian Gate, and beheaded.

In any case, at the end of this second letter to Timothy Paul reveals that his death is near. His whole letter has been leading up to this point. This situation adds urgency to his instructions to Timothy.

Paul uses two metaphors when he talks about his own death. The first one is from the language of sacrifice. Paul says that he is "being poured out like a drink offering." The drink offering was the offering of wine poured out around the base of the altar, and it was the last act of a sacrifice. Paul is so sure that death is near that he talks as if his death has already begun.

The second metaphor gives us a picture of Paul ready to move on, ready to set sail. Paul says, "The time has come for my departure." The Greek word for departure that Paul uses here means "loosing," implying taking down a tent or untying a ship from the dock. So in Paul's view, he's not at a dead end. He's setting out. He's departing from this earthly life to dwell with God.

And then comes a third metaphor. Paul had said earlier, "I consider my life worth nothing to me, if only I may finish the race and complete the task the Lord Jesus has given me—the task of testifying to the gospel of God's grace" (Acts 20:24). Now Paul looks back over his life. He looks back over 30 years of work as an apostle and says with good conscience that he has been faithful to the task. And now he continues the metaphor. Like an athlete in a competition, he has given it his all. Now the Olympic gold and the victory lap are waiting for him.

And with that Paul passes the baton to Timothy. "Preach the Word . . . keep your head in all situations . . . do the work of an evangelist, discharge all the duties of your ministry." It's your turn now, he says to Timothy.

This isn't quite goodbye, though. Paul hopes to see Timothy soon. "Do your best to come to me quickly," Paul says. And then his letter closes with a benediction, "The Lord be with your spirit. Grace be with you."

Did Timothy and Paul meet in Rome? Did the cloak arrive in time from Troas to protect Paul from the prison's winter cold? Did Paul have some time to read and study his scrolls? These and other questions are left hanging.

Dying We Live

You want to read a line that will pin your ears back? How about this: "When Christ calls a man, he bids him come and die."

You can spend a lot of time hanging around Christian people and never hear a line that makes you gulp quite so deeply.

That line came from Dietrich Bonhoeffer, a young German pastor who dared to oppose Hitler. For Bonhoeffer, opposing the Nazi mob on the basis of God's command to love was an invitation to die for Christ.

When Hitler rose to power in 1933, some members of the German church supported him. At the same time, Bonhoeffer and some others broke away to form what came to be called the "Confessing Church."

Twice during those years Bonhoeffer could have escaped the ugliness of Nazi Germany: once when he took a pastorate in London and later when he accepted an opportunity to study in America after the Nazis forbade him to speak publicly in Germany in 1939.

Dietrich Bonhoeffer.

But escaping the evil mushrooming in his native land wasn't what Bonhoeffer wanted. He believed that anyone who ran away during the horror had no right to be a part of the rebuilding when Hitler was finally defeated. Twice he left, and twice he went back into the fire.

Some people who hated Hitler learned to keep their mouths shut and lay low. Not Bonhoeffer. When he returned to Germany, he worked hard for the resistance. To the Nazis, he was a traitor. But there was no question for Bonhoeffer, his obedience was pledged not to the Führer but to God.

Bonhoeffer paused when he learned of an attempt to assassinate Hitler, for even in this situation, he questioned murder. But finally he concluded that the Christian's obligation in Nazi Germany was more than to comfort the sorrowing; it was to end the suffering. Some Christians may well disagree with Bonhoeffer's opinion, but he stood firmly behind it.

The plot to kill Hitler failed. And, under torture, one of the conspirators gave Bonhoeffer's name to the SS, Hitler's security forces. He was taken to Tegel prison, tortured, interrogated, and then isolated in solitary confinement.

On April 5, 1945—the day Hitler decided that none of those who had conspired to kill him would live—Bonhoeffer was sent to a detention camp at Schonberg. On April 8 he began to preach a sermon in the prison. He was interrupted by guards, who ordered him to collect his things. Taken to Flossenburg concentration camp, Bonhoeffer was sentenced to death. He was hanged on April 9, 1945.

There was no funeral. There is no stone. Bonhoeffer's body was burned, his ashes flung to the wind. But his story is not forgotten.

Letters and Poems from Prison

Like Paul, Bonhoeffer was also a prisoner for Christ, and, like Paul, he fully accepted death as an outcome of his commitment to Christ. He didn't want death to catch up with him by chance, or suddenly, without any significance. "It will not be external circumstances," he wrote, "but we ourselves who make of our death what it can be, a death freely and willingly accepted."

Dietrich Bonhoeffer was held in Nazi prisons for two years before being executed. After the war, his letters and papers from prison were published. Here are excerpts from two letters.

To his parents   [Tegel] Easter Day, 25 April 1943

Dear parents,

At last the tenth day has come round and I'm allowed to write to you again; I'm so glad to let you know that even here I'm having a happy Easter. Good Friday and Easter free us to think about other things far beyond our own personal fate, about the ultimate meaning of all life, suffering, and events; and we lay hold of a great hope.

To Eberhard Bethge [Bonhoeffer's friend]   [Tegel] 23 [August 1944]

Dear Eberhard,

Please don't ever get anxious or worried about me, but don't forget to pray for me—I'm sure you don't. I am so sure of God's guiding hand that I hope I shall always be kept in that certainty. You must never doubt that I'm traveling with gratitude and cheerfulness along the road where I'm being led. My past life is brim-full of God's goodness, and my sins are covered by the forgiving love of Christ crucified.

—Dietrich Bonhoeffer, *Letters and Papers from Prison*.

11 — — — — ➤ Called to Suffering

> Bible Reference: The Book of 1 Peter

Transformed into a Rock

When you think of Peter, what pictures of him are the most real to you? The confident Peter who confessed, "You are the Messiah, the Christ" and promised Jesus he would never forsake him? The impulsive Peter who decided to step out of the boat and walk to Jesus on the Sea of Galilee and who later jumped out of another boat to get to shore as fast as he could in order to see the risen Jesus? Peter, the gutsy leader?

Or do you remember the other side of Peter? The know-it-all Peter saying to Jesus, "No, Lord, you'll never have to go to Jerusalem and be killed." Or, "No, you'll never wash my feet." Or (just before the cock crowed), "I don't know the man!"

In *The Message* Eugene Peterson writes that "from what we know of the early stories of Peter, he had in him all the makings of a bully. That he didn't become a bully (and religious bullies are the worst kind) but rather the boldly confident and humbly self-effacing servant of Jesus Christ" that we find in these letters of Peter is a strong witness to Peter's "brand-new life."

The letters of Peter show that he had grown up in every way. He had been shaped by the Spirit so that he was filled with Christ-like qualities. Christ had come alive in him.

The Crucifixion of St. Peter by Michelangelo Buonarroti, 1475–1564.

Tertullian says that Peter was martyred at Rome. Origen adds that Peter was crucified upside-down because he thought he was unworthy to die in the same way as Christ. Peter probably died not long after he wrote this letter. According to Christian tradition, Nero was the emperor who had Peter (and Paul) put to death.

Hope in the Middle of Trouble

As we read this letter of Peter (and Paul's pastoral letters too) we notice dark clouds gathering over the church. The persecution of the church was gathering momentum. Members of the Jewish community were increasingly hostile to Christians. As Christians grew in number, Roman society tolerated them less and less.

Both Peter and Paul saw the signs of trouble ahead for the church. Both saw that with such hostility surrounding them believers would be tempted to drift out of the Christian community and back into their old ways of living and thinking. Christianity was proving too costly.

So Peter writes to the Christian community: Remember that suffering is part of the Christian life. When you live in a Christ-like way, you're living at odds with the world's sinful pattern. And sooner or later you're bound to feel the sting of disapproval and pressure to conform. If we Christians never feel uncomfortable in the world, if we never suffer for Christ's sake, we aren't living as Christians.

Of course, there are also other kinds of suffering. Christians struggle with the same kinds of things all people struggle with: sickness, the death of loved ones, unemployment, disabilities, natural disasters. Other times Christians suffer through their own mistakes or sins or just plain foolishness.

Suffering isn't on our top-ten list. In fact, sometimes we think that Christians shouldn't have to suffer. If God is for us, then why this pain and trouble? Why does God leave us twisting in the wind?

Peter's answer is hard to accept, especially when we're the ones doing the suffering. Peter says that suffering has a purpose. God is shaping us, making us into what God wants us to be. And God wants us to be like Christ.

But Peter gives his Christian readers more than the promise that they'll suffer. He holds out living hope: Now it's Good Friday, but Easter is coming. Hang on! Be confident! Christ's victory is ours.

Lifestyle Again

Peter's letter also deals with Christian lifestyle. From the first to the last chapter, Peter weaves into his writing instructions on how to live the Christian life. Christians, says Peter, are called to be nothing less than holy.

Being holy isn't on our top-ten list either. But that's what God is and that's what we will be by the grace of God.

According to Peter, living a Christian lifestyle is a matter of growing up in our salvation. Frederick Buechner remembers that the great question when he was growing up was this: What am I going to be when I grow up? That question still haunted him at age 58. That question is for everyone, no matter what age. We're not talking about being computer programmers or pilots or teachers. The question is not, What are we going to do? but What are we going to be?

Peter answers this question. We're going to be holy, he says, like God wants us to be. When God is finished working on us, we will be holy. Being holy, Peter says, is what it means to grow up in our salvation.

This letter for first-century Christians is amazingly alive today. As you read it, look for what it has to say to you, remembering that although North American Christians may live without fear of persecution now, there's no guarantee for the future.

12 — — — — — — ➤ Be on Guard

Bible Reference: The Book of 2 Peter

Forewarned Is Forearmed

Peter's second letter has a different tone than his first. In his first letter Peter encourages believers who are facing persecution from a hostile environment. In this second letter Peter takes on false teachers who are undermining the church from within. Knowing something about what these people were teaching will help you understand his letter.

First, some people thought that salvation was a matter of proper knowledge. Knowledge was all-important; all that stuff about holy living wasn't necessary. Christians, they taught, were free to live as they pleased. (Where have we met this idea before in the New Testament?)

A second heresy, or false teaching, floating in the church was this: Christ had not come to earth in human form, and, in fact, Christ was not going to return to earth. This heresy denied Christ's incarnation—the very heart of the gospel. This heresy may have started when Christians who had expected Christ to return soon were disappointed.

Peter hits these false teachings hard. Peter, like Paul, raises his voice a notch to make sure his readers—including the false teachers—get the message. In chapter 2 Peter gives three Old Testament examples as a stern warning: angels rebelling against God were punished; people who laughed at Noah were punished while Noah was saved; and Sodom and Gomorrah were destroyed, yet God saved the righteous Lot. These situations, says Peter, show that God will rescue the godly, but those who oppose God will eventually be punished.

Our Times/God's Time

To understand Peter's meaning in 2 Peter 3:8–9, it helps to know two

God's Time

Almost certainly God is not in Time. His life does not consist of moments following one another. If a million people are praying to Him at ten-thirty tonight, He need not listen to them all in that one little snippet which we call ten-thirty. Ten-thirty—and every other moment from the beginning of the world—is always the Present for Him.

—C. S. Lewis, *Mere Christianity*

Greek words: *chronos* and *kairos*. *Chronos* is calendar time, our clock time. We get the word *chronology* from *chronos*. *Chronos* began with creation. *Kairos* is God's time, real time. *Kairos* is the right time in God's eyes. "When the fullness of *kairos* (God's time) had come," Paul says, "God sent his Son, born of a woman" (Galatians 4:4).

"But do not forget this one thing, dear friends," says Peter. "With the Lord a day is like a thousand years, and a thousand years are like a day. The Lord is not slow in keeping his promise, as some understand slowness. He is patient with you, not wanting anyone to perish, but everyone to come to repentance."

If we think of Christ's return in clock time, we feel disappointed. But God doesn't operate by our clock time. He operates by *kairos*. So a delay in Christ's return by our clock time doesn't mean that God is behind schedule. Rather, it means that God is merciful. God wants all to have time to repent.

With the Lord one *kairos* day is like 365,000 *chronos* days, and 365,000 *kairos* days are like one *chronos* day. The two don't compute. We can't measure God by our clocks. But the time (the *kairos*) will come when the earth shall be filled with the glory of God as the waters cover the sea.

Encouraging the Church to Stand Firm

1 — — — ➤ Good News in Hebrews

Bible Reference: Hebrews 1–10:31

A Unique Book

The Book of Hebrews is called a letter, but it doesn't fit the New Testament mold. It doesn't open with a greeting. The author doesn't identify himself or those to whom the letter is addressed. And the letter doesn't offer a prayer of thanks. Hebrews is different.

The Book of Hebrews, in fact, seems more like a sermon than a letter. The author refers to himself as speaking and to his audience as listening, and his language suggests an oral style. For example, he uses alliteration and unusual word order to catch his listeners' attention.

The subject matter of Hebrews is unlike that of other letters, too. Paul's letters emphasize Christ's death and resurrection, but the Book of Hebrews emphasizes the ascended Christ. It holds up the Christ, who is the perfect priest, and who stands before God on behalf of believers and intercedes for them.

Hebrews describes this priest as greater than any angel in heaven, greater than Moses, and greater than all the priests and high priests in the history of God's people. But still, Hebrews says, even though Jesus Christ is in the position of supreme power, he identifies completely with us. Because Jesus became human, he knows about temptation and suffering. He knows exactly what we're up against. And because Jesus identifies with us, he understands us.

The New Covenant

The author of the Book of Hebrews also explains the huge change

Christ's coming has meant for God's covenant with his people. The old covenant, he says, has been replaced with a new covenant.

Before Christ's coming, the covenant of the law was in effect. This was the covenant God had made with Moses on Mount Sinai. Under this covenant God's people were to obey God's law, the Ten Commandments. Obeying the law was the way to fellowship with God and to be made right with God.

But because the people were sinful, they were unable to perfectly obey God's law. That's why Israel needed the priests and sacrifices. The priests were the mediators between God and the people. They offered sacrifices in atonement for sin and brought the people's petitions before God.

But like Humpty Dumpty, Israel couldn't be put back together so easily. The old covenant just couldn't do it. So God drew up a new covenant. With Christ a new covenant replaced the covenant of the law. Christ replaced the endless round of offerings with the sacrifice of himself. That sinless, perfect sacrifice did what the blood of animals could never do. It paid for sins once for all. Out went the old temporary covenant, and in came a new permanent covenant. Christ became the High Priest who makes us right with God.

In the old covenant access to God was limited. Only priests could enter the Holy Place for certain assigned tasks. Only the high priest could enter the Most Holy Place—and only on one day of the year, the Day of Atonement. The people had to wait outside. But Christ changed all that, too. When Jesus died, the curtain of the temple between the Holy and Most Holy Place was torn in two from top to bottom as a sign that now believers can go directly into God's presence.

Here's another important difference between the old and new covenants. The laws of the old covenant were written on tablets of stone. But in the new covenant God has made it possible for his covenant people to live new lives of spontaneous obedience. God has written this new covenant on our hearts by the work of the Holy Spirit. We no longer serve under the old written code but in the new Spirit-filled

The Book of Hebrews

Who wrote it? The letter is anonymous. Early on, some scholars thought that Paul was the author, but now most agree that he probably wasn't. The letter's style is quite different from Paul's. Other suggestions are Apollos, Barnabas, the deacon Philip, or Aristarchus. Here are some facts about Hebrews that provide a few clues:

- Hebrews is written in the finest Greek in the New Testament.
- It was composed by someone who was well educated. The letter shows a broad vocabulary.
- The way the material is put together shows that the author was formally trained in rhetoric, in the art of putting words/material together for maximum effect.
- The letter reflects a deep knowledge of Jewish temple practices and beliefs.

But the conclusion of Origen, the third-century church father, still stands:"Who wrote the epistle God alone knows certainly."

Whom was it sent to? Full of references to Jewish history, the Scriptures, and temple worship, the letter was obviously meant for Jewish Christians. The earliest manuscripts of the letter have the inscription "to the Hebrews." Where these people lived is not known. The farewell (Hebrews 13:24) implies that they may have lived in Rome. The author sends greetings from his companions who are from Italy, suggesting that they're sending their hellos to their hometown friends.

The intended audience is a house church, a small group of Christians. They had come to the faith through the preaching of those who had heard Jesus (Hebrews 2:3). But now, perhaps because of persecution, they are tempted to drift away (Hebrews 10:32–36).

When was it written? The letter was probably written in the 60s. It probably wasn't written earlier because it addresses second-generation Christians who are being persecuted (serious persecution started under Nero after the year 64). And it most likely wasn't written before the year 70 because the temple was destroyed that year, a fact the writer doesn't mention.

life. Now God's people are able to be obedient to the will of God from the heart. We now have the possibility not to sin, not by our own power but by the power of God working in us. Through the power of Christ, given to us by the Spirit, we can lead a new life of obedience to God.

But God's promise of the new covenant is not fully fulfilled. The fulfillment is *already*, but also *not yet*. The new covenant is *already*, but also *not yet*.

What do you think those last sentences mean? When will the new covenant be fully fulfilled? What will that mean for you and for all of God's people?

2 ------→ Gallery of Faith

Bible Reference: Hebrews 11–12:3

A Matter of Faith

Looking at the gallery of faith heroes in Hebrews can jolt us with surprise. Some people whose pictures are hanging in the gallery seem a little out of place there.

Take Rahab, for example. A prostitute in the gallery? What's Rahab doing there? And Samson's another surprise. What did he do to earn a place? Samson's caper with Delilah alone should rule him out. But Father Abraham had failures, too. When he went to Egypt to escape famine, he passed off his beautiful wife as his sister. He was afraid that otherwise Pharaoh might kill him in order to get Sarah. And what about David's double sin of adultery and murder? Next to David, Rahab looks good.

The gallery of the faithful, someone said, might better be described as a "'rogues' gallery of the redeemed." But these people aren't in the gallery because of their upright lives. They're there in spite of their sins. They're there because they believed God's promises.

What Rahab had heard of the God of the Hebrews turned her into a believer. But she didn't leave it at that. She acted on her faith. With the king

"If you look at a window, you see fly-specks, dust, the crack where junior's Frisbee hit it. If you look through a window, you see the world beyond.

"Something like this is the difference between those who see the Bible as a Holy Bore and those who see it as the Word of God which speaks out of the depths of an almost unimaginable past into the depths of ourselves."

—Frederick Buechner, *Wishful Thinking*

of Jericho demanding that she turn over the spies, she calmly hid them on the roof of her place and sent the would-be captors in another direction.

All of the gallery heroes in one way or another staked their lives on God's grace. They counted on God's promises when they made choices.

Today many people think that being a Christian is dull. But Hebrews 11 says to think again. Martin Luther says that true faith is "a lively, reckless trust in the grace of God." It's that kind of recklessness that faith heroes show.

Why? With eyes of faith believers see beyond space and time. Through faith believers know that this isn't all there is. We're living the present in the presence of God.

Running the Marathon

Living by faith may not be boring, but it's not easy either. We hope, but we do not see. At times we may live with doubts—just like the Christians addressed in this letter.

Imagine your life as a marathon, Hebrews says. All along the route the faithful are cheering you on: "Hang in there!" "Don't give up!" "You can do it!" Looking at what the heroes of faith did gives you courage. It's like watching videos of great athletes for inspiration.

But to stay in the race, we have to make sure we've stripped our lives of everything that distracts or hinders us. What kinds of things do people carry that make it hard to live the life of faith? What effect would it have to dump these things?

Enduring in the life of faith is hard. The author of Hebrews doesn't gloss that over. But the passage ends with the most important thing we must remember in this race: to keep our eyes on Jesus, the One who is the beginning and the end of the race. Remember what Jesus went through. Remember that Jesus is sitting at the right hand of God.

How does knowing that Jesus is sitting at the right hand of God encourage you to live by faith?

3 ▬ ▬ ▬ ➤ No More Temple Worship

Bible Reference: Mark 13:1–2; Luke 19:41–44

When Time Ran Out

Sacrificing animals in the Jerusalem temple was no longer necessary, the author of Hebrews wrote, because Jesus himself was the once-for-all sacrifice for sin. Nor was the Most Holy Place, the temple, the place to meet God. Jesus himself had become the temple. Jesus, not the temple, was now the place for believers to meet God. The author didn't know that not long after he sent off his letter, the temple itself would be leveled. Temple worship ended for all Jews in a way the author of Hebrews never expected.

But Jesus had dropped some clues about the temple's future. Once as Jesus and his disciples were leaving the temple, one of his disciples said, "What massive stones! What magnificent buildings!" But Jesus told him, "Not one here will be left on another; every one will be thrown down."

The very idea must have seemed absurd to the disciples. Members of the

Sanhedrin would have been outraged. To them, the very idea was blasphemy. But in the year 70 the Romans reduced the temple to a pile of rubble.

The Jewish War

The trouble started in Caesarea in the year 66 when Flores became procurator. A lawless ruler, he teamed up with outlaws to get a cut of their spoils. He stripped whole cities of their wealth and committed many atrocities.

When the Jewish leaders in Jerusalem complained about Flores, he plotted revenge. He schemed to drive the Jews into open revolt against Rome. A war would be a great coverup for his own crimes. The last thing he needed was a complaint against him brought to Caesar.

The war was triggered by this incident. A Greek owned the land next to the synagogue in Caesarea. The Jews had offered him a high price for his land, but he wouldn't sell. To irritate them, he began putting up some workshops along the entrance to their place of worship, blocking easy access. Some angry young Jews stopped the building. But Flores stepped in and stopped the fight. The Jews, in turn, bribed Flores to stop the builders. Although Flores accepted the bribe, he left the city and then waited for things to heat up.

Flores didn't have to wait long. The next Sabbath, troublemakers mocked the Jews by sacrificing birds near the synagogue. When a young man attacked the troublemakers, a riot started. During the riot, some Jews took a copy of the Law with them and fled the city. They contacted Flores to remind him of his promise to help them, but instead he put them in prison for taking a copy of the Law from Caesarea. To insult the Jews further, he also helped himself to money from the temple treasury.

Then, still baiting the Jews, Flores marched on Jerusalem. Incensed by the way he was received, he ordered his troops to sack the market and kill anyone they met. Thousands of men, women, and children were killed; some were even crucified.

At the time King Agrippa was away in Egypt, but Bernice, who was in Jerusalem, went to Flores barefooted, begging him to stop the killing. But it was no use. In fact, she had to hurry back to the palace to save her own life.

The frightened population tried not to provoke Flores, but he continued to engineer more clashes and kill more people. Flores finally left Jerusalem with his troops, but only after Jewish rebels cut off the connecting porticoes between the Fortress Antonia and the temple to keep him from seizing the temple and its treasures.

Meanwhile Agrippa returned to Jerusalem. He tried to calm the people, arguing that just because Flores was brutal didn't mean all Romans were brutal. Agrippa warned them, "By your actions you are already at war with Rome." He urged them to rebuild the porticoes. At first the people followed his advice, but when he tried to convince them to submit to Flores, they told him to get out of the city. Agrippa angrily retreated to the north.

Looking down at the circular middle palace of Masada.

The Zealots, who had always stood for armed resistance against Rome, now spearheaded an open revolt. Some of them captured the Masada, the huge rock-fortress south of Jerusalem near the Dead Sea. Others took command in Jerusalem. Moderate leaders were powerless to stop them.

All this happened between May and August of the year 66. In just a few months Flores had succeeded. Now the Jews were in a full-scale war with the Romans, a war they couldn't win.

Nero responded by sending his veteran commander Vespasian to put down the rebellion. By the spring of 67 Vespasian was in Syria in command of the Roman army and auxiliary forces of neighboring princes. He launched his attack on Galilee. Some Galilean towns submitted and were spared; others, like Jotapata, resisted and were razed. The siege of Jotapata took 47 days and cost 40,000 Jewish lives. By November of 66 the Romans had subdued all of Galilee. Jerusalem was the next campaign.

War in Jerusalem

Meanwhile, Jerusalem was already at war—civil war. Bands of robbers had entered Jerusalem. These bands called themselves Zealots, but they were outlaws.

These Zealots openly robbed and killed respected citizens of Jerusalem. They even made the Holy Place their headquarters and mocked the priesthood, choosing their own high priest and putting sacred vestments on him.

Outraged, the citizens of Jerusalem held an assembly to organize a counterattack. The Romans, they said, had never defiled the temple as these Jews had. Ananias, the high priest, agreed to lead them in their holy fight against the Zealots.

But the Zealots, getting wind of what was going on, rushed out of the temple. The two sides fought furiously, and many people were killed. Finally, the Zealots retreated to the temple's inner courts. Ananias, not wanting to fight on sacred ground, placed a guard of 6,000 men around the temple.

But the situation worsened. The Zealots tricked the Idumeans (who lived to the south of Judea) into helping them. Once the Idumean force of 20,000 broke into the city at night, they and the Zealots looted and killed thousands of people. When the Idumeans got fed up with the Zealots' atrocities and left the city, the Zealots became even more brutal.

Meanwhile, Vespasian had put the Jerusalem campaign on hold when he heard of Nero's violent death. The political situation in Rome was too uncertain to go off to war. Vespasian waited for news.

News came: Nero's successor was Galba. Then Galba was murdered. More news: Otho, the next emperor, committed suicide when Vitellius marched into Rome to assume power. Eight months later, a mob killed Vitellius. And finally this good news: Vespasian was proclaimed emperor and called to Rome.

In December of 69, before leaving for Rome, Vespasian gave his son Titus command of the troops and the order to crush Jerusalem.

The Siege of Jerusalem

Titus advanced on Jerusalem with four Roman legions plus auxiliary troops from allied kings. He systematically destroyed the suburbs and then constructed earthwork embankments to protect his troops and allow them to approach the city.

The Zealots, in turn, stood on the city walls shooting arrows and hurling firebrands down on the Romans. The Jews also dashed out of the city to make daring raids.

But next the Romans built siege towers plated with iron. Standing on the high towers, archers and stone-throwers could shoot into the city. Then the Romans brought up battering rams and relentlessly beat on the north tower of the city until it tottered and fell. But behind the first wall was a second to be breached.

The Jews fought with everything they had. Titus wanted to spare the city and the temple, so more than once he tried to negotiate a peace. But the Zealots refused.

Siege tower

At one point the Zealots completely surprised the Romans by cleverly tunneling under Roman embankments and collapsing and burning them.

Titus abruptly decided to change tactics. He built a siege wall around Jerusalem, making it impossible for anyone to leave and cutting off any food supplies. Jerusalem would submit or starve.

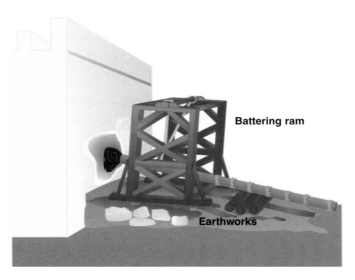

Battering ram

Earthworks

Famine was the killer in Jerusalem as Titus waited for surrender. A scary silence hung over the city. The Roman troops, though, were in good spirits. They had plenty of food—and rest.

But when Titus saw the dead bodies being thrown from the city walls into the ravines, he felt pity for Jerusalem. He had his men build earthworks again, and this time they were successful, breaking down the outer wall of the Antonia and then entering over a second wall.

Once inside the city, Titus gave the Zealots a chance to come out of the temple and fight elsewhere so as not to defile the temple. But the Zealots flatly refused. Titus reminded them that the Romans had allowed the Jews to put up signs in Greek and Hebrew warning that no Gentile could pass into the inner court or be put to death. And now Jews themselves were profaning the temple. According to the historian Josephus, Titus said, "Fight in any other place and no Roman shall profane your holy places. Rather, I will save the sanctuary for you, even against your will."

But the Zealots were not leaving. Instead, they lured the Romans into the temple complex and set up deadly fire traps in the temple's corridors.

Although Titus wanted to spare the magnificent temple, his soldiers were fighting for their lives in the temple area. Finally, in the heat of battle a soldier pursuing Jews up to the sanctuary snatched a burning brand. Josephus writes, "Hoisted up by one of his comrades, he threw the brand through a small golden door on the north side which gave access to chambers surrounding the sanctuary. As the flames caught, a fearful cry welled up from the Jews, who rushed to the rescue, caring nothing for their lives."

The soldiers launched an all-out fire attack, throwing torch after torch into the sanctuary. Titus, alerted to what was going on, made a last attempt to save the temple. But he was unsuccessful, and the Romans torched the sanctuary and all of the surrounding buildings.

With that, the back of Jewish resistance was broken. The Romans went on to take the rest of the city. Pouring into the streets, they massacred the people and burned houses, some with people still in them. "So great was the slaughter that in many places the flames were put out by streams of blood. Towards evening the butchery ceased, but all night the fires spread, and when dawn broke, all Jerusalem was in flames."

It was September 26 in the year 70 when Jerusalem fell to the Romans. Later, Titus ordered his soldiers to raze the whole city, including the temple and the city walls. But to show what strong defenses of Jerusalem the Roman army had overcome, he ordered part of the Western wall and three of the mighty city towers to be left standing.

The next spring Titus joined his father and brother Domitian in Rome. A splendid procession celebrated Titus's victory. Among all the spoils of war paraded before the people were treasures from the temple in Jerusalem— among them a golden table, a menorah, and a copy of the Law.

No More Temple Worship

What Jesus foretold in Mark 13 had come true: the temple was gone. Temple worship was over. The priesthood was finished. The animal sacrifices for sin ceased. The unthinkable had happened.

The temple was central to the Jews—to their worship and to their nation. It was so central that Jewish proverbs said that when the temple fell, the world would end. To the Jews, it was as if an atomic bomb had fallen in the middle of their world.

Imagine the news spreading through the Jewish communities around the Mediterranean. Imagine the tears and the shock as Jews gathered in their synagogues, remembering how they had gone up to the house of the Lord. Jews from all over had flocked to Jerusalem for Passover. "Next year in Jerusalem" was the common saying.

The destruction of Jerusalem and the temple was a body blow to Judaism. From that time on, the new center of Judaism was the Law of Moses, the Torah. In synagogues throughout the world today, the scrolls of the Torah have the central place in Jewish worship.

Now that you know this history, can you better understand why Jewish people worldwide rejoiced when Israelis captured the Western Wall in 1967?

Flavius Josephus

This account of the Jewish War is based on the report of an eyewitness,

Josephus. Josephus gives many more details in his report than you have here, about 90 pages more. Since he took part in the events he wrote about, the history comes alive. But his point of view isn't completely objective, and you should be aware of how he himself fits into the events:

Flavius Josephus.

- When the revolt started, Josephus joined the Jewish rebels—but reluctantly. He was made a commander in Galilee and led the defense of Jotapata. When the city fell, everyone around him vowed to die rather than be taken. To keep the vow, they took turns killing each other. But when Josephus and one other remained, Josephus talked him into breaking the vow. Both of them surrendered to the Romans.

- After being taken into custody by the Romans, Josephus changed sides and supported Rome. When he was given an audience with Vespasian, Josephus predicted that Vespasian would become emperor. That pleased Vespasian and probably saved Josephus's life. When some months later Vespasian actually was proclaimed emperor, he cut off Josephus's chains. In fact, Vespasian became the patron of Josephus. Josephus even took on the family name Flavius.

During the siege of Jerusalem, Josephus worked for the Romans as an interpreter and a negotiator. More than once he was sent to offer terms to the Jews and urged them to surrender. After the war, Josephus moved to Rome, where he lived in comfort on a generous pension and wrote the histories for which he is famous.

How does knowing these facts influence what you think of his report? Do you think that his account shows bias? Whom does he appear to favor—the Romans or the Jewish Zealot leaders?

4 ▬ ▬ ➡ Unmasking False Teachers

Bible Reference: 1 John 1–3:10

Saved by Secret Knowledge

At the end of the first century a false teaching appeared in the church. This teaching said that only a few people who knew secret knowledge about Jesus could be saved. The Greek word for knowledge is *gnosis*, and the people who believed this false teaching later came to be called Gnostics. Their false teaching was called Gnosticism. Gnosticism was one of the most dangerous false teachings in the first two centuries of the church. Here's what Gnostics taught:

- Spirit is entirely good, and matter (everything physical) is entirely evil. In other words, our bodies are evil but not our spirits. Because the world is physical, it's evil too. God is good because he is all spirit.
- Salvation is escaping our evil bodies. It comes through knowing secrets from Christ, not from believing that Jesus died for our sins.
- Jesus didn't become truly human. Some said that Christ had a kind of artificial body. He only seemed to have a body because God simply couldn't have an evil body. One early Gnostic, Cerinthus, taught that Christ descended on the man Jesus at his baptism but left him before his crucifixion.
- As "insiders" advance in knowledge (not faith) they become higher, more spiritual beings.
- Since our bodies are evil, it doesn't matter what we do with them. Besides, some said, sin won't affect the spirit within.

Those who taught beliefs like these in the churches in the first centuries claimed that Christ himself originated the ideas. Christ, they said, secretly taught these ideas to a chosen few who kept them quiet until the time was right to make them public.

Links to New Age

Would it surprise you to know that some people today say that the Gnostics pretty much had it right? The New Age movement, although not a copy of Gnosticism, is strongly influenced by it. According to J. William Smit in *Where Do We Draw the Line? The Seductive Power of New Age* the Gnostics and New Agers both separate Jesus from the Christ. Jesus is a Christ, they say. And like the Gnostics, New Agers believe that salvation is possible only through knowledge and not through faith in God's grace in Christ.

One big difference between Gnostics and New Agers is this: Gnostics wanted to separate good spirit from evil matter, while New Agers believe that the physical universe is good and it is one with God. So, although they may talk about God, in their thinking a rock, a tree, a crocodile, a person, and God are all essentially one. God is in everything, and everything is God. To them, "God is not a personal being, but rather a sort of impersonal force that holds the universe together."

The tricky thing about both Gnostic and New Age ideas is that they often sound Christian. When we hear the words *Jesus* and *Christ* and *God,* we tend to think the ideas must be Christian. But that's not true if people put unbiblical meanings into the words. Be critical and check out ideas against biblical teachings.

That You May Know

The letter of the apostle John was written sometime around A.D. 85–95 to explode false teachings in the church. John hit hard the idea that Jesus was not fully human. In the opening verses John testifies that he heard with his own ears and saw with his own eyes and touched with his own hands the Word of Life—Jesus Christ. Later he writes: "Every spirit that acknowledges that Jesus Christ has come in the flesh is from God, but every spirit that does not acknowledge Jesus is not from God" (1 John 4:2–3). John's testimony is that Jesus Christ is fully human and fully God.

Being both God and man,
Jesus is the only Mediator
between God and his people.
He alone paid the debt of our sin;
there is no other Savior!
In him the Father chose those
whom he would save.
His electing love sustains our hope:
God's grace is free
to save sinners who offer nothing
but their need for mercy.
—"Our World Belongs to God," 28

But John also wrote to encourage the Christian believers. In effect he says, remain true to faith in Jesus Christ, stay with what you have heard "from the beginning." And he says, "My purpose in writing is simply this: that you who believe in God's Son will know beyond the shadow of doubt that you have eternal life, the reality and not the illusion" (1 John 5:13, *The Message*).

5 ‑ ‑ ‑ ‑ ➤ God's Love and Ours

Bible Reference: 1 John 3:11—4:21

Love in Action

John's letter is crammed with the word *love*. John's favorite theme is the love of God that shone in the life and death of Jesus, the Son of God, and that also must shine in our lives.

A famous story says that when the apostle John was in his nineties, he used to be carried into the congregation by his disciples. To everyone he saw, he said over and over, "Little children, love one another. Little children, love one another. Little children, love one another." His disciples finally asked him why he always repeated the same words. He said, "Because this is the Lord's command, and if this alone be done, it is enough."

God is love, John says. And this is the proof of love: Jesus Christ laid down his life for us. The cross that most likely hangs somewhere in your church is there to always remind you of God's love. That's a comforting thought.

But John follows his words about the proof of God's love with these words: "And we ought to lay down our lives for our brothers." That's not so comforting.

The first-century people who read those words must have immediately thought of martyrs of the faith. Most of them probably knew someone who had been killed for refusing to deny Christ. In a real sense these people laid down their lives for other Christians. They knew that standing by their faith strengthened others.

The burning of Christian martyrs in Rome (19th century engraving).

And that same kind of total self-giving love is still going on today. In today's world even more Christians than in the first century are dying for the faith.

Still, those of us living in North America can be pretty sure that we aren't going be called to die for our faith. Not soon, anyway. So we're back in our comfort zone. But John is ready for us. Just when we think we're off the hook, he writes, "If you see some brother or sister in need and have the means to do something about it but turn a cold shoulder and do nothing, what happens to God's love? It disappears. And you made it disappear" (*The Message*).

God's love is made visible in us. No one has ever seen God, but God is seen in us if we love—because that means God lives in us. The Scripture won't let us separate our beliefs from our daily lives. Being a Christian is costly. It will cost us something to put love into action.

6 ▬ ▬ ➤ Looking Behind the Scenes

Bible Reference: Revelation 1

The Bible's Last Word

Revelation is the last word in the Bible on the story of God and his people. And what a strange word it is! Twenty-two chapters full of wild pictures: four living creatures with eyes in front and back, locusts in armor that can sting like scorpions, an enormous red dragon with seven heads, burning lakes, fighting angels, and much more. Revelation ends the Bible with a series of word pictures that are like a burst of fireworks. Each new picture is a surprise, each a shining explosion.

In Revelation, John is putting on a dazzling display to get our attention. He's not adding any new facts about Jesus Christ or about living the Christian life. And he's not telling us anything that we can't find in the 65 Bible books we've already studied. Instead, John tells the old, old story in a new way.

John translated the story into language that's full of strange word pictures, full of symbolism and imagery. He called his writing Revelation, or Apocalypse. *Apocalypse* means literally "to uncover" or "to unveil." In other words, "to look at what we can't ordinarily see."

In *Reversed Thunder* Eugene Peterson uses this analogy to describe the meaning of the word *apocalypse:*

St. John on the island of Patmos (19th century engraving).

> A person enters the house and becomes aware of rich aromas coming from the kitchen. The smells are inviting. He guesses at some of the ingredients. He asks others in the house what is in the pot and gets different opinions. The cook doesn't seem to be anywhere around. Finally, everyone troops into the kitchen. One of the company takes the lid from the pot; they all crowd close and peer into it. Uncovered, the stew with all its ingredients is exposed to the eye: Apocalypse! What was guessed at is now known in detail and becomes food for a hearty meal.

Apocalyptic literature, then, looks at what's going on behind the scenes in the universe. Here are some basic features of this kind of writing:

- It's usually written under a pseudonym. The authors assumed the name of an ancient authority.
- It divides the world into two camps, good and evil. These two are struggling to dominate the world. Behind this conflict are God and Satan.
- It deals almost exclusively with events that will mark the end of history, when good will triumph and evil will be judged.

- Created in difficult times, it explains why God's people suffer and encourages them with the vision of God's ultimate triumph.
- It's full of symbols and images, many of them belonging to fantasy (for example, a woman clothed with the sun).

The Book of Revelation is certainly apocalyptic. It has many of the basic features of this kind of literature. But it doesn't neatly fit the pattern of apocalyptic literature either.

- Revelation clearly states the author. John writes in his own name and with the authority of Christ.
- The author calls his writing prophecy more than once. And he emphasizes the point by putting statements at the beginning and end of the book. (Look, for example, at 1:3 and 22:7, 10, 18, and 19.)
- Revelation blends prophecy and apocalyptic writing. It's written in apocalyptic style, using rich imagery and symbolism, and it's written in a time of persecution, pointing to the ultimate triumph of Christ. But it's also prophecy. It calls the church to repent and warns of judgment. It also addresses the here and now.
- Revelation is written in the form of a letter. It was sent by John to the seven churches of Asia Minor.

So, although Revelation uses apocalyptic language, it's more than an apocalypse. John doesn't just look to the future. He unveils Christ's hidden rule right now. He encourages the church to see that behind all things is Jesus Christ in control. And someday it won't be invisible anymore. At the right time Jesus will return in glory, and then everyone on earth will bow down to him and confess his kingship.

A Time of Trouble

When John wrote Revelation, God's people were going through a dark period. The Roman emperor Domitian (A.D. 81–96) was demanding that Christians worship him. When the world has the emperor, he said, it needs no more light from heaven. The emperor alone is Lord forever. Domitian's imperial commands began, "The Lord our God demands . . ."

Gradually, Domitian turned more and more to punishing anyone who didn't bow to his power. Domitian was the first emperor to understand that behind the Christian faith stood a figure who threatened the power of all emperors. When he understood that Christians refused to worship him

The temple of Hadrian in Ephesus.

because they confessed Jesus as their world ruler, he declared all-out war.

In Domitian's time Ephesus was the center of emperor worship in Asia Minor. But Ephesus was also the center of the Christian church after Jerusalem's destruction. And John, the writer of the Book of Revelation, was the head of the church there and in the surrounding area. Domitian had John brought to Rome, where he was cross-examined and tortured. Then he was sent to live on Patmos, an island in the Aegean Sea.

From this living tomb John wrote a letter to encourage the Christians of the province of Asia. He wanted them to see beyond the darkness, beyond the persecutions, beyond the legions of Rome, and beyond Domitian. John wanted them to see the vision of the Christ who had already won the victory.

The Vision of Jesus Christ

How do you picture Jesus? Most likely you picture him as the person who walked on earth. You think of the man who lived in Nazareth and walked the roads of Palestine. That's natural. And John must have thought of Jesus like that, too.

But when John is in the Spirit on the island of Patmos, he has a vision of Jesus Christ. What he sees isn't the lowly Jesus in the manger in Bethlehem or Jesus on the cross. The Jesus Christ of John's vision is magnificent. This Christ is a blazing, commanding figure with a voice like the

The Island of Patmos

John, the author of the book of Revelation, was exiled to Patmos "because of the word of God and the testimony of Jesus" (Revelation 1:9). Patmos is a rocky island about 50 miles off the coast of the province of Asia, southwest of Ephesus. The island is small, about eight miles long and six miles wide at its widest point. It was

The coast of Patmos.

one of the islands where Romans sent prisoners. According to one writer, "Prisoners were left to rot and bleach upon the rocks."

Eusebius, an early historian, says that Emperor Narva (96–98) permitted John to leave Patmos.

The island of Patmos today has many shrines, including a grotto where John supposedly had his vision. There is also an ancient monastery to St. John the Theologian, founded in 1088.

sound of Niagara Falls. John's book is the revelation of this Christ, the ruler of the world.

That's a picture of Jesus Christ to carry with you. What difference do you think that picture could have on your life?

7 ▪ ▪ ▪ ▪ ▪ ▪ ➔ Seven Churches

Bible Reference: Revelation 2–3

A Dialogue: Seven Messages

In John's vision Christ orders him to write down everything he sees: things that are and things about to be. And he is to write a message to each of these seven churches in the province of Asia: Ephesus, Smyrna, Pergamum, Thyatira, Sardis, Philadelphia, and Laodicea.

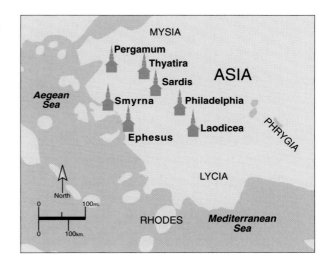

Your job is to understand what these messages are all about. Imagine that John is here to talk with you and clue you in.

You: Now, sir, you say there are seven messages to seven churches because there are seven lampstands. Lots of sevens, I'd say.

John: Good observation. You'll notice that the number seven pops up a lot in Revelation. There are seven stars, seven lampstands, seven churches, seven messages, seven seals, seven visions, seven bowls. Seven, you see, is a very special number in the Bible. It means that something is complete, all-inclusive.

You: Well, then, writing to seven churches means writing to all churches?

John: You've got it. Of course there were more than seven churches in Asia Minor. The ones I chose were places on a Roman postal route. Just look at a map. You'll see that the seven churches make a circle—that is, if you start in Ephesus and end up in Ephesus. You know, you should take a trip to Turkey and have a look. All those ancient cities have been excavated by archaeologists.

You: To get back to Revelation and those messages . . . the vision of Christ in the middle of the lampstands is awesome . . .

John (interrupting): Not everyone thinks that. Some people want Christ but not the church. Christ standing in the middle of the lampstands, his churches, tells us that that's where Christ is to be found. Christ isn't seen apart from those who gather to listen, pray, and praise God. Christ loves the church.

You: Never thought of it quite like that myself. That sounds tough . . . you know . . . harsh. Is the church that important?

John: You'd better believe it!

You: To get back to the Book of Revelation and those messages to churches in Asia . . . you know, I thought Revelation was about end times. I thought it was apoca . . .

John: Apocalyptic literature?

You: Right. Apocalyptic literature.

John: But don't forget Revelation is more than that. It talks about end times, but it's also prophecy, and it calls people to repent. It has things to say about how Christians should live here on earth, too. Before we can start getting excited about what's going to happen in the future, we've go to get straight in the present.

You: To get back to Revelation and those messages . . .

John: Yes. The messages follow a basic pattern. It helps to know that. Each one begins by identifying the Christ of the vision as the one who is speaking to the churches. But each uses a different feature of the vision. For example, one describes Christ with sharp sword.

You: I'll look for that, a description of Christ in each message. Anything else?

John: Each message also has the statement: "He who has an ear to hear, let him listen to what the Spirit says to the churches."

You: That sounds simple enough.

John: Does it? I pray that you find it so. In the first century I found that people were often conveniently deaf to what the Spirit was saying. Or

Ephesus was the chief city of Asia minor with a population 250,000, Ephesus was a cosmopolitan place. Its main attraction was the Temple of Artemis, which was one of the Seven Wonders of the Ancient World. The message to Ephesus mentions false teachers. When Paul bade farewell to the elders of the church in Ephesus, he had warned them about false teachers.

Smyrna (today's Izmir) was 35 miles north of Ephesus. Smyrna was a center of emperor worship, and here Christians were being persecuted for not participating in this worship. Besides, some Jews in the city were falsely accusing them of being trouble-makers. Revelation's message to them has only affirmation.

Pergamum (modern Bergama) was located about 50 miles north of Smyrna and set on a cone-shaped hill. The city was famous especially for its great library of scrolls. It was also known for its collection of shrines to pagan gods. The enormous altar to Zeus stood on a huge platform erected behind the city on a hill. Pergamum was also known for the worship of Asclepius, the god of healing.

Thyatira (modern Akhisar), some 45 miles southeast of Pergamum, was a center for traders and artisans. Archaeological inscriptions show that there were guilds of potters, bakers, slave traders, leather workers, bronze workers, dyers, and makers of linen and wool. These guilds were something like our trade unions, but they also held banquets in pagan temples or shrines "where an animal was offered to the gods and then eaten by the members of the guild."

Sardis (modern Sart), which was at a junction of five roads 35 miles south of Thyatira, was a busy commercial city. In the 6th century B.C. it had been one of the greatest cities of the world. Sardis was a natural citadel. It was set on a hill "with sheer cliffs on three sides that dropped some 1,500 feet to the valley below." Leveled in A.D. 17 by an earthquake, it was rebuilt and became a center for trade in wool. Revelation's message to Sardis is sharp.

Philadelphia was on the Roman road another 35 miles to the southeast. Founded in the 2nd century B.C., the earthquake that leveled Sardis did the same to Philadelphia. But by the 90s Philadelphia had been rebuilt with Roman help. Here the church was not only small and poor but also under attack by the synagogue. The message to this church has only encouragement.

Laodicea (near today's Denizli) was about 40 miles southeast of Philadelphia. The city, dating from the middle of the 3rd century B.C., was a was rich trading center. When it was destroyed by earthquake in A.D. 61, its citizens rebuilt without help from Rome. Its riches came chiefly from textiles and its world-famous eye salve. It was also known for banking. The severest message goes to the church in this city. But its call to repentance is one of the most loved in the Bible. And it too receives a rich promise.

else their ears were already so filled with noise that they couldn't hear the Spirit.

You: Oh. I wasn't thinking about it like that. I just meant . . .

John: Well, *do* think about it like that. Let's go on.

You: So it seems the pattern is the same but different. This isn't turning out to be all that basic.

John: Listen, there's more. The body of each message follows a pattern too. This pattern: first, an affirmation, or what's right about the church; second, a call to repent or change; third, a promise of eternal life to encourage the church.

You: In other words the message is what's good about the church, what's bad, and what the hope is for the future?

John: Neat summary! Each church is given a different picture, or image, of that promise. And what pictures! I tell you those are pictures to remember and carry with you all your life!

You: You probably won't like this question, but I can't help thinking it: Why should I read these messages? After all, those churches and people are long gone. They didn't have TV or cars or computers or anything. Things weren't like they are today.

John: Some things don't change. The times do, but people don't. And churches haven't changed either. If you picked seven churches at random from your city or area, I'm sure you'd find that they're pretty much like those seven in Asia. So . . . I'll meet you in the Book.

8 ━ ━ ━ ━ ➤ Worthy Is the Lamb

Bible Reference: Revelation 4–5

The Center

If someone asked you why you worship, what would you say?

People have said things like this:

"I worship because it gives me inner peace."

"I worship because I like a sermon that tells me what's right and wrong."

"I worship because I need strength to live—it's a jungle out there."

You've probably already noticed that all these answers have one thing in common: they focus on the I—on my feelings or needs or wants.

Measured against Revelation 4 and 5, these answers are out of kilter. In Revelation's scene of worship God is at the center. God gathers his people. And the people fall down before him saying,

"You are worthy, our Lord and God,

to receive glory and honor and power."

Here no one is centered on self. The focus is on God, from whom and through whom and to whom are all things.

The vision in the Book of Revelation begins with John seeing an open door and being invited to look into the throne room of God. It's a dazzling scene full of splendor and color.

Worthy Is the Lamb

The throne room scene ends with the song of praise sung by every creature that exists, "Worthy is the Lamb . . . ."

"Think of Handel's *Messiah*. Now imagine that whole oratorio as just one of many lines of music, with hundreds of other lines being sung alongside, and all blending together into a huge swelling harmony. And imagine every creature in heaven and on earth—penguins and peacocks, guinea pigs and gorillas, as well as children, women, and men—all singing this extraordinary song. That is how Easter is celebrated in God's dimension of reality. What we Christians do on earth is to add our line to that total harmony. We celebrate together the fact of a world reborn."

—N. T. Wright, *Following Jesus*

The Gathering

The throne of God is at the center of the room. The throne is magnificent, a rainbow of emerald circles it. The One on the throne is radiant, shining with the brilliance of amber and deep red precious stones. Around the throne are 24 thrones with 24 elders seated on them. The 24 elders are a double 12—the 12 Hebrew tribes and the 12 Christian apostles. They stand for Israel and the church, the old covenant people and the new covenant people.

Also around the throne are four living creatures: one like a lion, one like an ox, one with a face like a human, and one like an eagle. They represent all of creation, and they too are centered in God.

The whole scene is bathed with light, with shining lamps and lightning flashes and reflections from a luminous sea of glass. And all creation breaks out in praise to God, the Creator:

> "Holy, holy, holy,
> is the Lord God Almighty,
> who was, and is, and is to come."

The Scroll and the Lamb

As John looks at this spectacular scene, he notices a sealed scroll in the hand of God. No one is able to open it because no one is worthy. And John weeps.

But then the Lamb appears. As soon as he takes the scroll from the right hand of God, another song of praise again breaks out from the 24 elders, that is, from the whole church. This time the song celebrates Jesus Christ, the Lamb of God.

Then countless angels circle the throne and join the worship. This time the theme is the miracle of salvation in Christ.

The scene closes with every creature in heaven and on earth and under the earth and on and in the sea joining the angels in a final burst of worship:

"For the King! For the Lamb!
The blessing, the glory, the honor, the strength
For age after age after age." (*The Message*)

And to the songs of praise, the living creatures respond, "Yes!" "Amen!"
Yes to God. Yes to Jesus Christ. Yes! Yes! Yes!

9 ‒ ‒ ‒ ‒ ‒ ‒ ➤ War in Heaven

Bible Reference: Revelation 12–13:1

The Woman, Her Child, and the Dragon

Reader 1: Then a great and mysterious sight appeared in the sky.

Reader 2: There was a woman, whose dress was the sun

Reader 3: and who had the moon under her feet

Reader 4: and a crown of twelve stars on her head.

All: She was soon to give birth, and the pains and suffering of childbirth made her cry out.

Reader 1: Another mysterious sight appeared in the sky.

Reader 2: There was a huge red dragon with seven heads

Reader 3: and ten horns

Reader 4: and a crown on each of his heads.

Reader 1: With his tail he dragged a third of the stars out of the sky

Reader 2: and threw them down to the earth.

Reader 3: He stood in front of the woman,

Reader 4: in order to eat her child as soon as it was born.

All: Then she gave birth to a son who would rule over all nations with an iron rod. But the child was snatched away and taken to God and his throne.

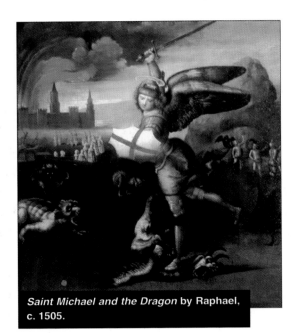

Saint Michael and the Dragon by Raphael, c. 1505.

Reader 1: The woman fled to the desert, to a place God had prepared for her,

Reader 2: where she would be taken care of for 1,260 days.

All: Then war broke out in heaven.

Reader 3: Michael and his angels fought against the dragon,

Reader 4: who fought back with his angels,

Reader 1: but the dragon was defeated,

Reader 2: and he and his angels were not allowed to stay in heaven any longer.

All: The huge dragon was thrown out—that ancient serpent, named the Devil, or Satan, that deceived the whole world. He was thrown down to earth, and all his angels with him.

Reader 3: Then I heard a loud voice in heaven saying,

Voice in heaven: "Now God's salvation has come!
Now God has shown his power as King!
Now his Messiah has shown his authority!
For the one who stood before our God
and accused our people day and night
has been thrown out of heaven.
Our people defeated him
by the blood of the Lamb
and by the word of their testimony,
which they proclaimed.
They were willing
to give up their lives.

"Be glad, you heavens,
and all you that live there!

But how terrible for the earth
and the sea!
For the devil was thrown down to you,
and he is filled with rage.
He knows that he has
only a little time left."

Reader 4: When the dragon realized that he had been thrown down to the earth,

Reader 1: he began to pursue the woman who had given birth to the boy.

All: She was given the two wings of a large eagle in order to fly to the desert, where she would be taken care of for a time, safe from the dragon's attack.

Reader 2: And then from his mouth the dragon poured out water like a river, to overtake the woman and sweep her away.

Reader 3: But the earth helped the woman by opening its mouth

Reader 4: and swallowing the water that had come from the dragon's mouth.

All: The dragon was furious with the woman and went off to fight against the rest of her descendants, all those who obey God and are faithful to what Jesus did and taught.

Reader 1: And the dragon stood on the shore of the sea.

10 — — — — → The Last Battle

> **Bible Reference: Revelation 13:2–18;**
> **19:11—20:15**

The Counterfeit Trinity

In Revelation 13 two beasts appear who are agents of the dragon Satan. One beast comes out of the sea, and the other rises out of the ground. The

The Beast Comes Out of the Sea
by Giusto di Giovanni Menabuoi,
1363–1393.

beast from the sea is a monster—part leopard, part bear, and part lion. The second beast looks like a lamb but speaks like a dragon. Both serve the dragon. Together the three make up an unholy, counterfeit trinity.

According to many, the first beast symbolizes the world powers opposing Christ. Some call the beast Antichrist. It uses power to frighten people into submission. In John's day this was the Roman Empire. The emperors, beginning with Julius Caesar, were worshiped as gods. Domitian even made others address him as "our Lord and God." The power of the state was openly setting itself up against God's kingdom. It was holding up a god other than the Lord God to worship. John accuses this beast of blaspheming against God.

The second beast pretends to be a lamb, but its voice gives it away. In other words, it pretends to be of God, but it lies. (Chapter 19 calls it a false prophet.) Its main task is to win people over to the worship of the first beast. This lying beast uses trickery—and people get taken in by it. It marks the first beast's followers on the right hand or on the forehead, showing that they're part of the "in" group.

This counterfeit trinity tries to make us worship the powers we can see instead of worshiping God. It's well-organized. It has ways of convincing us to buy into things that bring quick rewards. It presses us to go along. "Everybody's doing it." And if we don't bow as it wishes, it has ways of liquidating us. It has ways of leaving us out and making life difficult.

Although John doesn't want us to underestimate the power of these beasts, he also unmasks them. They're just a hoax, John says. Don't be taken in. Use your head. Just figure out the riddle of the number of the beast. That will tell you that what's going on is not of God. The beast's number is a human number: 666.

The Millennium

The 1,000 years, or millennium, that John talks about in Revelation 20 has long been a hot topic of discussion among Christians. Some understand the 1,000 as a literal number and others as a symbolic number.

- **Amillennialists** take the view that the 1,000 years are symbolic and not literal. In their view the number stands for the ascended Christ's present reign between his first and second coming. Amillennialists quote Jesus' parable in Matthew 13 about the wheat and weeds growing side by side until the harvest, the end of the world.
- **Premillennialists** believe that Christ will return to earth before the millennium begins. Before Christ's return, things on earth will get worse and worse. The Antichrist will assume power. Then Christ will come, take control, and usher in 1,000 years of peace here on earth.
- **Postmillennialists** maintain that Christ will return after the 1,000 years. In their view God's kingdom is gradually coming in the world through preaching and the Holy Spirit's work. Christ is already reigning through his church and will bring spiritual prosperity and peace to the world 1,000 years before he returns at the end of history.

Does John's clue help you? Did you expect anything else in apocalyptic literature?

The Last Battle

In Revelation 19–20 John again takes us behind the scenes. In these chapters John describes a series of seven short visions. Each one begins with the words *I saw*.

The first vision begins with Christ, the Warrior-Messiah-King riding out to war. Now the time for the last battle has come, the time to defeat evil for all eternity. Although salvation means saving those who in faith accept the grace offered in Christ Jesus, it also means ending evil. In John's visions Christ takes on the two beasts and the dragon, Satan. In other words, Christ battles every evil power.

People in the ancient world loved riddles with numbers. In Greek and Hebrew, letters of the alphabet were used not only for vowels and consonants but also for numerals. It was common to code names by adding up their letters. In the ruins of Pompeii, for example, these words were found written on a wall: "I love thee, whose number is . . . "

So, for example, if we did the same thing using the English alphabet, the name *Abe* would have a number of 8 (figuring $A = 1$, $B = 2$, and $E = 5$). What would your number be?

Number codes were also used for serious messages—as in the Book of Revelation. Over the centuries many have tried to solve the cryptogram 666. Some think that "Nero Caesar" is the answer. The letters of "Nero Caesar" add up to 666 using the Hebrew alphabet.

Others think the number 666 has a deeper meaning. You know that seven is the number for perfection, or the number for God. So 777 is the number of the Trinity. In contrast, 666 is the number of imperfection. "In the language of numbers 666 is a triple failure to be 777, the three-times perfect, whole number," explains Eugene Peterson.

John description is full of details, many that we can't begin to understand. But the final outcome is clear. The two beasts are thrown alive into the "fiery lake of burning sulfur." Then when the dragon is finally thrown in the same lake 1,000 years later, Satan's rule is totally and finally over.

Revelation 20 ends with the last of the seven visions, an apocalyptic description of the last judgment. John sees a great drama unfold. A great white throne appears in the heaven, and all humanity stands before God. No exceptions, no excuses. Books are opened. Tension crackles as the books tell everything that has happened on earth. With the opening of these books John is telling us that what we do or don't do here on earth is important. Our decisions and actions have eternal meaning.

Then one more book is opened: the book of life. The opening of this book tells us that God has the final word. God is the final judge. But we know that those who have new life in Christ will find God merciful. Another name for this book might be the book of amazing grace.

11 ━ ━ ━ ━ ━ ➤ All Things New

Bible Reference: Revelation 21–22

The New World

In *Following Jesus* N. T. Wright tells about the first time that he read a book of the Bible from beginning to end. It was the Book of Revelation: "I was fourteen at the time. The New English Bible had just come out, and I'd been given a copy; and at school there was an hour when we had to read something religious, and I was curious about this strange book at the end of the New Testament. I started it without knowing if it was even readable; I finished it without the question even occurring to me. The funny thing is that I am quite sure I didn't understand what on earth it was all about, but I can still remember the explosive power and beauty of it, the sense that the New Testament I held in my hands had a thunderstorm hidden inside it that nobody had warned me about."

The "most thunderous moment" of the Christian year is Easter, when Christians celebrate Jesus Christ's resurrection. Because Jesus is alive today, we Christians can be sure that there's life beyond death. That's wonderfully true. But that's just the beginning of the power of Jesus' resurrection, because the resurrection means much more than our personal experience of Jesus and our hope for the future.

In fact, Jesus' resurrection is the beginning of God's new world. God is making all things new—not only us but also the whole world. Salvation is not just for us, not just for human beings. Salvation is for the whole creation. Jesus' resurrection brings new life, but it also brings a new world. In Christ the world is being reborn.

In the Book of Revelation John is telling us this good news, the same news that the whole Bible has been telling. The Old Testament prophets—Paul, Peter, and the other apostles—all have been telling about the new things God is doing. The Gospels use the words of Jesus himself to tell about it.

But John gathers all these voices together. And to do justice to something this big, he reaches for "big" language. He reaches for beasts and thunder and lightning, for thrones and stars and echoing music—all to paint a huge picture of the new thing God is doing in the resurrection. Now—in the same big language—John gives one final picture. He shows us a picture of the final outcome. He shows where Jesus' death and resurrection will finally lead: to a new world.

The New Jerusalem by Gustave Doré.

John's picture of the world finally and completely reborn tells what won't be there as well as what will.

- no sea
- a holy city coming down to earth
- no temple
- the kings of the earth bringing their splendor into the new city
- no death or crying or pain
- a river of the water of life
- two trees of life
- no need for sun or moon/no night
- the everlasting light of the Lord God

But reading this list is about as far from John's picture in Revelation as reading a list of baseball statistics is from watching the final inning of an exciting baseball game. Read Revelation 21 and 22, and be carried along by John's vision of how God is making all things new.

Soon and Very Soon

Suddenly, John's visions come to an end. John closes the Book of Revelation with a series of promises and warnings. Looking at them closely, we can see that John is rounding off his book by returning to what he said at the beginning. He says once more that his book is to be read aloud in the churches, that what he has to say is authentic, and that it is true prophecy.

But the important thing to notice is the urgency in John's voice. In the first chapter John says his vision is of what will take place soon. Now at the end of the book three times Christ says, "I am coming soon." *Soon*, says Eugene Peterson in *Reversed Thunder*, is a pale word compared with the original. The tone of the original word is closer to what we do when we step to the curb in a city and call, "Taxi! Taxi!" We grab the cab and tell the driver where we're going and we're off.

Christ's second coming is urgent. It requires our attention. But John isn't trying to scare us. Knowing that Jesus Christ is coming gives our lives meaning and shape. It helps us clear the "junk" out of our lives and live in the awareness of life's purpose. Then when Christ says, "I am coming soon," we can answer with a confident "Yes!"

1 ━ ━ ━ ━ ━ ━ ➤ Moving Forward

Beginnings

The church began in Jerusalem around A.D. 30 on the day of Pentecost. That was the day that Jesus' followers, in the power of the Spirit, announced the good news: "Jesus, whom you crucified, God raised from the dead. That same Jesus is the Savior, the Messiah that you have been waiting for." Three thousand were baptized that day, and the church was born.

The members of First Church in Jerusalem were Jews. Even though they were Christians, they continued to live like Jews—going to the temple to pray, eating according to strict Jewish laws, and observing Jewish religious days. But they were baptized in Jesus' name, they broke bread and drank wine together, and they followed Jesus' teachings.

Jewish authorities helped the church to expand by trying to squash it. After Stephen was stoned, the Christians had to flee for their lives. Most of them went north from Jerusalem into Samaria, up along the Mediterranean coast, and to Antioch. The scattered Christians scattered gospel seed. The gospel was no longer tied to Jerusalem.

The second and much bigger expansion occurred when the church opened its doors to Gentiles as well as Jews. Peter's vision and his witness about the Spirit coming upon Cornelius, a Gentile, were crucial to this. Paul was absolutely convinced that the good news of the gospel meant that baptism had replaced circumcision as the mark of a believer. This shocked many Jewish Christians. Some dragged their feet, not wanting to give up their favored status with God. But the Jerusalem Council, held in A.D. 50, finally settled the matter: Gentiles were welcome in the church without having to be circumcised or obey Jewish religious laws.

The next expansion was largely the result of Paul's mission. God called

Paul for the specific purpose of preaching to the Gentiles, and Paul threw himself into the task with every ounce of energy he had. Antioch, the third largest city in the Roman Empire (after Rome and Alexandria), became Paul's home base. From there Paul took the gospel to Cyprus, to the province of Asia (modern Turkey), and to Greece.

But the church's continuing growth was mainly due to the many Christians who took the news of the gospel with them wherever they went. Typical converts probably heard about the faith through ordinary Christians—neighbors and friends or traveling merchants and tradespeople—or through being slaves or workers in Christian households.

Consequently, in the four or five decades following its birth on Pentecost, Christianity spread throughout much of the eastern Mediterranean region, from Jerusalem to Rome. Some nonbiblical writings claim that churches were also started in the East, in what is now Iran and even as far as India.

Two Markers

One important marker in the history of the early church was the destruction of Jerusalem and the temple in A.D. 70. The end of the temple meant the end of temple worship, and Christians made a final break with Jewish religious practices. The destruction of the temple showed that the temple-centered era was past and that the Christ-centered era had begun.

Jews also gradually became more hostile to Christians, so that toward the end of the first century, Christians were expelled from the synagogues. The Christian faith became largely a Gentile faith.

Another marker was the death of the apostles. By A.D. 70 the era of the apostles was over. In 41 James, the brother of the apostle John, had been murdered by the command of Herod Agrippa I. According to tradition, Peter and Paul were martyred in Rome during Nero's persecution of Christians after the fire in 64. James, "the brother of the Lord," was murdered in 62 at the high priest's command. And John most likely died in exile on the island of Patmos.

The death of the apostles naturally left a huge gap in the church. The apostles had seen and heard and touched and talked with Jesus. They were the eyewitnesses. Jesus had sent them out as his representatives, and the apostles had spoken and written with Jesus' authority. When disagreements cropped up, the church could ask one or more of the apostles for guidance. But now, with the apostles gone, who would have the authority in the church? Who would decide if teachings were false or true?

Forming the Christian Scriptures

One way the church responded during the last decades of the first century was to gradually gather Christian writings. Churches began exchanging and collecting letters of the apostles and other writings. The Gospels, the accounts of Jesus' life and ministry, were composed between the years 50 and 90. Luke contributed a history of the church's beginnings called The Acts of the Apostles. Toward the end of the first century written accounts replaced the eyewitnesses themselves. But at this time the writings had not yet been collected and defined as "Scripture."

The Apostolic Fathers

Another thread connecting the church with the apostles was a group of men who seem to have known and talked with the apostles. These leaders, who wrote during the first half of the second century, are called the apostolic fathers. The most important of these leaders were Polycarp of Smyrna, Ignatius of Antioch, Clement and Hermas of Rome, Papias of Hieropolis, and Barnabas, probably of Alexandria.

In this excerpt from a letter written about 190, Irenaeus, a well-known church leader, tells about Polycarp's link to the apostle John.

> "I can describe the place where blessed Polycarp sat and talked, his goings out and comings in, the character of his life, his personal appearance, his addresses to crowded congregations. I remember how he spoke of his [talking] with John and with the others who had seen the Lord; how he repeated their words from memory; and how the things that he had heard them say

about the Lord, his miracles and his teaching, things that he had heard direct from the eyewitnesses of the Word of life, were proclaimed by Polycarp in complete harmony with scripture. To these things I listened eagerly at the time . . . learning them by heart." (Reported by Eusebius of Caesarea)

You can see that this connection to the apostle John was of immense importance to Irenaeus. It must have been important to the church too.

The apostolic fathers haven't gotten high marks for their writings. Their works are generally poorly organized and don't show much depth of thought. But these leaders were Christians who were trying to keep the faith alive in their time. Their writings are valuable to us today because they give us a glimpse into the life of Christians during the period following the apostles.

Ignatius

Ignatius was the bishop, or leading elder, of the church in Antioch. According to legend, he was the little child that Jesus had picked up and placed in the middle of his disciples. Ignatius was about 70 (around the year 107) when he was arrested, tried, and condemned to die in Rome. As he traveled to Rome through the province of Asia, Christians living along the route were able to visit and talk with him. During this trip Ignatius wrote seven letters to churches and individuals. In his letter to Rome he asked the Christians to pray that he might have the strength to face his coming trial "so that I may not only be called a Christian, but also behave as such. . . . I am God's wheat, to be ground by the teeth of beasts, so that I may be offered as pure bread of Christ."

Ignatius.

Polycarp

We know about Polycarp's death from a letter from the church at Smyrna to the church at Philomelium. This letter, known as "The Martyrdom of Polycarp," is the oldest nonbiblical account of a martyr's death. Written shortly after the event, it tells "in gruesome detail the pursuit, arrest, trial, and execution of Polycarp, the beloved 86-year-old bishop of the church of Smyrna."

On February 22, 156, when Polycarp was brought into the open arena, the authorities threatened to throw him to the lions. But they preferred that he deny that he was a Christian.

The Roman proconsul urged Polycarp to deny Christ and join the crowd's yells of "Away with atheists!"

But Polycarp looked straight at the yelling crowd, pointed his finger at them, and said, "Away with atheists!"

"Denounce Christ, and I'll let you go," said the proconsul.

Polycarp answered: "Eighty and six years have I served him, and he has never done me wrong. How can I blaspheme my King, who has saved me?"

"Simply swear by Caesar," the proconsul said.

"I am a Christian," said Polycarp. "If you want to know what that is, set a day and listen."

Finally the proconsul told the crowd, "Polycarp has confessed he is a Christian."

The crowd roared in anger, "Burn him alive!"

Quickly people collected sticks and firewood from the shops and baths. Polycarp asked not to be nailed to the stake. "Leave me as I am," he said. "He who enables me to endure the fire will also make me able to stand firm at the stake."

Then Polycarp prayed with a loud voice, "Lord God Almighty, Father of our Lord Jesus Christ, I praise you for thinking me worthy of this day and hour, to be among your martyrs and to share in the cup of Christ." When he said Amen, the men lit the fire.

But, according to the witnesses, the flames arched over Polycarp "like the sail of a ship filled by the wind" and "made a wall" around him. At last Polycarp was killed with a dagger.

Polycarp being burned at the stake.

Then his body was put in the flames and burned. Later, Christians took his bones and buried them.

2 ━ ━ ➤ Christians in a Hostile World

Persecutions in the Early Church

When we think of the early church, we think of martyrs. We think of Christians being thrown to wild animals like Ignatius or being burned at the stake like Polycarp or crucified like Peter or beheaded like Paul.

Christians were martyred in the early church, but in the first and second centuries Christians were not widely, systematically persecuted. Nero had used Christians as scapegoats for the fire in Rome. Later Domitian savagely turned against Christians because they resisted worshiping Roman gods and Domitian himself. But this persecution was centered mainly in Rome and in the province of Asia.

The Christians' lifestyle differed from that of people around them. Christians didn't participate in the rituals of beginning meals with offerings to pagan gods. They couldn't join parties held on temple grounds and starting off with animal sacrifices. They refused to attend arena events in which prisoners and slaves fought to the death. Their attitudes toward slaves and family life reflected Christian views. In these and many other ways Christians lived distinctive lives.

Many people disliked Christians because they were different. Somehow the Christian lifestyle was a judgment on their own lifestyle. So although Christians weren't persecuted in an organized way, persecution was never far off.

Accusations against Christianity

Various accusations sprang up against the Christians. Some of these accusations have been discovered in copies of anti-Christian writings from the early centuries.

One accusation was that Christians were atheists; Polycarp was accused of this. Because they refused to worship pagan gods or the emperor,

Christians were thought to have no god. This idea frightened pagans, who thought that the gods would get even. They feared that the gods would inflict earthquakes, fires, illnesses, or other punishments on their cities.

Christians were also accused of being superstitious. The Roman writer Suetonius (writing around 120) wrote that the Christians were "given to a new and dangerous superstition." The historian Tacitus wrote about the Christian faith's "detestable superstition." And Pliny, writing to Emperor Trajan, warned of an "unreasonable and limitless superstition." To some, superstition was worse than atheism. Plutarch, for example, said that although atheists didn't believe in any god, superstitious people were "moved as they ought not to be, and their minds are perverted."

Other, more surprising accusations were that Christians were cannibals and were sexually immoral. The charge of cannibalism came from the words of the Lord Supper, "Take and eat, this is my body broken for you." Christians, they said, were eating flesh. And the charge of immorality came from the Christian love feast and the holy kiss exchanged by Christian "brothers and sisters."

Porphyry

Porphyry, a philosopher who lived from 234–305, published an attack on the Christian faith called *Against the Christians*. He thought that Christian beliefs were simply absurd. Here are some of the things that he wrote.

"Even supposing that some Greeks were stupid enough to think that gods dwell in statues, this would be a purer idea than to accept that the divine had descended into the womb of the Virgin Mary, that he had become an embryo, that after his birth he had been wrapped in swaddling clothes, stained with blood, bile and worse . . .

"Why, when he was taken before the high priest and governor, did not the Christ say anything worthy of a divine man . . . ? He allowed himself to be struck, spat upon the face, crowned with thorns. . . . Even if he had to suffer by order of God, he should have accepted the punishment but should not have endured his passion without some bold speech . . . instead of allowing himself to be insulted like one of the rabble from off the streets."

Around A.D. 170 Celsus wrote against Christian beliefs and practices in *The True Doctrine*. He wrote that "The assertion that some God or son of God has come down to the earth as judge of mankind is most shameful, and no lengthy argument is required to refute it. What is the purpose of such a descent on the part of God? Was it in order to learn what was going on among men? Does he not know everything? If then he does know, why does he not correct men, and why can he not do this by divine power, without sending someone specially endowed for the purpose?"

Celsus also accused Christians of being bad citizens of the Roman Empire. "If everyone were to do the same as you," he wrote, "there would be nothing to prevent the emperor from being abandoned, alone and deserted." As a result, he said, savage barbarians would come into power—and then what would Christians do?

These accusations weren't hard to refute. But as time passed and Christianity was taken more seriously, well-educated people studied Christian beliefs and then wrote their objections. Two of the best-known of these writers are Celsus and Porphyry. Some of their arguments are still put forward today.

Apologists

Christian writers came to the defense of the Christian faith. These writers are known as the apologists. The term *apology* comes from a Greek word

Justin.

meaning "defense." These Christians tried to give a defense such as a lawyer might give at a trial.

Apologists addressed their writing to the emperor. But they wanted to reach the educated people of their culture. They hoped to change opinions about the Christian faith and convince people to convert.

One of the first apologists of the second century was Justin. Justin was educated as a Greek philosopher, and he had looked for truth in many different

To Diognetus

This is an excerpt from one well-known apology called *To Diognetus*, which was written around 200. The author is anonymous.

"Christians are no different from the rest in their nationality, language or customs. . . . They live in their own countries, but as sojourners. They fulfill all their duties as citizens, but they are treated as foreigners. They find their homeland wherever they are, but their homeland is not in any one place. They marry, like everyone else, and they beget children, but they do not cast out their offspring. They share their board with each other, but not their marriage bed.

"They are in the flesh, but do not live according to the flesh. They live on earth, but their citizenship is in heaven. They obey all laws, but they live at a level higher than the laws require. They love all, but all persecute them."

schools of philosophy. One day he was walking along the seashore, thinking about how his study of philosophy had left him with more questions than answers about life. An old Christian man struck up a conversation with him. As they walked and talked together, the man convinced Justin to read the Scriptures. Justin came to recognize that Jesus was the Truth.

After he became a Christian, Justin used his education to make a defense of the faith. Justin argued that Christians should not be condemned unless it could be proved that they were criminals. He was sure, he said, that facts would prove that Christians were law-abiding citizens of the empire. He also tried to clear up misunderstandings by explaining exactly what happened during a typical worship service, during baptism, and during the Lord's supper. Justin came to be called Justin Martyr because he was beheaded for his faith.

Tertullian was another famous Christian apologist. Although most apologists wrote with careful tact, Tertullian mocked some of the wild charges against Christians. Tertullian, for example, said that it was absurd to think that Christians even wanted to drink blood—or had Romans found that human blood was drinkable?

Tertullian.

The Christian apologists of the second and third centuries showed that the Christian faith couldn't simply be dismissed as superstition. Christianity was reasonable. It was not a religion for simple-minded people. The apologists used logical arguments to convince Romans to believe in the Christian faith. They did a great service to the church. Still, most people came into the church through the ongoing life and outreach of the local church. For although some took offense at the distinctive Christian lifestyle, it attracted others.

The Church Fathers

Later apologists and leaders of the church (during the last part of the second and on through the fourth century) are called the church fathers. Many, but not all, were bishops.

- Irenaeus was born in Smyrna around 130. He was a student of Polycarp. Irenaeus became a missionary to southern France and later became bishop of Lyons. In his apologies he instructed believers and refuted false teachings. His most famous apology, written against Gnostic ideas, is *Against Heresies*.

Irenaeus.

- Tertullian (150–220) was from Carthage, North Africa. Converted in Rome when he was 40, Tertullian was a fiery, fearless champion of Christianity. In *Apology* he argued that Christianity should be encouraged because of its benefit to the empire.

- Origen (185–254), who came from a Christian home, was a scholar and teacher in Alexandria, Egypt. He is considered the most brilliant thinker of the church in its first 300 years. Origen had seven writers working in relays to write down his ideas. Origen produced versions of the Old Testament, studies of the Bible, sermons, and hundreds of apologies against both pagans and heretics.

Origen.

3 ▬ ▬ ▬ ▬ ➤ Good News in Action

Love and Mercy

The good news of the gospel was, of course, the message of God's offer of grace in Jesus Christ. But along with that good news came the good news of a Christian community. The church was like a light beaming out in darkness, like yeast working through a batch of dough.

In a time when no government offered social services, Christians made sure that no one in their community was homeless or hungry. According to a letter written by the bishop of Rome in 251, the church there was caring for "more than 1,500 widows" and others who needed help. Tertullian wrote that Christians gave money to "support and bury poor people, to supply the wants of boys and girls destitute of means and parents, and of old persons confined to the house."

"The willingness of Christians to care for others was put on dramatic public display when two great plagues swept the empire, one beginning in 165 and the second in 251," says Rodney Stark in *Christian History*. "Mortality rates climbed higher than 30 percent. Pagans tried to avoid all contact with the afflicted, often casting the still living into the gutters. Christians, on the other hand, nursed the sick even though some believers died doing so."

Clearly, Christian love shown in acts of mercy to others was one of the most powerful witnesses to the gospel. Christians visited people who were sentenced to prisons or to work in mines and helped others during earthquakes, wars, or other disasters. They also buried the poor. One Christian scholar named Lactantius wrote that Christians could not allow the creation of God to be thrown out like garbage for wild animals and birds to eat.

Even Emperor Julian, one of the Christian faith's enemies, noticed what Christians were doing. He wrote that the cause of Christianity had been helped by "the loving service rendered to strangers, and through their care for the burial of the dead. It is a scandal that there is not a single Jew who is a beggar, and that the godless Galileans care not only for their own poor but for ours as well."

Equal before God

Celsus, a critic of the church, accused it of appealing only to people who were "idiots, slaves, poor women, and children." These were the only ones, he claimed, who were interested in becoming Christians.

There was something to what Celsus said. Jesus had preached to crowds of ordinary people. Most Christians in the early centuries were have-nots. But that was also the beauty of the Christian faith. All were welcome to Christ's family. As Paul said, "There is neither Jew nor Greek, slave nor free, male nor female, for you are all one in Christ Jesus" (Galatians 3:28).

The Christian community showed a new way. Christian attitudes sharply contrasted with the attitudes of pagan society.

In the church women and girls had more dignity than they did in pagan society. In fact, they had more chance of living. The Roman Empire had many more men than women. In Rome the ratio was about 131 men to 100 women. In other places in the empire the ratio of men to women was even higher. The difference in numbers was due to the practice of killing baby girls. A letter from one Roman to his wife instructs her, "If it's a boy, keep it; if it is a girl, discard it." But the Christian community welcomed girls and women and treated them with respect. Young girls, often treated as property and married off without their consent in pagan society, had more freedom of choice. Women had influence and responsible roles in the Christian community.

Along with that came the Christian view of marriage. Both men and women were expected to keep their marriage vows and treat each other in Christ-like ways. (One complaint against the church was that Christianity undermined the authority of husbands and fathers!)

Similarly, slaves found a home in the Christian community. In pagan society slaves were at the mercy of others. Here they were brothers and sisters in Christ's family.

Celsus was blessedly right. Those who were desperate for respect and dignity discovered that in God's eyes they had great worth. In God's sight, they discovered, all believers are equal.

4 ━ ━ ━ ━ ➤ The Need for a Creed

Who Is Jesus Christ?

My name is Alexander, and I live in Smyrna. This has not been a peaceful day at my home. My parents are more upset than I've ever seen—or should I say, heard—them.

You see, we invited a traveling preacher to stay at our place. But this morning when the preacher spoke in church he said that Jesus had never been a real human being. If Jesus was the Son of God, he told us, then he couldn't have been a real person like you or me. Jesus may have seemed to be human, but he wasn't.

I'd never heard anyone say that before, so I turned to see how my father was taking it. I watched as his face first turned pink, then red, and then dark purple.

I looked around to check how others were reacting. Many, I saw, were listening closely and with great interest. My friend's mother was even nodding her head, urging the preacher on.

As soon as the service was over, I went home, picked up some bread and fresh figs, and then went off to find my friends. It would be wiser, I thought, to stay out of my parents' way.

Later, quite a bit later, as I approached home, I could hear a loud voice—my father's. "Paul would have none of what you are saying! Don't you remember what he wrote? God has reconciled us by Christ's physical body! Read his letter to the Colossians. If you don't have a copy, I'll get one for you. But how dare you come around and spout lies!"

I decided not to go in the house but to stay outside. And that's where

I've been ever since. Sitting outside under the window—listening. Now they've got me wondering. Who exactly was Jesus Christ anyway?

Rule of Faith

Alexander's problem was very real in the early church. Believers had a cafeteria of teachings set before them. And some people started believing a little of this and a little of that. Were there three gods—Father, Son, and Holy Spirit—or one God? Was Jesus fully God? Was Jesus fully human?

The Rule of Faith and Baptism

Hippolytus, a leader in the church in Rome, described what took place during a baptism there in about the year 200.

When the person being baptized goes down into the water, he who baptizes him, putting his hand on him, shall say: "Do you believe in God the Father Almighty?"

And the person being baptized shall say: "I believe."

Then holding his hand on his head, he shall baptize him once. And then he shall say:

"Do you believe in Christ Jesus, the Son of God,

who was born by the Holy Spirit of the Virgin Mary,

and was crucified under Pontius Pilate,

and was dead and buried,

and rose again the third day, alive from the dead,

and ascended into heaven,

and sat at the right hand of the Father,

and will come to judge the living and the dead?"

And when he says: "I believe," he is baptized again.

And again he shall say: "Do you believe in the Holy Spirit, in the holy church, and the resurrection of the body?"

Then person being baptized shall say: "I believe," and then he is baptized a third time.

—Hippolytus of Rome, *Apostolic Tradition*

How could Christians know what to believe? What teachers and leaders could Christians trust? The church had to set some standards, some beliefs to serve as the rule of faith.

In answer to this problem some church leaders began making short summaries of the apostles' teachings about Jesus. These simple statements of the main points of Christian belief were used at first to prepare persons for baptism. A new Christian was taught about the Father, Son, and Holy Spirit. Then during baptism he or she was quizzed on the rule of faith.

Some churches began asking converts to memorize the rule of faith in question and answer form. At baptism the new believers recited the questions and answers as a confession of faith.

The Apostles' Creed

As time went on, the rules of faith took on another role: they were used to defend against false teachings (especially Gnostic ideas). Although at first the rules had been transmitted orally, now they were carefully written down. Irenaeus in France, Tertullian in North African, and Origen in Egypt were among those composing written summaries of the Christian faith.

A written rule of faith always began with the Latin word *credo*, meaning

Ichthus

The fish, one of the earliest Christian symbols, expresses one of the earliest Christian creeds. The Greek word for fish, *ichthus*, creates an acrostic meaning "Jesus, Christ, Son of God, Savior."

Iesous Christos	*I CH* (one letter in Greek)
Theou	*TH* (also one letter in Greek)
Huois	*U* (there is no *H* in Greek)
Soter	*S*

In times when being a Christian was dangerous, drawing a fish in the dust was a secret, safe way to communicate that you were a Christian.

Baptism Standards

Hippolytus set strict standards for being baptized:

- If a man be a priest of idols or a keeper of idols either let him desist or let him be rejected.
- A soldier of the government must be told not to execute men; if he should be ordered to do it, he shall not do it. He must be told not to take the military oath. If he will not agree, let him be rejected.
- A military governor or a magistrate of a city who wears the purple, either let him desist or let him be rejected.
- If a baptized Christian wishes to become a soldier, let him be cast out. For he has despised God.

—Apostolic Tradition

Hippolytus also excluded people in other professions—gladiators, astrologers, magicians, and teachers in pagan schools. To be baptized, all these people had to change their line of work.

"I believe." Soon a rule of faith became known as a credo, or creed. So a creed is a statement of a group's set of beliefs.

Eventually some churches combined their creeds into one common creed. The creed used in the church in Rome became the most widely accepted. Later this creed became known as the Apostles' Creed. The apostles didn't write it, but it summarized what the apostles had taught.

By the year 340 most of the articles of the Apostles' Creed were decided. But the creed as we have it wasn't completely developed until about 700. "He descended into hell" was the last article to be included.

You can find a contemporary translation of the Apostles' Creed on page 91 of this book. Maybe you know this creed well. Maybe you've recited it many times in worship services. Maybe you've even learned to say it easily, almost without thinking of its meaning. But if you've ever said the Apostles' Creed while standing next to an open grave, you'll know—in a powerful way—its meaning. Saying "I believe" in God's presence is something to do mindfully.

5 ━ ━ ━ ━ ━ ➤ Forming the New Testament Canon

Testing, Testing

"Jesus was going through the village and a lad ran and knocked against his shoulder. Jesus was exasperated and said to him, 'You shall not go further on your way,' and the child immediately fell down and died."

How does this story about Jesus strike you? Do you think it's true? The story is from *The Infancy Gospel of Thomas*, a book that was circulated in the early church.

In early times Christians often read letters from the apostles in worship services. They also read accounts of what Jesus had said and done on earth and of Jesus' death and resurrection. As time went on more and more writings circulated in the church. Remember Luke's comment that many had written an account of "things that have been fulfilled among us," and that now he was writing his own "orderly account"?

Out of all these writings how did 27 books come to be set apart in what we know as the New Testament? How did they come to be called the Word of God?

Keep in mind that the process of organizing the New Testament in its present form took centuries. It was nearly 300 years after the last New Testament book was written before the 27 books of the New Testament were accepted as Scripture. Three things especially influenced whether books were eventually included in the New Testament.

First, books that are the Word of God have power to change people's lives. The books themselves have a quality that shows that they are authentic. By reading these books people came to believe and their lives were changed.

Second, some books had become a vital part of Christian worship. We know from the New Testament that letters from the apostles were read in the churches. Justin Martyr, who gives the first description of a Christian service around the middle of the second century, says that "the memoirs of the apostles [gospels] or the writings of the prophets are read."

Third, books directly linked to an apostle had the mark of being authentic. This was the most important qualifying test: a book had to be written by an apostle or by someone with close contact to an apostle.

What's In, What's Out

The word *canon* describes the unique place of the books included in the Bible. *Canon* comes from a word meaning "measuring rod," what we today would call a ruler. A ruler is used for drawing lines, for keeping things straight. And the list of books in the canon became the rule of the church. These are the books the church has discovered to be the Word of God.

Tracing how the canon was formed is difficult because history doesn't give much exact information, but we know that it was not a neat process. Church leaders like Justin Martyr, Irenaeus, Tertullian, and Origen began making lists of which books they thought had God's authority. One reason for doing this was to help Christians distinguish between Christian and Gnostic writings.

The lists of these men were not exactly alike, but they all included the four Gospels, Acts, Paul's 13 letters, John's first letter, and Revelation. The writings of those who were not apostles or writings with unknown authorship caused the most debate.

The earliest list of New Testament books is in a document written about the year 190. It's called the "Muratorian Canon" after L. A. Muratori, who discovered it and first published it in 1740. Two of the books found in Muratori's list—the Revelation of Peter and the Wisdom of Solomon—were later dropped.

Shortly after the year 300 Eusebius, the first church historian, wrote a list of the books that churches in the Roman Empire were ready to include in the canon. The list included all but five of our present New Testament books. These books were accepted by some, but "spoken against" by others.

In an Easter letter written in 367 Bishop Athanasius of Alexandria first wrote a complete list of the 27 books of the New Testament. Some years

Books of the New Testament as They Gained Acceptance by the Early Church

100	200	250	300	400

Different parts of our New Testament were written by this time but not collected and defined as Scripture.
 	
Early Christian writers such as Polycarp and Ignatius quote from the Gospels and Paul's letters, as well as from other Christian writers and oral sources. Paul's letters were collected late in the first century. The writings of Matthew, Mark, and Luke were brought together by 150.
	New Testament used in the church at Rome (the Muratorian Canon)
	
	Four Gospels
	Acts
	Paul's letters:
	  Romans
	  1 & 2 Corinthians
	  Galatians
	  Ephesians
	  Philippians
	  Colossians
	  1 & 2 Thessalonians
	  1 & 2 Timothy
	  Titus
	  Philemon
	James
	1 & 2 John
	Jude
	Revelation of Peter
	Revelation of John
	
	Wisdom of Solomon
		New Testament used by Origen
		
		Four Gospels
		Acts
		Paul's letters:
		  Romans
		  1 & 2 Corinthians
		  Galatians
		  Ephesians
		  Philippians
		  Colossians
		  1 & 2 Thessalonians
		  1 & 2 Timothy
		  Titus
		  Philemon
		
		1 John
		
		1 Peter
		Revelation of John
			New Testament used by Eusebius
			
			Four Gospels
			Acts
			Paul's letters:
			  Romans
			  1 & 2 Corinthians
			  Galatians
			  Ephesians
			  Philippians
			  Colossians
			  1 & 2 Thessalonians
			  1 & 2 Timothy
			  Titus
			  Philemon
			
			1 John
			
			1 Peter
			Revelation of John
			(authorship in doubt)
				New Testament fixed for the West by the Council of Carthage
				
				Four Gospels
				Acts
				Paul's letters:
				  Romans
				  1 & 2 Corinthians
				  Galatians
				  Ephesians
				  Philippians
				  Colossians
				  1 & 2 Thessalonians
				  1 & 2 Timothy
				  Titus
				  Philemon
				James
				1, 2, & 3 John
				Jude
				1 & 2 Peter
				Revelation of John
				
				Hebrews

	Used in private but not public worship The Shepherd of Hermas	**Disputed** Hebrews James 2 Peter 2 & 3 John Jude The Shepherd of Hermas Letter of Barnabas Teaching of Twelve Apostles Gospel of the Hebrews	**Disputed but well known** James 2 Peter 2 & 3 John Jude	**Excluded** The Shepherd of Hermas Letter of Barnabas Gospel of the Hebrews Revelation of Peter Acts of Peter Didache

later two church councils meeting in North Africa at Hippo (in 393) and Carthage (in 397) accepted the same list of books. The New Testament you have today has those 27 books in it.

The church, through a long process, decided the canon of the New Testament. That's a historical fact. But it's also true that the church was simply identifying the writings that had shown authority in the various Christian communities. The Holy Spirit, who influenced the minds and

The canon of the Old Testament was generally formed by the time of Jesus. Jesus clearly accepted these Scriptures as God's Word. "Everything written about me in the law of Moses and the prophets and the psalms must be fulfilled," he said (John 10:35; Luke 24:44).

A council of Jewish rabbis meeting at Jamnia in A.D. 90 settled the debate about two questionable books—Ecclesiastes and Song of Songs.

hearts of those who wrote the New Testament, also led the church to recognize the books as God's Word.

6 — — — ➤ Changes in the Church

Scene 1

Sometime around the middle of the first century it was the custom for small groups of Christians to meet at a believer's house on Sunday, the Lord's Day, for a service much like the Jewish synagogue services. They came together to read the Scriptures and pray. One believer started singing a psalm, and others joined in. Then someone from the group stood to talk about the resurrection of Jesus Christ and to encourage everyone to have faith.

Then it was time to eat. Believers brought out their food and gathered for a meal. Near the end of the meal, they joined in the love feast. They drank wine and broke bread together and joyfully celebrated their new life in Christ. Their service closed with thanksgiving.

In these early years Christian groups were loosely organized. Elders taught and made decisions for the church. Deacons took care of the needs of the poor. Although sometimes visiting leaders or travelers brought news, generally churches had little contact with each other.

Scene 2

Shortly after the year 100 the believers started coming together at someone's home for worship. Someone read and also commented on Christian writings—maybe from a letter of Paul or one of the apostles' memoirs. Because this was the only way for believers to come to know the Scriptures, sometimes the reading went on for a long time. The believers sang Christian hymns as well as psalms.

The Lord's Supper followed. Bread and wine were brought forward. The person leading the service prayed a long prayer that listed the saving acts of God. The service closed with a benediction. The service had become somewhat more formal, and the Lord's Supper was no longer part of a common meal.

One of the biggest changes was in the running of the church. There were still elders and deacons, but in the cities there were also bishops, who had been chosen by the elders and deacons to make sure that things were done in order.

The bishop supervised the elders and deacons and made decisions about what should be taught in the church and how money should be distributed. He also instructed converts who wanted to be baptized, using an oral summary of faith.

House Churches

From the end of the second century, Christians donated houses which were used solely as places of worship. Actual churches were built from the middle of the third century. The oldest known Christian building is the house-church of Dura Europos on the Euphrates (about 250).

—Jean Comby, *How to Read Church History*

Floor plan labels: font, baptistery, assembly hall (formerly the dining area), courtyard, stairs to upper level, dais, portico, entrance to house

In some places the bishop also supervised churches springing up in outlying areas. Because traveling teachers and missionaries circulated through these churches, the bishop carefully checked on what was being taught.

The people greatly respected and loved these pastor-bishops. Polycarp, for example, was the bishop of Smyrna, and Irenaeus was the bishop of Lyons.

Scene 3

In the early part of the third century believers gathered in worship halls. First the appointed reader stood, took up the scrolls, and read selections from the prophets and from the writings of the apostles. After the reading the choir, seated apart, began to sing. The songs were either directly from the writings (like the Song of Mary) or from the 300 approved hymns. The people joined in, as invited, for some refrains. After the singing ended, the bishop rose and delivered the sermon. All listened quietly, although if the sermon was good the congregation perhaps applauded at the end. Then a priest asked those who were not baptized to leave. Baptized Christians stayed to take part in the Lord's Supper. After prayers of thanksgiving, the congregation was dismissed.

This service was startlingly different from the gatherings of the church in the first century. Instead of an informal service with many believers taking an active part, now believers watched as priests led. Those who weren't baptized weren't allowed to even see the breaking of bread and pouring of wine. In fact, the Lord's Supper and baptism had become complicated and very solemn rituals in the worship service. And the bishop gave a formal sermon.

You can see that church leadership had an added layer. Now along with bishops, elders, and deacons, there were priests.

Clergy Power

During the third and fourth centuries the church continued to become more structured. As time passed, ordinary church members, called the laity, had less and less to say in the church. And the leaders, the clergy, had more and more to say.

Among the clergy, gradually the bishops had the most authority. People started thinking of bishops as carrying the same authority as the apostles. Eventually, bishops in the biggest cities—Rome, Alexandria, Constantinople, and Antioch—ended up with the most power and influence in the church.

So from loosely organized groups of Christians led by the apostles, the church had become a large organization of carefully governed churches. By the year 300 bishops ruled the churches in all major cities of the Roman Empire.

One reason for these changes was the number of Christians. The church had grown so much that it needed more organization. Other reasons were the threat of persecution and paganism from the outside and the threat of heresy from the inside.

The changes weren't all good; the bishops had become very powerful. Still, the church had survived many outer and inner threats. The church still held fast to the faith and preached the gospel.

7 — — — — — → Persecution Plus

On the Firing Line

In 250 a violent persecution, the most violent the church had ever faced, was ordered by Emperor Decius. Decius, who became emperor in 249, was an old-style Roman, a general who had fought on the frontier. His great dream was to restore the empire's glory. He blamed the empire's troubles on the neglect of Roman gods.

Determined to change that, Decius commanded all subjects of the empire to sacrifice to Roman gods and to burn incense before a statue of Decius himself. Those who followed the order were given certificates proving their obedience. Those who did not have a certificate faced torture and death.

Suddenly Christians throughout the empire had hard choices to make. Some squirmed out of the tight spot by managing to buy false certificates. And a good many saved their lives and property by offering the sacrifices to Roman gods. These Christians were called the "lapsed" because they had fallen away or lapsed in their faith.

But Decius wasn't so much interested in killing Christians as in making them worship Roman gods. So when Christians were arrested, they were tortured to force them to confess "Caesar is Lord." A number refused to deny Christ and were imprisoned or martyred. The believers who stayed firm in their faith—and survived—were called "confessors." Both the martyrs and the confessors were highly respected in the church.

This persecution continued until 251, when Decius was killed in battle. For a while anyway, the assault on the church had stopped.

What about the Lapsed?

Once the crisis was over, some Christians who had lapsed asked to be readmitted to the church. In some churches many had lapsed—sometimes as many as three-quarters of a congregation, according to one scholar.

Sharp disagreement arose over the question of whether those who had denied Christ should be allowed back into the church. Absolutely not, answered one group; for them, what the lapsed had done was unforgivable. They pointed to Hebrews 6:4–6 for support. It isn't possible, Hebrews says, for those who have shared the Holy Spirit and then fallen away to be brought back to repentance.

But those taking the other side pointed to Peter, who had denied his Lord three times. The Lord forgave Peter and made him an apostle, they said.

Most of the church agreed with this latter opinion. But one group still objected. Rather than forgive the lapsed Christians, members of this group formed their own church. This splinter group continued into the fifth century before it died off.

The Great Persecution

Except for a time under Emperor Valerian, a friend of Decius, the church enjoyed a long period of relative peace. But shortly after the turn of the fourth century, Christians again felt the intense heat of persecution. This time the persecution led to a bloodbath.

When Diocletian came to power in 285, the empire was in bad shape, sliding into ruin. So far in the third century no fewer than 30 men had reigned as emperors. Would-be emperors were seizing power only to be killed off by rivals. No one bothered waiting anymore for the Roman Senate's stamp of approval.

Emperor Diocletian.

When Diocletian seized power, he decided that the empire was too large for one person to manage. Diocletian decided that the way to hold power was to "divide and rule." He reorganized the government, inviting three others to share his power. Two of the four men sharing power were "senior" emperors with the title of augustus: Diocletian himself in the East, and Maximian in the West. Two other younger men, called caesars, ruled under them: Galerius under Diocletian and Constantius Chlorus under Maximian. Diocletian made Nicomedia in the province of Asia his capital.

Diocletian's plan was effective. Galerius could be off defending the empire's borders while Diocletian tended the home front. The empire was shaping up.

But after ruling effectively for many years, Diocletian suddenly turned against Christians towards the end of his reign—even though his wife, Prisca, and their daughter, Valeria, were Christians.

The trouble started in the army. In 295 a group of Christian soldiers were condemned to death for trying to leave the army. Galerius convinced Diocletian to expel all Christians from the army because they were unreliable.

Then from February 303 to February 304 Diocletian issued a series of

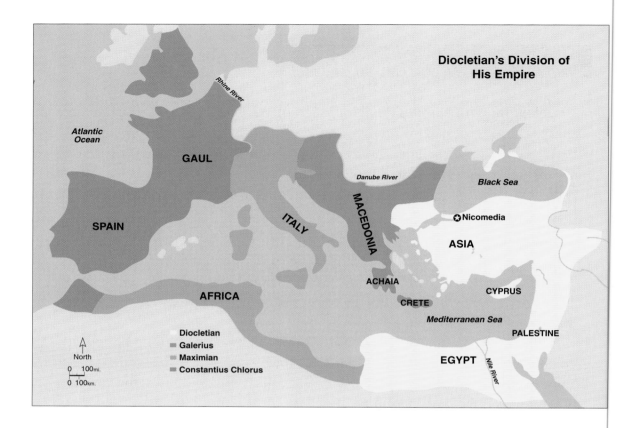

Diocletian's Division of His Empire

Atlantic Ocean

Rhine River

GAUL

Danube River

Black Sea

MACEDONIA

⊛ Nicomedia

SPAIN

ITALY

ASIA

ACHAIA

CYPRUS

AFRICA

CRETE

Mediterranean Sea

PALESTINE

North

0   100mi.

0   100km.

■ Diocletian
■ Galerius
■ Maximian
■ Constantius Chlorus

EGYPT

Nile River

decrees throughout the empire. The authorities were commanded to destroy places of worship and burn the Scriptures; to take the property of Christians, and to torture, execute, or send to the mines anyone who did not sacrifice to the Roman gods. Christians were burned, drowned, and beheaded. Bishops were especially singled out; they were put in prison and tortured, and many were killed. Although how Diocletian's decrees were carried out varied from one place to another, many local authorities carried them out to the letter.

Unexpected U-Turn

In 305 both Diocletian and Maximian, the other augustus, stepped down. The two junior emperors, Galerius and Constantius Chlorus, stepped up to take their places.

Constantius Chlorus, who had always been half-hearted about enforcing the decrees, stopped persecuting Christians. But in the East Galerius continued the persecution full force. More and more Christians joined the long list of martyrs. Even though thousands had died, Galerius was not able to stamp out the church.

Many pagans were starting to question why Christians should be treated so cruelly. How could killing so many people be justified? Besides, they were impressed that so many Christians stood firm and died for their faith. Gradually, public opinion did a U-turn.

In *Christian History* William Frend says, "'Great numbers are driven from the worship of the false gods by their hatred of cruelty,' Lactantius wrote. Still more onlookers marveled at Christians who would rather die than worship Roman gods and wondered if their own gods were worth dying for: 'The people who stand around hear them saying . . . that they do not sacrifice to stones wrought by the hand of man but to the living God, who is in heaven; many understand that this is true.'"

Finally on April 30, 311, Galerius unwillingly sent out a decree called the edict of toleration. "Moved by mercy," he said, he was extending a pardon to Christians. They were allowed "to be Christians once again, and once again gather in their assemblies." In return, they were "to pray to their god for us, for the public good, and for themselves." Galerius died five days later.

Celebrating the Martyrs

The respect for the martyrs and confessors was tremendous. Churches

Prayers of the Martyrs

We pray that the God whom the enemies
    of the church are always provoking
    would tame their unruly hearts.
May their rage subside and peace
    return to their hearts;
May their minds, clouded by sin,
    turn and see the light;
May they seek the prayers of the bishop
    and not his blood.
           —Cyprian of Carthage

Blessed are you Lord,
    and may your Son's name
    be blessed forevermore.
I can see what those who
    persecute me cannot:
On the other side of this river
    there is a multitude
Waiting to receive my soul
    and carry it to glory.
           —Sabas the Goth

A ladder is before me, surrounded by light, stretching from the earth to heaven.
I am called by my friend to climb and not to fear.
I shall not die, but live and reign eternally with you, O God, and Jesus Christ your Son.
           —Sadoth of Seleucia

kept lists of their martyrs and began celebrating their death days with annual services. They gathered at the tomb on the martyr's heavenly "birthday" to pray, recite the martyr's sufferings, and share the Lord's Supper.

This practice began innocently enough, but it led to excesses. The idea grew that martyrs had special influence with God. And in the following centuries churches competed to get relics of the martyrs—bones, pieces of hair, or belongings—to place in their church altars. Church leaders strongly opposed such superstitions. Although they were thankful for the witness of the martyrs, they saw dangers in thinking that dead believers had power. The emphasis belonged not on the work of the martyrs but on God in Jesus Christ.

Worship service in the catacombs of St. Calixtus.

The Catacombs of Rome

From the third century, Christians, like other groups, were given their own burial grounds. Roman Christians' burial grounds were underground tunnels called catacombs. Outside the city of Rome archaeologists have discovered catacombs that wind for miles and miles, almost like an underground city. They run through red volcanic rock that's solid but easy to dig out with spades. If the catacombs were laid out end to end, they would stretch several hundred miles.

In the walls of these tunnels are shelf-like compartments sealed with marble slabs, which are the graves of about 6 million people buried here during the time of the Roman Empire.

The catacombs tell us a lot about the early church. Visitors can still see names, dates, sayings, and pictures telling of Christian faith and hope scratched into the walls. These burial grounds have some of the first Christian art: paintings of scenes from the Gospels and drawings of Christian symbols.

Symbols for Christ include the lamb, the good shepherd,

Visitors can still see these symbols on a wall in the Domitilla catacomb in Rome.

and the dolphin (believed to save people from drowning). The Holy Spirit is pictured as a dove, and the church as a ship. There are drawings of a cross—in the shape of a three-pronged fork—but no pictures of Jesus on the cross.

There are pictures of a peacock, which is a symbol of eternal life (supposedly eating its meat gave immortality), and a ship with an anchor above, which is a symbol of faith and hope. Other symbols are a fish with a loaf of bread (communion) and a man with outstretched arms (unity of the Christian community).

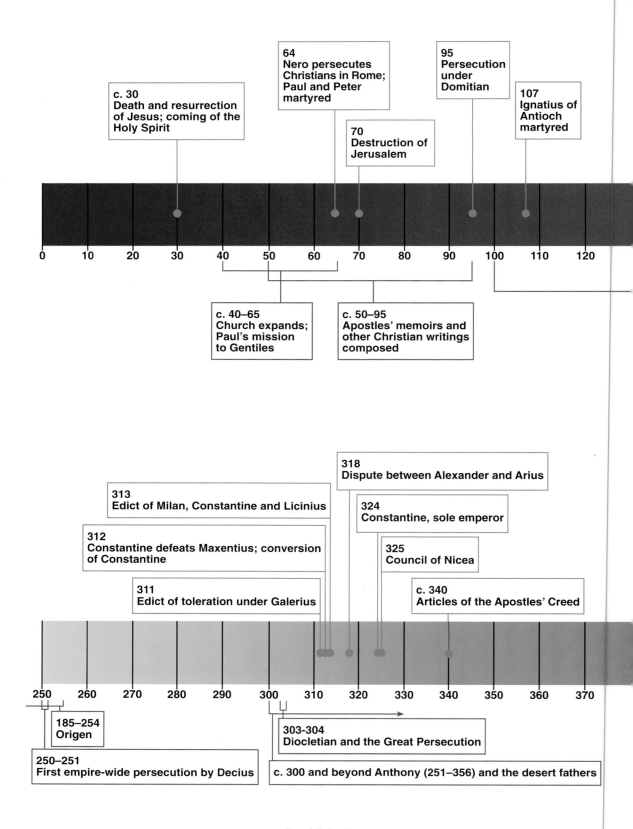

c. 30
Death and resurrection of Jesus; coming of the Holy Spirit

64
Nero persecutes Christians in Rome; Paul and Peter martyred

70
Destruction of Jerusalem

95
Persecution under Domitian

107
Ignatius of Antioch martyred

0 10 20 30 40 50 60 70 80 90 100 110 120

c. 40–65
Church expands; Paul's mission to Gentiles

c. 50–95
Apostles' memoirs and other Christian writings composed

318
Dispute between Alexander and Arius

313
Edict of Milan, Constantine and Licinius

324
Constantine, sole emperor

312
Constantine defeats Maxentius; conversion of Constantine

325
Council of Nicea

311
Edict of toleration under Galerius

c. 340
Articles of the Apostles' Creed

250 260 270 280 290 300 310 320 330 340 350 360 370

185–254
Origen

303-304
Diocletian and the Great Persecution

250–251
First empire-wide persecution by Decius

c. 300 and beyond Anthony (251–356) and the desert fathers

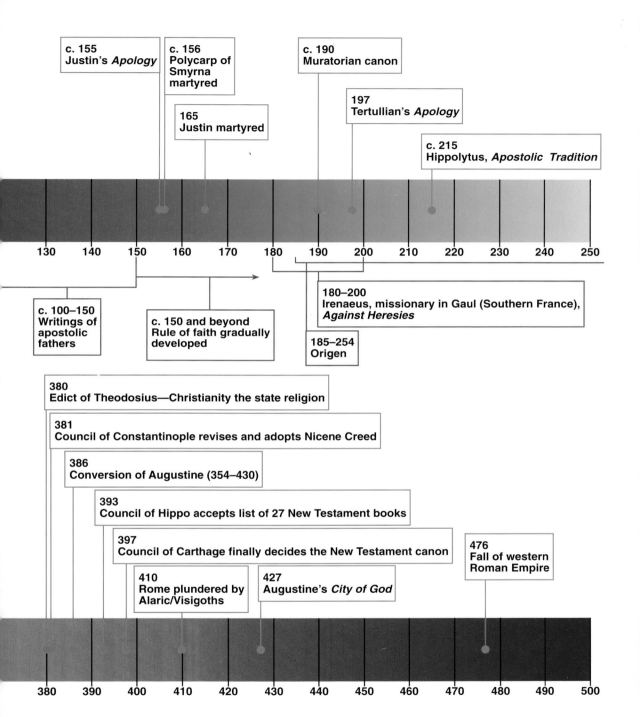

c. 155
Justin's *Apology*

c. 156
Polycarp of
Smyrna
martyred

165
Justin martyred

c. 190
Muratorian canon

197
Tertullian's *Apology*

c. 215
Hippolytus, *Apostolic Tradition*

130 140 150 160 170 180 190 200 210 220 230 240 250

c. 100–150
Writings of
apostolic
fathers

c. 150 and beyond
Rule of faith gradually
developed

180–200
Irenaeus, missionary in Gaul (Southern France),
Against Heresies

185–254
Origen

380
Edict of Theodosius—Christianity the state religion

381
Council of Constantinople revises and adopts Nicene Creed

386
Conversion of Augustine (354–430)

393
Council of Hippo accepts list of 27 New Testament books

397
Council of Carthage finally decides the New Testament canon

410
Rome plundered by
Alaric/Visigoths

427
Augustine's *City of God*

476
Fall of western
Roman Empire

380 390 400 410 420 430 440 450 460 470 480 490 500

8 ━ ━ ━ ━ ➤ The Sign of Victory

The Vision and Victory

A power struggle followed Galerius's death. In the year 312 Constantine, the son of Constantius Chlorus, rode toward Rome with his army of 40,000. His aim was to defeat Maxentius, his rival, and become the sole emperor of the West. But this was a daring scheme because Maxentius had at least four times as many soldiers. Constantine's victory was not a sure thing.

Battle of Constantine and Maxentius by Peter Paul Rubens, 1577–1640.

The two armies met just outside the walls of Rome. The night before the battle Constantine was wondering to himself whether or not Mithras, the sun god, would give him victory. Then he found himself turning to the God of the Christians for help. In a vision he saw a cross in the sky with the words "In this sign you will conquer." Then in a dream he was told by Christ to place the cross on the standards of his soldiers.

Constantine obeyed the command. On October 28, 312, he and his soldiers went into battle with the chi-rho symbol marked on their shields and standards. And Constantine did win the battle.

As the retreating army pushed across a narrow bridge, Constantine's enemy, Maxentius, fell into the river and drowned, weighed down in his armor.

The victory convinced Constantine that the Christian God was more

powerful than pagan gods. From that time on, Constantine considered himself a Christian. His conversion changed the whole Roman Empire and the church.

Edict of Milan

Soon after the defeat of Maxentius, Constantine met in Milan with Licinius, a ruler in the East, to form an alliance. Together they issued an decree, known as the Edict of Milan. This decree in 313 gave freedom of worship to everyone in the empire. The Christian faith was no longer outlawed. It was equal with other religions. In addition, authorities were ordered to restore the property taken from Christians and from the church during Diocletian's persecution.

Constantine quickly followed with more decisions that favored Christians. He paid for the Scriptures to be recopied. He provided transportation for bishops who were traveling to Arles in 314.

Imagine the reaction in the Christian community to these decisions. This attitude toward Christians was unheard of. Eusebius describes the how Christians sang and danced with joy at the unexpected turn of events. Some said that the kingdom of God had come down to earth.

Is He or Isn't He?

Was Constantine a Christian? Or was he a sharp politician who saw advantages in supporting the Christian church? Those questions have no clear answers.

Although Constantine had converted, he actually knew little about the Christian faith, and he held on to many pagan practices. He kept his sun god alongside of the Christian God. He also kept his title of High Priest of the traditional religion of the empire and took part in pagan ceremonies. Constantine didn't see a problem with this; he thought that this role went with being emperor.

Although Constantine was friendly toward Christians and his policies favored Christians, he didn't take the step of joining the Christian community. He surrounded himself with Christians and later provided his children with a Christian education, but he never put himself under the church's discipline.

When Licinius, now the emperor in the East, began taking his disagreements with Constantine out on the Christians, Constantine went to war as their champion. He gave the impression that he was fighting to defend Christians. But once he defeated Licinius in 324, Constantine became the sole ruler of the whole empire.

Many of Constantine's actions were obviously self-serving, even brutal. He murdered rivals and even some members of his family, among them a father-in-law, a few brothers-in-law, and his son Crispus. In many ways he was a typical Roman emperor.

Still, Constantine expressed his faith many times. Writing to the bishops meeting in Arles, he said, "The eternal, holy and unfathomable goodness of God does not allow us to wander in darkness, but shows us the way of salvation. . . . This I have seen in others as well as in myself. . . . The Almighty God . . . granted what I did not deserve."

A New Capital

After defeating Licinius, Constantine made a surprising move. He left Rome and set up a new capital for the empire. He chose the small city of Byzantium (modern Istanbul), which was strategically located. It was a wise choice. Set on the narrow straits of the Bosporus, the city could be reached by water or by land. Constantine said the credit wasn't his: he was following instructions God had given him in a dream.

At first the city was called New Rome, but soon it became known as Constantinople, or the City of Constantine. Constantine built up the capital into a large and splendid city. His agents traveled throughout the empire to find materials and art for his city. To draw more people to his city, Constantine offered free oil, wheat, and wine.

A Mixed Blessing

Under Constantine, for the first time in the history of the church, Christians could feel secure from persecution. In earlier centuries Christians had always been on the fringes of society. But under Constantine all that changed: the Christian religion was officially favored.

With a Christian emperor in power Christians not only had freedom of worship, they also enjoyed special privileges. The result was that Christianity became popular. People left their pagan religions and streamed into the church. It paid to be a Christian now. Gradually, Christians changed from a persecuted minority to a privileged majority.

The church was rapidly growing, but many who came into the church were Christians mostly in name. Anyone wanting to get ahead in the world could see the advantage of belonging to the church. The narrow gate of Jesus had grown wide—wide enough for crowds of people to enter without thinking much about the meaning of the cross. The persecutions had been horrible, but they had made the biblical picture very clear: to be a disciple of Christ was costly. Now the costs weren't so obvious.

Was Constantine's victory a victory for the church or not?

9 ▬ ▬ ▬ ▬ ▬ ➤ How Constantine Changed the Church

Imperial Favor

Constantine had given Christians complete freedom of worship, but his favor didn't stop there. He generously supported the church. He built churches all over the empire, and he also built shrines to martyrs. He gave the church official buildings and even palaces for their use. He also passed a law giving the church the property of anyone who died without an heir. With all Constantine's generosity the church was becoming wealthy.

Under Constantine the church developed great influence in public life. Christians filled high government positions. Bishops had increasing power as advisors to the emperor. One result was that Constantine created laws that Christians wanted.

- Sundays and Christian festivals were made holidays.
- Divorce was made more difficult.
- Prisoners could not be starved to death, and they were entitled to sunlight once a day. Clergy could visit the prisons.
- Gladiator fights and crucifixions were outlawed.
- Killing babies was against the law.
- Breaking up families of slaves was illegal.
- Slaves could be set free by reading a statement before a member of the clergy.

The new freedom also gave the church unlimited opportunity to teach and preach the gospel. Christians wondered, Was this the time when the whole world would be converted?

Constantine's favor brought immense advantages to the church.

Favor for a Price

But the advantages were not free. Constantine was the emperor, and he made it clear that the bishops did not rule him. He ruled the bishops. For example, he took them along to battles to make sure that God's power was on his side.

Constantine also concerned himself with church affairs. Because his main interest was his empire's peace and unity, he disliked disagreements within the church. He did all he could to help solve these problems.

Sometimes the church asked him to intervene. From 313 on, the churches in Africa had been asking Constantine to help them settle a problem. A difference of opinion had led to two sets of rival bishops in many cities. Constantine placed the problem before bishops meeting in both Italy and France. They ruled against one of the bishops, Donatus. When his followers refused to accept the ruling, Constantine sent his soldiers to remove them from churches where they were holed up.

You can see from these brief examples that the church and the state had become intertwined. One hand washed the other. Constantine expected the church to bless his policies and wars. And the church looked to Constantine to advance its cause.

Changing Worship and Church Life

Ordinary Christians probably noticed the emperor's influence on the church when they went to worship services. Worship had become more splendid. Some of the trappings of emperor worship had been introduced. Incense, a sign of honor for the emperor, now filled the church. The services began with a procession. Now choirs did much of the singing. The clergy wore grand robes. The Lord's Supper was celebrated with special pomp.

Baptism had always been taken seriously by the church as the sacrament marking a person as part of God's family. But now many had only basic instruction in the faith, were "marked with the sign of the cross," and then considered themselves Christians. They put off being baptized until they were very old or were going to die. Constantine, for example, was baptized on his deathbed.

But why? The church at this time taught that all sins were forgiven at baptism. If a person died after baptism, how could his or her sins be forgiven? Well, the church had thought of that. It also allowed a person to do penance (acts of atonement) for sin, but only once in a lifetime. It made a certain sense, then, for people to wait as long as possible to make a commitment. After all, no one wanted to die with unforgiven sins. So the situation was partly the church's fault. The church allowed a person to be considered a Christian and yet escape the responsibility of Christian living.

Cross section of Old Saint Peter's Basilica.

Other changes were seen in the church buildings. They had become much larger and much more elaborate. The church in Dura-Europos, the oldest church archaeologists have found, was simple and unassuming. In contrast, many of the churches built under Constantine and later emperors were large basilicas (named for their basic rectangular plan).

Inside were polished marble and rich tapestries. And in many churches the walls were covered with mosaics (art using very small pieces of colored stone or glass). Usually the mosaics showed Christian symbols or scenes from the Bible.

Another development was building churches at places where martyrs had been buried or at other "holy" places. The idea was that worshiping in these places had a special effect.

Constantine's mother, Helena, who had made a pilgrimage to Palestine,

From Outlaw Religion to State Religion

Constantine's edict in 313 gave Christians equality with other religions. All were legal in the empire.

But Constantine soon showed that he favored the Christian faith above paganism. That change made it possible for people who had sacrificed only to the gods as a patriotic duty to quit the practice. Traditional paganism still had strength in many parts of the empire, though.

Then as Christians gathered more power, laws unfavorable to the old religions were passed. In 319, for example, Constantine outlawed several magical practices. "Ceremonies of a bygone perversion" could not be openly conducted, he ruled.

By the time Constantius, Constantine's son, was emperor (337–361) Christians outnumbered non-Christians in some parts of the empire. Now Christians began doing the persecuting, and they urged the emperor to outlaw paganism altogether. Not all Christians agreed with this move. But in 356 Constantius passed a decree forbidding sacrifices and threatening capital punishment to those who disobeyed. Many pagans resisted the law and Constantius didn't strongly enforce it.

In 380 Emperor Theodosius made being a Christian the law of the empire with this edict: "It is Our Will that all peoples we rule shall practice that religion that Peter the Apostle transmitted to the Romans. We shall believe in the single Deity of the Father, the Son, and the Holy Spirit."

Now paganism had become illegal. The power of the state had changed sides. Religion was still the foundation of the empire, but now the religion was Christianity. By the beginning of the fourth century Christianity had changed from an outlaw religion to a state religion.

Sad to say, Christians thought they had the right to use violence against pagans. Most were happy to have the state enforce their wishes.

---

developed a great interest in the places connected with the events of Jesus' life. She persuaded Constantine to build churches in Bethlehem and Jerusalem. The Church of the Nativity was placed over the cave where Jesus was believed to have been born and the Church of the Holy Sepulcher over Jesus' tomb.

You can see that Constantine's conversion made an enormous impact. The church had to struggle with the question of how to be obedient in this new environment. How could Christians remain faithful to Jesus Christ in a church of wealth and power?

Retreating to the Desert

A number of Christians began to answer that question by retreating from the world—or rather, by retreating from what they saw of the world in the church.

The first to retreat were hermits in Egypt who went off into the desert to live. These Christians were the beginning of the monastic life, or the life of monks and nuns totally set apart from the ordinary world.

Anthony (251–356) was one of the first and best-known hermits of the desert. At 20 Anthony gave away all of his wealth. At first he lived in a tomb, but later he withdrew into the desert, where he tried to live a holy and simple life. As part of his self-denial, he "neither bathed his body with water to free himself from filth nor did he ever wash his feet."

Hundreds followed Anthony into the desert. These desert fathers, as they are called, lived simple, and in some cases strange, lives. Some made baskets for a living, trading them for bread and other simple foods. They had few belongings: usually just a mat for sleeping and a few pieces of basic clothing. They spent their time praying and memorizing whole books of the Bible. Sometimes they exchanged sayings of wisdom from the most respected among them.

Simeon Stylites on top of a column (16th century Russian icon).

Certain desert fathers earned a reputation for holiness and wisdom. As a result, people from the cities went looking for them—which did not please the hermits. Anthony, for example, moved over and over again trying to find peace and quiet.

Another well-known hermit, Simeon Stylites, found a unique way out. To escape the crowds around his cave, Stylites moved to the top of a high rock. Later he made his home on top of a pillar 24 meters high, where he lived on a platform measuring 2 square meters. He stayed up there for more than 30 years. His followers kept him alive by sending food up to him in a basket. Sometimes Simeon preached to the people gathered below or yelled at them to quiet down. Sitting on pillars caught on (mostly in Syria) among hermits. These high-minded types came to be called pillar saints.

The hermits lived dedicated but strange lives. They showed their disappointment with the wealth and lack of commitment in the church by escaping to caves, huts, trees—and pillars.

10 ------→ Is Jesus God?

The Dispute

One of the distinctive beliefs of the Christian faith is the Trinity. Probably every Sunday you confess that God is three-in-one. We know that what we confess is a mystery. But in the early church this belief in the Trinity wasn't so clearly spelled out. In fact, in the fourth century the Trinity was a hot topic in the streets.

"Every part of the city," wrote a bishop, "is filled with such talk: the alleys, the crossroads, the squares, the avenues. It comes from those who sell clothes, money changers, grocers. . . . When you ask the price of bread, the baker will say, 'The Father is greater and the Son is less.'"

All the talk had started some years before, around 319, in the city of Alexandria. A popular pastor named Arius and his bishop, Alexander, disagreed sharply about the person of Jesus.

Jesus is a half-god, said Arius. God the Father created Jesus before anything else, and then Jesus helped God create the rest of the universe. Jesus is better than we will ever be, but God the Father is the only true God. The Arians made up a little jingle: "There was a time when the Son was not."

Bishop Alexander knew heresy when he heard it. No, said Alexander, Christ is God. Christ is eternal with God. Christ is not a created Being. Alexander had long discussions with Arius, trying to convince him of his errors.

Alexander finally called a meeting of the area bishops. Agreeing with Alexander, they excommunicated Arius.

Arius, in turn, asked other bishops for support. And he made up more catchy jingles and put them to music. Before long his songs were everywhere.

Soon Christians in Alexandria and other cities were taking sides. The church was splitting into two groups, some following Arius and some following Alexander.

Constantine was concerned about this conflict in his empire. So he fired off an angry letter ordering Arius and Alexander to end the quarrel. These matters are "deep and hidden mysteries," he wrote, and who is capable of understanding them? He went on to say that they were fighting about "these small and very insignificant questions."

But to the church these matters were not small and insignificant. Besides, Constantine's letter came too late. The quarrel had spread far beyond Alexandria. And there was no easy way to put out the fire that had started.

Constantine saw that the issue had to be settled. He called all of the bishops together in Nicea, a small city in the province of Asia. He wanted unity in the church.

The Council of Nicea

The Council of Nicea, held in 325, was the first empire-wide council. About 300 bishops came to the meeting, the largest share from the East, where the dispute was the hottest. Most of these bishops had lived through the great persecutions; many had scars from torture. But now they were gathered as guests of the emperor!

The group assembled in a marble hall close the edge of a lake. Honor guards and officers of the court announced Constantine's arrival. The bishops stood as he strode into the room.

The Council of Nicea.

Over six feet tall, with long wavy hair and a short beard, Constantine was a strong, energetic figure. He presided over the first meetings, sitting on a throne that was a little higher than those of the bishops.

After some polite remarks, Constantine told the bishops that he had not expected divisions among them. He said that he expected them to come to agreement and restore peace. Then he let the discussions begin.

Arius was allowed to explain his position. At one point he broke into one of his popular chants. Those who opposed him covered their ears until they had a chance to speak. The emperor seemed to take it all in stride.

The bishop who backed Arius stepped forward to explain the view. But his explanation infuriated the others. They shouted, "Heresy! You lie!" And in the heat of the moment someone even grabbed the paper on which the bishop's speech was written and tore it up. Now even bishops who had been ready to compromise were determined to utterly reject the views of Arius.

The debates and discussions continued with no solution in sight. Then one bishop suggested that the council adopt a creed he had learned as a child. The creed was beautiful but didn't address the specific heresies of Arius. Finally they made changes to make the creed clearly state that Christ was true God, of the same essence as the Father. Constantine was pleased.

Council members, though, continued to debate. Becoming impatient, Constantine ordered the bishops to stop talking and adopt the creed. They obeyed. The result was the Nicene Creed, one of today's ecumenical creeds.

Setting the Date for Easter

The Council of Nicea did more than debate the heresy of Arius. The bishops discussed 84 different topics. One was the date of Easter. They set the day as the first Sunday after the first full moon following the vernal equinox.

Bishop Alexander had won the argument. The bishops deposed Arius. But Constantine added additional punishment: he sent Arius and some of his followers into exile.

Happy that unity had been restored, Constantine threw a banquet for the bishops. On July 25, the emperor and church leaders celebrated together. Constantine passed out gifts and compliments. After seven weeks of meetings the council was over. Mission accomplished.

Not Over Yet

But in spite of the decision at Nicea, the matter was not finally settled. Arius and his followers kept fighting for their beliefs, even from exile. They continued their struggle after Alexander died and Athanasius became bishop of Alexandria. Then bishops who had influence with Constantine got him to change his mind—more than once. Sometimes the emperor pardoned Arius and exiled Athanasius; sometimes it was the other way around. Athanasius was sent into exile five times. The argument was going still strong even after Arius and then Constantine himself died in 337.

Finally, 50 years later Emperor Theodosius called another church council, the Council of Constantinople in 381. This council revised and polished the Nicene Creed, adding a statement about the Holy Spirit and making it a beautiful and strong summary of the faith.

The Nicene Creed declares that Christ and the Holy Spirit are true God, equal with God the Father. It also confesses that God is three Persons—Father, Son, and Holy Spirit—but one God. In other words, it confesses the

Trinity. The word *trinity* isn't found in the Bible. It comes from *tri* ("three") and *unity* ("one"), and it means that God is three in one. This is one of the central beliefs of the church.

The Nicene Creed is truly a creed for all Christians and for all ages.

> We believe in one God,
> > the Father almighty,
> > maker of heaven and earth,
> > of all things visible and invisible.
> And in one Lord Jesus Christ,
> > the only Son of God,
> > begotten from the Father before all ages,
> > > God from God,
> > > Light from Light,
> > > true God from true God,
> > begotten, not made,
> > of the same essence as the Father.
> > Through him all things were made.
> For us and our salvation
> > he came down from heaven;
> > he became incarnate by the Holy Spirit and the virgin Mary,
> > and was made human.
> > He was crucified for us under Pontius Pilate;
> > he suffered and was buried.
> > The third day he rose again, according to the Scriptures.
> > He ascended to heaven
> > and is seated at the right hand of the Father.
> > He will come again with glory
> > to judge the living and the dead.
> > His kingdom will never end.
>
> And we believe in the Holy Spirit,
> > the Lord, the giver of life.
> > He proceeds from the Father and the Son,

and with the Father and the Son is worshiped and glorified.
He spoke through the prophets.
We believe in one holy catholic and apostolic church.
We affirm one baptism for the forgiveness of sins.
We look forward to the resurrection of the dead,
and to life in the world to come. Amen.

11 ▬ ▬ ▬ ▬ ▬ ▬ ➡ Augustine and the Crumbling Empire

The Eternal City

Rome was the heart of the Roman Empire—and had been for more that 600 years. It was the invincible eternal city until the Visigoths under Alaric broke through the Roman defenses in 410. They stormed into Rome and tore it apart, destroying buildings, killing, looting, and taking prisoners. After holding the city for a short time, the Visigoths abruptly retreated, moving on to the West.

The whole empire was shocked and frightened. If Rome could be captured and sacked, then anything could happen! Romans blamed the destruction in Rome on the new religion. The old Roman gods had done a better job of protecting Rome. Now the angry gods were punishing the empire for neglecting them.

Christians were full of questions. Why had God let Rome fall? Why hadn't the apostles and martyrs protected the city? How could the church survive if the empire collapsed? Was the end of the world coming soon?

Augustine, bishop of Hippo in North Africa, thought about these questions. His answers gave Christians in the collapsing empire new understanding of the kingdom of God and its relation to the empires of this world.

Coming to Faith

Augustine of Hippo was born in 354 in Tagaste, a small village in North Africa. His father, Patricius, was a Roman official. His mother, Monica, was a devout Christian. Monica brought up her son in the faith. Of the two parents, Monica had more influence on Augustine.

At 17 Augustine was sent to school in Carthage. Soon he had a live-in girlfriend. And at 18 he had a son, whom he greatly loved.

Augustine was a brilliant scholar, and he spent many years searching for a philosophy more satisfying than Christianity. The Christian faith, he thought, was too simple for his questioning mind. Through all his years of searching, Augustine's mother continued praying for him.

When Augustine was 32 and a teacher of public speaking in the city of Milan, he began going to hear Ambrose preach. Actually, at first he went to study Ambrose's skill in public speaking. But as he listened to Ambrose, he rediscovered the Christian faith. His objections crumbled. Augustine began to

St. Augustine by Sandro Botticelli, 1500.

admit to himself that his heart was empty in spite of his education and free lifestyle.

But Augustine didn't want to become a Christian if he couldn't do it with his whole heart. And he didn't want to give up his ambitions and pleasures—at least not yet. Then one day a friend told Augustine about two men who had recently given up high government positions to follow the example of Anthony the hermit. Augustine found himself moved and ashamed. Why wasn't he able to commit himself to God? Suddenly he was caught up in a battle with himself.

Going into the garden, he talked with God for a long time. As he was struggling, he heard a voice coming from the house next door. It was a child's voice saying, almost like a chant, "Take and read it. Take and read it." Turning to the New Testament, Augustine read these words: "We can't afford to waste a minute, must not squander these precious daylight hours in frivolity and indulgence, in sleeping around and dissipation, in bickering and grabbing everything in sight. . . . Dress yourselves in Christ" (Romans 13:13–14, *The Message*).

When he came to the end of this sentence, Augustine was ready to commit his life to Christ. He later wrote that instantly "the light of peace poured into my heart and all doubt disappeared."

Augustine, the Bishop

On the Easter after Augustine's conversion, Ambrose baptized Augustine and his son. Soon after that, Augustine returned to North Africa to the farm that he had inherited from his parents. He had decided to enter the monastic life when the church in Hippo chose him to be their priest. Then in 395 he became bishop of Hippo.

Augustine used his gifts of writing and speaking to advance God's kingdom. As bishop he preached, traveled widely, and argued—both in person and in his writing—against heresies. He had to deal with several serious disputes within the church. We still have many of his writings: sermons, catechisms, commentaries, many papers, and several books. Two of his best-known writings are *Confessions* and *The City of God*. *Confessions,* one of the masterpieces of world literature, is Augustine's account of his inner life.

Augustine's Confession

When I thought of devoting myself entirely to you, my God . . . it was I that wished to do it, and I that wished not to do it. It was I. And since I neither completely wished, nor completely refused, I fought against myself and tore myself to pieces.

—Augustine of Hippo, *Confessions*, Book 8

Augustine wrote *The City of God* to answer the Christians' questions about the capture of Rome by Alaric. Augustine was in his fifties when the Visigoths took Rome. During the years that followed, the empire continued to weaken and barbarian tribes began occupying more Roman territory. In his book Augustine reflects on history and assures Christians that God has not abandoned them. From the beginning, Augustine explains, there have been two cities: the city of God—whose citizens are born of God's grace and love the things of God—and the city of the world—whose citizens are godless and love things of this world. These two cities are mixed together on earth, but only the city of God will last forever. Augustine said that even if the barbarians destroyed the Roman Empire, the church would not be destroyed. In the middle of changing empires, the church would continue. God would not abandon his people. Certainly their eternal city would never be destroyed.

By the year 430 Hippo, Augustine's city, was under siege by Vandal barbarians who had entered Africa over the Straits of Gibraltar. Augustine died at the age of 76, shortly before Vandals took the city.

Acknowledgments

"The Divine Campout," page 36, from *Home Link: When Advent Doesn't Feel Like Christmas* by Scott Hoezee. ©1997 by CRC Publications, Grand Rapids, MI 49560. Used by permission.

"Finding God in Unexpected Places," page 39, adapted from "Career Dividends" in *Finding God in Unexpected Places* by Philip Yancey. ©1995 by Moorings/Ballantine.

"Going to the Dogs," page 55, adapted from *Daily Study Bible Series: Mark* by William Barclay. ©1975 by Westminster John Knox Press.

"Fire!," page 96, adapted from a sermon by Rev. David Deters. Used by permission.

"Keeping the Faith," page 105, adapted from *Speaking as One: A Look at the Ecumenical Creeds* by Scott Hoezee. ©1997 by CRC Publications, Grand Rapids, MI 49560. Used by permission.

"What's Freedom," page 141, from *ACTS* (Interpretation Series) by William H. Willimon. ©1988 John Knox Press. Used by permission of Westminster John Knox Press.

"The Greatest of These," page 157, from *Intermission: Breaking Away with God* by James C. Schaap. ©1985, 1987, 1997 by CRC Publications, Grand Rapids, MI 49560. Used by permission.

"Fortress Antonia," page 174, adapted from *Jerusalem: City of Jesus* by Richard M. Mackowski. ©1980 by Wm. B. Eerdmans Publishing Co.

"Ready with Your Own Defense?," page 181, from *Your Questions, God's Answers* by Peter Kreeft, p. 101–102. ©1994 by Ignatius Press, San Francisco. All rights reserved; used by permission of Ignatius Press.

"Rough Sailing," page 185, adapted from *The Book of Acts* by F. F. Bruce. ©1988 by Wm. B. Eerdmans Publishing Co. Used by permission.

"Basil," page 187, adapted from "Russia's Untold Story" in *Finding God in Unexpected Places* by Philip Yancey. ©1995 by Moorings/Ballantine.

"First-Century Letters," page 190, from *Selections from the Greek Papyri* by G. Milligan in *The All-Sufficient Christ*, by William Barclay. ©1974 by Westminster Press.

"Dying We Live," page 200, from Meditation 56, "Greater Love Hath No Man or Woman . . ." in *The 40-year Campout* by James C. Schaap. ©1993 by CRC Publications, Grand Rapids, MI 49560. Used by permission.

"Worthy Is the Lamb," page 235, from *Following Jesus: Biblical Reflections on Discipleship* by N. T. Wright. ©1994 by Wm. B. Eerdmans Publishing Co.